ENGLISH LAW UNDER TWO ELIZABETHS

Comparative legal history is generally understood to involve the comparison of legal systems in different countries. This is an experiment in a different kind of comparison. The legal world of the first Elizabethans is separated from that of today by nearly half a millennium. But the past is not a wholly different country. The common law is still, in an organic sense, the same common law as it was in Tudor times and Parliament is legally the same Parliament. The concerns of Tudor lawyers turn out to resonate with those of the present and this book concentrates on three of them: access to justice, in terms of both cost and public awareness; the respective roles of common law and legislation; and the means of protecting the rule of law through the courts. Central to the story is the development of judicial review in the time of Elizabeth I.

SIR JOHN BAKER is Emeritus Downing Professor of the Laws of England, University of Cambridge. His recent publications include *The Reinvention of Magna Carta 1216–1616* (Cambridge, 2017) and *Collected Papers on English Legal History* (Cambridge, 2013).

ENGLISH LAW UNDER TWO ELIZABETHS

The Late Tudor Legal World and the Present

SIR JOHN BAKER
University of Cambridge

CAMBRIDGE
UNIVERSITY PRESS

CAMBRIDGE
UNIVERSITY PRESS

University Printing House, Cambridge CB2 8BS, United Kingdom

One Liberty Plaza, 20th Floor, New York, NY 10006, USA

477 Williamstown Road, Port Melbourne, VIC 3207, Australia

314–321, 3rd Floor, Plot 3, Splendor Forum, Jasola District Centre, New Delhi – 110025, India

79 Anson Road, #06–04/06, Singapore 079906

Cambridge University Press is part of the University of Cambridge.

It furthers the University's mission by disseminating knowledge in the pursuit of education, learning, and research at the highest international levels of excellence.

www.cambridge.org
Information on this title: www.cambridge.org/9781108837965
DOI: 10.1017/9781108936705

First published 2021

A catalogue record for this publication is available from the British Library.

Library of Congress Cataloging-in-Publication Data
NAMES: Baker, John H. (John Hamilton), author.
TITLE: English law under two Elizabeths : the late Tudor legal world and the present / Sir John Baker, University of Cambridge.
DESCRIPTION: Cambridge, United Kingdom ; New York, NY : Cambridge University Press, 2021. | Series: The Hamlyn lectures | Includes index.
IDENTIFIERS: LCCN 2020047380 (print) | LCCN 2020047381 (ebook) | ISBN 9781108837965 (hardback) | ISBN 9781108947329 (paperback) | ISBN 9781108936705 (ebook)
SUBJECTS: LCSH: Common law – England – History. | Law – England – History. | Statutes – England. | Elizabeth I, Queen of England, 1533–1603. | Elizabeth II, Queen of Great Britain, 1926– | Great Britain – History – Tudors, 1485–1603.
CLASSIFICATION: LCC KD671 .B353 2021 (print) | LCC KD671 (ebook) | DDC 349.4209/031–dc23
LC record available at https://lccn.loc.gov/2020047380
LC ebook record available at https://lccn.loc.gov/2020047381

ISBN 978-1-108-83796-5 Hardback
ISBN 978-1-108-94732-9 Paperback

CONTENTS

CONTENTS

The Hamlyn Trust owes its existence today to the will of the late Miss Emma Warburton Hamlyn of Torquay, who died in 1941 at the age of eighty. She came from an old and well-known Devon family. Her father, William Bussell Hamlyn, practised in Torquay as a solicitor and was a Justice of the Peace for many years, and it seems likely that Miss Hamlyn founded the trust in his memory. Emma Hamlyn was a woman of strong character who was intelligent and cultured; well versed in literature, music and art; and a lover of her country. She travelled extensively in Europe and Egypt, and apparently took considerable interest in the law, ethnology and culture of the countries that she visited. An account of Miss Hamlyn may be found, under the title 'The Hamlyn Legacy', in volume 42 of the published lectures.

Miss Hamlyn bequeathed the residue of her estate on trust in terms that, it seems, were her own. The wording was thought to be vague, and the will was taken to the Chancery Division of the High Court, which, in November 1948, approved a scheme for the administration of the trust. Paragraph 3 of the scheme, which follows Miss Hamlyn's own wording, is as follows:

> The object of the charity is the furtherance by lecturers or otherwise among the Common People of the United Kingdom of Great Britain and Northern Ireland of the

knowledge of the Comparative Jurisprudence and Ethnology of the Chief European countries including the United Kingdom, and the circumstances of the growth of such jurisprudence to the Intent that the Common People of the United Kingdom may realise the privileges which in law and custom they enjoy in comparison with other European Peoples and realising and appreciating such privileges may recognise the responsibilities and obligations attaching to them.

At present, there are eight trustees:

From the outset, it was decided that the objects of the trust could be best achieved by means of an annual course of public lectures of outstanding interest and quality by eminent lecturers, and by their subsequent publication and distribution to a wider audience. The first of the lectures was delivered by the Rt Hon. Lord Justice Denning (as he then was) in 1949. Since then, there has been an unbroken series of annual lectures published until 2005 by Sweet & Maxwell and from 2006 by Cambridge University Press. A complete list of the lectures may be found on pages x to xiv. In 2005, the trustees decided to supplement the lectures with an annual Hamlyn seminar, normally held at the Institute of Advanced Legal Studies at the University of London, to mark the publication of the lectures in printed book form. The trustees have also, from time to time, provided financial support for a variety of projects that, in various ways, have disseminated knowledge or promoted, to a wider public, understanding of the law.

This, the seventy-first series of lectures, was delivered by Professor Sir John Baker at the University of Cambridge, the University of Reading and Senate House, University of London. The board of trustees would like to record its gratitude to John Baker and also to the three venues that generously hosted these lectures.

AVROM SHERR
Chair of the Trustees

THE HAMLYN LECTURES

In 1983, at the end of the thirty-fifth series, Lord Hailsham expressed confidence that 'in 2018 (or thereabouts) Miss Hamlyn's seventieth lecturer will be preparing to deliver his own series of lectures'. That must have seemed very far in the future, but it has indeed now come to pass, and it has been my privilege to make this contribution to what is now a venerable collection. Underlying Lord Hailsham's remark was the concern that new ways would have to be found of carrying out Miss Hamlyn's intentions, as the law of this country receded further from her understanding of it. Certainly, in common with most of the previous lecturers, I have had to adopt a free interpretation of her stipulations. Her will provided for 'the furtherance by lectures . . . of the knowledge of the comparative jurisprudence and ethnology of the chief European countries . . . and the circumstances of the growth of such jurisprudence . . .', with a view to demonstrating to the general public ('the common people') the superiority of our law. Although she indicated that comparison was to be made with other 'European peoples', few of my precursors have tried to tackle legal history from a comparative, let alone an ethnological, perspective. I hope it was not too far ultra vires for me to attempt a different kind of comparison, for which I can find no precedent. I have sought to say something about the jurisprudence and legal system of England, and the circumstances of its growth, from a comparative angle but by making a comparison across time rather than space.

Comparison over time can tell us at least as much about where we are now as the kind of ethnological comparison over space proposed by Miss Hamlyn; and it may also assist a reciprocal understanding of the past. Historians often like to think that they study the past in isolation, with protective social distancing, uninfected by preconceptions picked up in today's world. Sometimes, however, they make comparisons with the present covertly, while pretending not to; and sometimes they do it inadvertently. In truth, if only through the limitations of language, comparison is unavoidable. Insofar as historical scholarship involves the study of change over time, or just the differences due to time, it must deal with the evolution of ideas, sentiments and institutions which keep their old names as they mutate in reality. Our understanding of former societies and modes of thought can therefore be enhanced, rather than distorted, by occasionally venturing to discuss the longer-term changes – and also the continuities – more openly.

I have spent much of my career working on the sixteenth century, and so it seemed natural to choose the long reigns of two admired queens four centuries apart. The world of the first Elizabethans[1] is sufficiently different from our own, while being at the same time organically connected with it, to have made this an intriguing and challenging exercise. Some

---

[1] To avoid circumlocution, I have throughout used the word 'Elizabethan' (unless with qualification) to refer to the period of Elizabeth I (1558–1603).

features of the Elizabethan legal world are already well known, but others, particularly in relation to public law, have had to be exhumed from long-dormant manuscript materials. Several major differences, some striking resonances and perhaps even a few potential lessons emerge from the comparison.

Miss Hamlyn's will spoke of 'this country', almost certainly meaning England, though the Chancery Division saw fit to reword it as 'the United Kingdom'. Since there was no United Kingdom in the time of the first Elizabeth, I have had to limit myself to the original intent. With respect to another aspect of that intent, it will be evident from some contemporary passages cited at the end of Chapter 2 that our Elizabethan forebears were as eager as Miss Hamlyn was to compare the happy state of the English with the misery of those less fortunate 'European peoples' who lived outside the common law. For practical reasons, however, I have not attempted to assess how right or wrong they were with regard to the multifarious continental legal systems of the sixteenth century, and certainly not to make any comments on the European laws of today.

This book goes into more detail than the lectures as delivered in November 2019, but it does not pretend to be a comprehensive outline of the legal history of either Elizabethan period. I have confined it to some salient features that lend themselves to comparison, and tried to avoid too much technicality. In that connection, I am grateful to my wife Liesbeth for her valuable comments on the draft lectures. I also acknowledge the helpful comments received at an early stage from the anonymous referees. Quotations from law-French texts have been translated into English, and original

English texts have been transposed into modern spelling with modern punctuation, even when taken from printed editions. I have nevertheless provided full references, many of them to unpublished Elizabethan manuscripts, for those who wish to know my sources.

Unless otherwise stated, all books cited here or in the footnotes were published in London.

Att.-Gen.	Attorney-General
B. & M.	J. H. Baker and S. F. C. Milsom ed., *Sources of English Legal History: Private Law to 1750* (2nd edn by Sir John Baker, Oxford, 2010).
Baker, *Collected Papers*	Sir John Baker, *Collected Papers on English Legal History* (Cambridge, 2013), three volumes.
Baker, *Magna Carta*	Sir John Baker, *The Reinvention of Magna Carta 1216–1616* (Cambridge, 2017; reissued in paperback 2018).
Briggs Report (2016)	Lord Justice [Sir Michael, now Lord] Briggs, *Civil Courts Structure Review: Final Report* (2016).
Brooks, *Pettyfoggers and Vipers*	C. W. Brooks, 'Pettyfoggers and Vipers of the Commonwealth': The 'Lower Branch' of the Legal Profession in Early Modern England (Cambridge, 1986).
Burrows, *Thinking about Statutes*	A. Burrows, *Thinking about Statutes: Interpretation, Interaction, Improvement* (Hamlyn Lectures: Cambridge, 2018).

CB	chief baron of the Exchequer
Ch.	chapter (in this book)
CLJ	*Cambridge Law Journal*
Co. Inst.	Sir Edward Coke, *Institutes of the Laws of England (1628–44)*, four volumes. The first volume (the commentary on Littleton's *Tenures*, 1st edn, 1628) is cited as Co. Litt. Quotations are here modernised.
Co. Litt.	See Co. Inst.
Co. Nbk	Edward Coke's manuscript notebooks and commonplace, BL MSS. Harley 6686A-B, 6687A-D. An edition of the cases from 1572 to 1600 is in preparation for the Selden Society.
Co. Rep.	*The Reports of Sir Edward* Coke, first published in French in eleven separate parts (1600–15), with two posthumous volumes in English translation (1658–9). Quotations are here translated.
CP 40	Public Record Office, plea rolls of the Court of Common Pleas.
CUL	Cambridge University Library
Dyer	Sir James Dyer, *Ascuns Novel Cases* (1585; 1586 new style). Quotations are here translated.

Dyer's Notebooks	*Reports from the Lost Notebooks of Sir James Dyer*, ed. J. H. Baker (109–10 Selden Soc., 1994–5). References in Roman numerals are to the introduction in vol. i.
Dyson, *Justice*	J. [Lord] Dyson, *Justice: Continuity and Change* (Oxford, 2018).
Emmison, *Elizabethan Life: Disorder*	F. G. Emmison, *Elizabethan Life: Disorder* (Essex Record Office Publications no. 56, Chelmsford, 1970).
Fleetwood, *Discourse*	[W. Fleetwood], *A Discourse upon the Exposicion & Understandinge of Statutes*, ed. S. E. Thorne (San Marino, CA, 1942). Unknown to Thorne, this had first been printed at the end of Fleetwood's *Justice* (1658). Quotations are here modernised.
Genn, *Judging Civil Justice*	Dame Hazel Genn, *Judging Civil Justice* (Hamlyn Lectures: Cambridge, 2010).
Hailsham, *Hamlyn Revisited*	[Q. Hogg], Lord Hailsham, *Hamlyn Revisited: The British Legal System Today* (Hamlyn Lectures, 1983).
Hake, *Epieikeia*	E. Hake, *Epieikeia: A Dialogue on Equity in Three Parts*, ed. D. E. C. Yale (New Haven, CT, 1953). Quotations are here modernised.

Hawarde	J. Hawarde, *Reportes del Cases in Camera Stellata 1593–1609*, ed. W. P. Baildon (1894). An edition of the only known manuscript, now in the Carl H. Pforzheimer Library, University of Texas at Austin, MS. 36.
HLS	Harvard Law School Library, Cambridge, MA
IELH (5th edn)	Sir John Baker, *An Introduction to English Legal History* (5th edn, Oxford, 2019).
KB 27	Public Record Office, plea rolls of the Court of King's Bench.
Kesselring, *Mercy and Authority*	K. J. Kesselring, *Mercy and Authority in the Tudor State* (Cambridge, 2003).
Lambarde, *Charges*	*William Lambarde & Local Government: His 'Ephemeris' and Twenty-Nine Charges to Juries and Commissions*, ed. C. Read (Ithaca, NY, 1962), pp. 153–89.
Lambarde, *Ephemeris*	*William Lambarde & Local Government: His 'Ephemeris' and Twenty-Nine Charges to Juries and Commissions*, ed. C. Read (Ithaca, NY, 1962), pp. 67–149.
Laws, *The Common Law Constitution*	Sir John Laws, *The Common Law Constitution* (Hamlyn Lectures: Cambridge, 2014).
LI	Lincoln's Inn library, London
LK	Lord Keeper of the Great Seal

OHLE, vi	Sir John Baker, *Oxford History of the Laws of England*, vol. vi (1483–1558) (Oxford, 2003).
PC 2	Public Record Office, Registers of the Privy Council.
Plowd.	E. Plowden, *Les Comentaries ou Reports* (1571; second part 1579). Quotations are here translated.
Proc. Parl.	*Proceedings in the Parliaments of Elizabeth I*, ed. T. E. Hartley (Leicester, 1981, 1995), three volumes.
Scarman, *English Law – The New Dimension*	Sir Leslie Scarman, *English Law – The New Dimension* (Hamlyn Lectures, 1974).
Sedley, *Lions under the Throne*	Sir Stephen Sedley, *Lions under the Throne: Essays on the History of English Public Law* (Cambridge, 2015).
sjt	serjeant-at-law
Smith, *De Republica*	Sir Thomas Smith, *De Republica Anglorum* (1583). This was written in about 1565.
Sol.-Gen.	Solicitor-General
SP 12	Public Record Office, State Papers (Domestic), Elizabeth I.
Star Cha. Rep.	*Star Chamber Reports: BL Harley MS. 2143*, ed. K. J. Kesselring (List & Index Society, Kew, 2018).
tr.	translated, translation

YB	Year Books, Edw. III to Hen. VIII. Passages are translated from the latest black-letter edition (1679–80).
Zander, *The State of Justice*	M. Zander, *The State of Justice* (Hamlyn Lectures, 2000).

Printed law reports are cited by the standard abbreviations currently in use, which may be found in P. Osborn, *A Concise Law Dictionary for Students and Practitioners* (12th edn, 2013).

1

The English Legal System under Elizabeth I

I have lived through one Elizabethan age – so far – and spent part of my career time-travelling in the other. I can still dimly remember the euphoric optimism in the 1950s greeting the new Elizabethan age, and it has certainly proved as transformational a period in the nation's history as that of the first Elizabeth. Both queens have been greatly admired, and their loving subjects have seen changes beyond all imagination when they acceded to the throne. Their reigns are separated by an enormous distance of time. In theory, though, England was subject in both periods to the same common law. One does not need to be a historian to appreciate that this is the kind of theory which borders on fiction. After four centuries of evolution, the queen's courts and their proceedings look very different. But the theory does have a basis in truth. What it means is that there has been no sudden jurisprudential break, no Justinian or Napoleon, no Lenin or Mao, to disturb the legal continuity in England between the sixteenth century and the present. Elizabethan cases can still be cited, if they are relevant to some current question and have not been overruled or overtaken by later cases or statutes, though in the nature of things this is now rare.[1] Likewise, Elizabethan

---

[1] E.g. *Wood* v. *Ash* (1586) Godb. 112 (ownership of lambs born to leased sheep) was followed in *Tucker* v. *Farm and General Investment Trust Ltd*

statutes are still law if they have not been repealed, though most of them have been. The law actually is the same law, if we understand the word 'same' in the way that the present writer is the same John Baker as the boy of that name who was at primary school when the queen was crowned, even though there is little discernible similarity between the two entities and not one molecule remains of the earlier being. It is quite possible to be the same organically and yet to evolve and to grow, and also (eventually) to decline.

Although the common law of the two Elizabethan periods is the same law, in that sense, it has certainly grown much older. Whether that means it is more advanced or more decrepit, or just ageing gracefully, is a question which properly belongs neither with history nor with law. But perhaps the present experiment in comparative law may qualify as an approximation to the kind of enquiry which Miss Hamlyn wished to encourage. It might be objected that the sixteenth century is too remote from us to merit such attention. But we still learn and draw inspiration from the works of Shakespeare, even though the language and social context have moved on, because so much of the human experience is timeless. Tudor legal language does not usually match Shakespeare's, it is true, and it is a barrier to the uninitiated;

[1966] 2 QB 421, being the only previous English authority. For other modern citations see *Anon.* (1584) Ch. 2, n. 119; *Heydon's Case* (1584), Ch. 3, n. 17; *Rooke's Case* (1598), Ch. 3, n. 84; and *Semayne's Case* (1602), Ch. 2, n. 72. *Pinnel's Case* (1602) 5 Co. Rep. 117 is well known from textbooks on contract and has been cited in the Court of Appeal more than once in the present reign.

and yet the law which governs everyone's lives should surely be as interesting to us as war, intrigue and dynasties.

The Queen's Courts

The survey had best begin with the legal system. For the Elizabethans it was a medieval inheritance, and the concept of 'due process' – developed from Magna Carta – seemingly rendered it immune to alteration. In reality, there had been considerable alterations over the preceding century, mostly achieved by accretion or circumvention, without abolishing anything. There had long been three central common-law courts in Westminster Hall, the reason for which need not be explained here. The Common Bench (or Common Pleas) was historically the most important for civil purposes, though the King's Bench (as it was usually known) was gaining ground by offering more advantageous remedies.[2] The Exchequer was still principally a revenue court, assisted in relation to feudal revenue by the relatively new Court of Wards and Liveries. Alongside them were the Court of Chancery, no longer an extraordinary tribunal but a burgeoning court of equity; the Star Chamber, now in its heyday as an extraordinary court for civil disputes;[3] and the Court of Requests, notionally a court for poor people but increasingly concerned (like all the others) with real property.

---

[2] *IELH* (5th edn), pp. 48–52. King's Bench (more rarely Queen's Bench) was an informal name because in records it was 'the queen's court held before the queen herself'.

[3] I.e. civil in substance. In principle, 'every suit in the Star Chamber is for the queen': *Drywood* v. *Appleton* (1600) 5 Co. Rep. 48 (tr.).

There were no appeals in the modern sense, but the King's Bench could reverse Common Pleas judgments for errors on the face of the record, and after 1585 it was possible for King's Bench judgments to be similarly reviewed in a statutory Court of Exchequer Chamber.[4]

Counting cases in any of these courts is problematic for technical reasons, but in 1558 there were probably at least 10,000 cases commenced each year in the two benches alone, rising to around 20,000 by the end of the reign.[5] That is more than the figure for the Queen's Bench Division today. The number of Chancery cases was considerably smaller than the figure for the Chancery Division today,[6] though the present jurisdiction is too different from that of the Elizabethan Court of Chancery to be meaningfully compared.[7] However, there

---

[4] 27 Eliz. I, c. 8; first proposed in 1581: *Proc. Parl.*, i. 532. It had nothing to do with the Court of Exchequer but met in the conveniently large chamber. Exchequer judgments could be reversed in what a medieval statute called the Council Chamber (also, de facto, the Exchequer Chamber).

[5] Brooks, *Pettyfoggers and Vipers*, p. 51 (cf. *Lawyers, Litigation and English Society since 1450* (1998), p. 11), calculated that there were 13,300 cases 'in advanced stages' in the two benches in 1580, and 23,453 in 1606. Yet it was stated by a contemporary that 13,500 writs were issued in 1569, and almost twice that number by 1584: ibid. 76, 304; BL MS. Lansdowne 47, fo. 122. These figures are difficult to reconcile, because very few cases reached 'advanced stages' and many were commenced without writ.

[6] W. J. Jones, *The Elizabethan Court of Chancery* (Oxford, 1969), p. 304 n. 1, estimated that around 1,600 cases were commenced annually in 1600. In 2014 around 24,000 cases were commenced in the Chancery Division: Royal Courts of Justice Tables, published online by the Ministry of Justice.

[7] The majority of cases in the Chancery Division now are either in the Companies List (over 20,000 in 2008; just over 9,000 in 2014) or in the

was no County Court then, as we know it. Since actions for as little as 40s. – equivalent to between £300 and £1,000 today[8] – went to Westminster Hall, a true comparison would have to include today's County Court. Over one and a half million suits are commenced in the County Court every year,[9] seventy times the 1600 figure, whereas the population is only seventeen times the size. On the other hand, there is an unknown but enormous figure for the number of small claims which went to the myriad local jurisdictions, such as borough courts, manorial courts and ancient county courts, which still flourished in the Tudor period. Then, as now, only a tiny proportion in any court proceeded as far as a trial,[10] the great majority being merely uncontested steps in the process of debt collection. Even allowing for that, what must strike us as remarkable today is that all the trials and legal arguments in

Insolvency List (nearly 19,000 in 2008; around 7,000 in 2014). The peak in 2008 reflected the financial crisis. Another large part of today's business concerns intellectual property.

[8] The Currency Converter 1270–2017 on the National Archives website suggests that £1 in 1560 ≡ £233 today, while £1 in 1600 ≡ £138. The Bank of England Inflation Calculator suggests that £1 in 1560 ≡ £502 today, while £1 in 1600 ≡ £300. Halfway between these two, MeasuringWorth.com gives the corresponding figures as £355 and £219.

[9] The figure for 2015–16: *Briggs Report* (2016), p. 172. Only 50,638 resulted in hearings. In 2014 the county courts (created in 1846) were merged into a single County Court. It has nothing to do with counties. And its judges, now called circuit judges, do not go on circuit.

[10] Modern statistics fluctuate wildly. Between 1960 and 1990 the number of trials in the Queen's Bench Division fell from around 3,000 to nearer 500, representing 0.5% of suits commenced: Genn, *Judging Civil Justice*, pp. 33–5. In the County Court the proportion is only 0.03%: previous note. Figures for Elizabethan trials have not yet been ascertained.

common-law cases commenced in the central courts were dealt with by a mere ten to twelve judges, who also despatched all the most serious criminal cases at the assizes and the Old Bailey. Only forty judges were appointed during the entire reign. With three exceptions, they served till death, since there were no regular pension arrangements.[11] We now have over a hundred judges of the High Court at any one time, and over a thousand sitting in the County Court.

The courts in Westminster Hall sat for only around 100 days a year. Another fifty to sixty days were spent by the judges travelling on assize, a burdensome role which could leave them out of pocket.[12] The judges on circuit not only delivered the gaols but also conducted jury trials in civil cases begun in the two benches. Hardly any cases were tried in Westminster Hall, where the full courts sat. The usual procedure was to try issues of fact in the county where the cause of action arose, by a jury drawn from that county.[13] This system was crucial to the administration of justice, since it enabled cases to be tried within ready reach of the parties, witnesses

[11] Only one, John Clench, retired with a pension. By 1602, aged sixty-seven, he was so decrepit that he was unable to venture out of Suffolk: Yale Law School MS. G.R29.15, fo. 31. John Southcote was discharged in 1584, aged around seventy-four; he died in 1585. For Robert Monson's dismissal in 1580 see Ch. 5, n. 22.

[12] The allowance given to each pair of judges for 'the diets and charges of themselves, their assistants, servants and horses' ranged from £5. 14s. to £7. 2s. 8d. *per diem*: BL MS. Lansdowne 53, fo. 198 (1587); MS. Lansdowne 78, fo. 93 (1595). Catlin CJ complained in 1574 to Lord Burghley that this was insufficient: BL MS. Harley 6991, fo. 78.

[13] London cases were tried at the Guildhall, since there were no assizes in London.

and jurors. And it was relatively inexpensive to manage. There were no dedicated court buildings. The judges would sit in the castle or town hall, if there was one, or sometimes in a ramshackle court set up in the open air. Any inconveniences of the latter were offset by its being more salubrious than a packed courtroom with the ever-present risk of gaol-fever.[14] Trials were short, and there was no question of adjourning a hearing overnight. It would not have been possible to complete the circuit if trials had lasted more than half an hour on average. Even so, it was common to sit beyond sunset in order to get through the calendar.[15] The parties themselves were not allowed to give evidence, and the number of witnesses in most cases must have been small. Although counsel were allowed to conduct civil trials, direct evidence for the extent of their involvement in routine cases is sparse. There was enough work for Edward Coke at the height of his fame as a barrister to earn £80 at a single assizes, but he was exceptional;[16] indeed, he will feature prominently throughout this book.[17] Counsel seem not to have received trial briefs

---

[14] At Oxford's 'Black Assize' in 1577 both judges (Bell CB and Serjeant Barham) and hundreds of others died; at Exeter in 1586 Flowerdew B and eight JPs died; and in 1598 Beaumont J and Serjeant Drew both died of gaol fever caught on the Northern circuit.

[15] *Withers* v. *Drewe* (1599) Co. Nbk, BL MS. Harley 6686B, fo. 347 (tr.: 'the justices of assize are used to sit after the setting of the sun'). There was similar pressure at the Old Bailey. Serjeant Fleetwood reported that on 2 July 1585 he sat there from 7 a.m. to 7 p.m.: BL MS. Lansdowne 44, fo. 113.

[16] Holkham Hall 8014, endpaper (1587).

[17] Edward Coke (1552–1634), 'famous utter-barrister of the Inner Temple' (BL MS. Add. 25196, fo. 121v, tr.), was de facto leader of the Bar by the mid-1580s;

from attorneys at this date, since they were expected to draw briefs themselves from oral instructions.[18] There were no piles of lever-arch files, storage boxes or bulging trial bundles. If documents were put in evidence, they were likely to be single records, deeds or letters patent; and if anything turned on their wording, they could be copied into a special verdict and discussed later. In what must have been a longer than average trial at Nottingham assizes in 1584, the evidence consisted of court rolls, an exemplified verdict, a Chancery exemplification, a deed of conveyance, and eight witnesses, some of whom had apparently deposed written evidence upon interrogatories in the Star Chamber.[19] The common-law courts did not themselves take depositions or order the disclosure of private documents.

Although the Chancery could be asked to compel the production of title-deeds for use in a court of law, a suit for discovery was not aimed at producing heaps of documents. The Chancery was, nevertheless, foremost in the network of parallel jurisdictions which, while serving justifiable purposes in principle, caused much delay and harassment in practice. An action at law was very often met by suits in the Chancery and the Star Chamber, either seeking equitable relief or attempting to impeach the evidence; there might be parallel actions or cross-actions in the other two courts of common

in 1592 he became Sol.-Gen. and in 1594 Att.-Gen., being knighted by James I in 1603; he was CJCP 1606–13 and CJKB 1613–16, when he was dismissed.

[18] This remained so as late as 1640: Baker, *Collected Papers*, i. 65.

[19] Nottinghamshire Archives, DD/4P/79/8: 'A breviate for Howley More [Holymoor]'. This brief, a disorganised aide-memoire, was seemingly written by one of the parties.

law, or even in the same court; and after judgment there might be further actions involving other parts of the same property, or different parties (such as lessees or servants), with essentially the same issue. This was seen as a grievance, but it was difficult to see how to stop it. In 1599 Egerton LK cited an old precedent of punishment by the Star Chamber for suing in two forums, saying that it would be a good practice to follow; but there is no evidence that this happened.[20] One case concerning a disputed title was said to have been before all six courts at Westminster between 1556 and 1585, when it was still litigious.[21]

Legal Argument and Decision-Making

An important feature of the assize system was that in a civil case the trial judge did not give judgment, since he was merely a commissioner to take the verdict and return it to the court where the case began. The court of first instance, whether of King's Bench, Common Pleas or Exchequer, was not (as now) the single trial judge but a bench of three or four judges sitting 'in banc' in Westminster Hall.[22] This central court was fully

---

[20] BL MS. Add. 35947, fo. 179, referring to *Swadell's Case* (1506). For Egerton's transcript of the case see 75 Selden Soc. 45.

[21] Burghley Papers, BL MS. Lansdowne 44, fo. 44. The case concerned the queen's title to St Lawrence's Hospital, Canterbury, which had been bought by Serjeant Lovelace but was claimed to be 'concealed land'.

[22] Nevertheless, the reports sometimes mention judges' absences in the Chancery or Star Chamber, or on grounds of illness. It was not unknown for a single judge to sit in banc: e.g. CUL MS. Ff.2.14, fo. 23 (Gawdy J, 1598); BL MS. Add. 25203, fo. 409 (Fenner J, 1601). But it was then usual to adjourn for further argument.

insulated from the fact-finding process at the assizes. The parchment memory on which it relied deliberately excluded the evidence, since that was for the jury alone to assess. Unless a point of law could be taken on the Latin words entered on the roll, judgment followed automatically from the verdict. There was no need in routine cases for the judges to give reasons for such judgments, since they had no decision to make.

In medieval times most legal argument had taken place in banc before trial, in the course of framing the question to be tried in the country; once that had been done, the die was cast and it was all up to the laymen. But it had become usual by the second half of the sixteenth century for the trial to take place first, upon pleadings drawn up in writing out of court, and for any point of law arising from the facts to be argued after the trial. This was effected by a motion in arrest of judgment, which was an attempt to persuade the court in banc that judgment should not be entered despite a verdict for the plaintiff. Usually it had to be founded on the facts as summarised in the enrolled pleadings, fictions and all; but the Elizabethan judges facilitated the procedure by allowing parties to settle a 'special' verdict, so that detailed agreed facts could be placed on the record.[23] The result of all this was that legal argument now usually focused on facts which had already been established, instead of hypothetical propositions considered before trial. Even so, it was still constrained by the Latin formulae required for starting actions, defining the

---

[23] This had once been permissible only in special cases, but there were no restrictions by 1586: *OHLE*, vi. 400–3; *IELH* (5th edn), p. 91 n. 71.

issue, and recording all the steps in the action up to the trial and verdict.[24]

Motions after trial dominate the law reports of this period, although they were used in only a small proportion of cases. What made them interesting to the profession is that they were argued by counsel and called for reasoned resolutions of points of law or procedure. Not that the judges were keen to decide difficult questions. Deliberative delay was an accepted feature of the system. If there was any division of opinion on the bench, the parties might have a long wait before judgment was given, if indeed it ever was, and their counsel might have to return for repeated re-argument. For instance, in a case of 1593 an exasperated Coke Sol.-Gen. prayed a final resolution, saying 'he would not move it any more, inasmuch as he had moved it seventeen or eighteen times already'.[25] In really controversial cases, all twelve judges of the three central courts could be convoked in one of the Serjeants' Inns for a full-scale debate, which would be keenly observed and reported. In such cases it was not uncommon for the judges to divide more or less evenly, often with robust intransigence. Even so, unanimity was the goal. The judges reserved the right to withhold judgment indefinitely if they could not reach a consensus.[26] Since there was no court of appeal, it was thought unsafe to give judgment when the

---

[24] See also 'Law and Procedure' in Ch. 2.

[25] *Woodward's Case* (1593) BL MS. Harley 6745, fo. 17 (tr.). This time the court condescended to make up its mind.

[26] See e.g. *Stocke* v. *Lawraunce* (1587) HLS MS. 16, fo. 380 (tr.: 'the justices would not rule the case so as to make it a precedent either way, for it is a difficult case'); *Hulme* v. *Jee* (1593) BL MS. Harley 6745, fo. 21v (tr.: 'the

judges themselves were not fully agreed. While it was clearly wrong to delay judgment through indolence,[27] knowingly to risk a mistake was considered to be worse than indecision.[28] The judges were well aware that they were potentially creating precedents.[29] That was a particular concern when it came to deciding important questions of law which affected people generally.[30] In a case of 1594 Coke Att.-Gen. was asked by the court to go away and think of a better solution to the complex problem before them, since 'it touches the entire common weal'.[31] In other cases the judges withheld judgment for the

judges would not give their opinions ... Fenner thought it would be a hard case').

[27] Sir Nicholas Bacon said there would be 'great loss of time' if judges were neglectful, and that it would make suits more costly than they were worth: BL MS. Harley 396, fo. 37 (speech to a new judge, 1577).

[28] Baker, *Magna Carta*, pp. 181–4.

[29] See D. Ibbetson, 'Authority and Precedent' in *Law and Authority in British Legal History 1200–1900*, ed. M. Godfrey (Cambridge, 2016), pp. 60–84, at 69–83.

[30] E.g. *Verey v. Carew* (1597) Moo. 535 at 537 (tr.: '[Popham CJ] would be advised ... because the case was common and weighty ... throughout the realm'); *Collins v. Hardinge* (1598) BL MS. Hargrave 7B, fo. 146v, *per* Popham CJ (tr.: 'this is a notable case, and a case which much concerns the state of the common weal, and therefore it is meet that it should be argued now, and later also'); *Mildmay v. Mildmay* (1601) LI MS. Maynard 66, fo. 168, *per* Anderson CJ (tr: 'It is not the case of Sir Anthony and Humphrey Mildmay alone, but the case of the whole land').

[31] *Downhall v. Catesby* (1594) BL MS. Hargrave 7A, fo. 24 (tr.: 'Popham [CJ] said, "It is good to be advised as to this case, for it is of great consequence, not only between the parties, but it touches the whole common wealth; therefore, Mr Attorney, see if you can show us a better course" ... Coke: "So I will, if you will give me some time to do it." Popham: "You have it."').

different purpose of achieving equity, contrary to strict law, though it is impossible to know how normal this was.[32]

One way out of an impasse was to decide the case on some flaw in the pleadings and thereby avoid the substantive point altogether. Avoiding a decision could, on occasion, have the positive merit of concealing from people what the law was. For instance, in 1583 Anderson CJ tried to persuade the plaintiff in *Capel's Case* to reach a compromise with the defendant, 'because the precedent would touch all purchasers in England'; the parties declined the invitation, and it was ten years before the judges in the Exchequer Chamber finally brought themselves to sacrifice the old learning and put the law right.[33] In another leading case of 1586 the queen herself sought to induce a settlement, on the footing that it would affect many purchasers and it was sometimes better to let sleeping dogs lie.[34] One might have thought that purchasers would rather know the validity of what they were buying. When it came to litigation, however, a compromise was usually the best course for parties of comparable merit, and it incidentally helped discordant judges out of their predicament.

A different solution which became common in the 1590s was to tolerate majority judgments. This did not put an

---

[32] E.g. *Botye* v. *Brewster* (1595) BL MS. Harley 6745, fo. 105v; *Anon.* (1599) BL MS. Add. 25199, fo. 2 (inf. Dr P. Turner). For the enforced remission of damages see *IELH* (5th edn), p. 92. Another example is the decision of the Common Pleas in 1596 not to award costs where only nominal damages were recovered in trespass: BL MS. Hargrave 7A, fo. 194v. This anticipated a statute of 1601: 43 Eliz. I, c. 6; below, n. 93.

[33] *Hunt* v. *Gateley* (1581–92) *IELH* (5th edn), p. 302.

[34] *Chudleigh* v. *Dyer* (1586) Ch. 2, n. 157.

end to open dissents, which were often reported. One Common Pleas judge, Thomas Walmsley, was an habitual doubter and dissentient; an irritant, perhaps, but respected for his unwavering intellectual integrity.[35] But he was not alone to blame for the change of practice, since the Common Pleas on several occasions gave judgment despite a dissent by Anderson CJ.[36] The majoritarian principle bewildered some observers when they noticed that the prevailing opinion in the Exchequer Chamber might be that of a minority of the entire judiciary.[37] Their dismay no doubt strikes us as equally strange, but that is because we are accustomed to all judicial decisions being made by a minority; there is no mechanism today for ascertaining the majority opinion of the whole judiciary, or even of the Court of Appeal.

If and when judgment was eventually obtained, counsel might still have to press for some indication of the prevailing reasons, and the judges were not always willing to oblige.[38] The new Exchequer Chamber was particularly

---

[35] Baker, *Collected Papers*, i. 466–7. According to his epitaph, 'His inside was his outside. He ne'er sought | To make fair shows of what he never thought.'

[36] E.g. *Clerke* v. *Penruddocke* (1598) Co. Nbk, BL MS. Harley 6686A, fo. 288v; Coke edited this detail out of the printed report in 5 Co. Rep. 100. (The puisnes were upheld on a writ of error.) Other examples are *Bower* v. *Perman* (1599) MS. Harley 6686B, fo. 343; *Sparke* v. *Sparke* (1599) MS. Lansdowne 1061, fo. 33.

[37] *IELH* (5th edn), p. 148. In 1599 the King's Bench confirmed that a majority in the court of error was all the statute required: James Whitelocke's reports, CUL MS. Dd.8.48, p. 87.

[38] See e.g. *Shelley's Case* (1581) B. & M. 163 at 168; *Earl of Pembroke* v. *Berkeley* (1595) BL MS. Hargrave 7A, fo. 117v; MS. Hargrave 356, fo. 131;

complained of in the 1590s for not giving reasons in public as other courts did.[39] However, in difficult cases the judges usually made elaborately prepared speeches, doubtless from written notes. In ordinary cases in banc they spoke extempore. In neither kind of case was any official record made of what they said. The judgment was minuted on the roll in the short form, 'Therefore it is considered that the plaintiff recover' his property, his debt or his damages, without reasoned explanation. It was nevertheless useful to know what had been argued, and what principles the judges had agreed off the record. For this information the profession was dependent on unofficial reporters, of whom there were many, from judges down to students,[40] all writing in abbreviated law-French hieroglyphics. The lawyers' version of French was no longer spoken in court but had developed over the centuries to provide a useful form of shorthand in which to summarise arguments delivered in English. Only two extended series of reports were published in print in the second half of the sixteenth century, those of Edmund Plowden (1571) and Sir James Dyer (1585/6), though at the end of the reign Edward

Callard v. *Callard* (1596) MS. Hargrave 7A, fo. 21 (tr.: 'Coke asked the reason of this, for his learning. Popham [CJ]: "Be content."'); *Downhall* v. *Catesby* (1598) MS. Add. 35947, fo. 123v (Coke again). The reasons given in *Slade's Case* (1602) B. & M. 460, at 474, were extremely brief.

[39] Sir Thomas Heneage to Lord Burghley concerning *Finch* v. *Throckmorton* (1592): BL MS. Lansdowne 38, fo. 14; *IELH* (5th edn), p. 148.

[40] Student reporters stood at the sides of the court. See W. Burton, *The Description of Leicester Shire* (1622), p. 271 ('I was then standing by, being a reporter in the same court': referring to *Corbet's Case* in the Common Pleas, 1600).

Coke saw the first three volumes of his *Reports* through the press (1600, 1602). All of these were printed in black-letter type in French; Roman type was reserved for Latin. Many other series circulated within the profession in manuscript, sometimes posthumously, as in the case of Bendlowes[41] and the unprinted residue from Dyer's notebooks,[42] and sometimes contemporaneously, as when Coke allowed access to his own notebooks in the 1580s and 1590s. The genre was of variable quality and no innate authenticity, a defect which justified a greater flexibility than today in the treatment of precedents. Coke himself dealt with an unprinted report cited by opposing counsel by saying it was 'as easy to deny as to affirm'.[43] Although the judges were free to ignore or overrule decisions which they considered wrong,[44] especially when they had not been unanimous, it was easier to reject the reports instead, on the footing that opinions they disagreed with were probably misreported.

In theory, according to Francis Bacon, there were three sources of common law: usage, inference from statutes declaring what the common law was, and – in third place, be it noted – 'the

---

[41] William Bendlowes (d. 1584), whose reports circulated widely but were not printed until the seventeenth century, and then inaccurately.

[42] They belonged at one time to Coke. What survives was printed in *Reports from the Lost Notebooks of Sir James Dyer*, ed. J. H. Baker (109–10 Selden Soc., 1994–5).

[43] Godb. 84 (1586) ('As to the reports which are not printed, vouched by Tanfield, *eâdem facilitate negantur quâ affirmantur*').

[44] See e.g. Ducke's reports, BL MS. Hargrave 51, fo. 19v (tr.), where Anderson CJ 'denied the book, and said that even if his authority was but yesterday he would not obey it'.

authorities and books of our law'.[45] This hierarchy made philosophical sense, since written materials could serve only as evidence of the unwritten law, which was usage, and public statutes had evidential priority over private writings. But in reality the books of cases, ancient and modern, were the principal source of the common law and were routinely cited to 'prove' the common law, though not conclusively.[46] And it is from the same books that we are able to ascertain today, as best we can, the law of the sixteenth century.

Accessibility of the Law

The workings of the law were more accessible and familiar to the Elizabethan public than they are today,[47] and there was more general awareness of the content of the law.[48] There were no newspapers yet, but most people became involved in the law from time to time, whether in local

---

[45] *Corbin's Case* (1599) BL MS. Lansdowne 1061, fo. 30. He was arguing against Coke Att.-Gen.

[46] For the treatment of decided cases as authority in this period see I. Williams, 'Early-Modern Judges and the Practice of Precedent' in *Judges and Judging in the History of the Common Law and Civil Law*, ed. P. Brand and J. Getzler (Cambridge, 2011), pp. 51–66; Ibbetson, 'Authority and Precedent' (n. 29 above).

[47] See 'The Operation and Public Perception of the Law' in Ch. 4. This seems to have been true throughout Europe: G. Vermeesch, 'Reflections on the Relative Accessibility of Law Courts in Early Modern Europe' (2015) 19 *Crime, History & Societies* 53–76.

[48] J. Walter, 'Law-Mindedness' in *Law, Lawyers and Litigants in Early Modern England: Essays in Memory of Christopher W. Brooks*, ed. M. Lobban, J. Begiato and A. Green (Cambridge, 2019), pp. 164–84 (mostly referring to the early seventeenth century).

courts,[49] or in ecclesiastical courts, or through attendance at the assizes or quarter sessions of the peace. They could be involved not only as parties but as witnesses or jurors, or indeed as spectators. At the sessions, it was common for statutes to be read out for the information of the many people present.[50] Assize towns were always crowded when the judges were sitting, and gaps in jury panels were frequently made up from those standing around. One of the merits of the assize system was that no one engaged in litigation, or in criminal prosecutions, had to travel outside their county to reach court. Indeed, it was one of the complaints against the High Commission and the provincial councils that they forced people to attend at great distances from their places of residence, and then often adjourned them without prior notice and required them to remain in attendance from day to day; this was thought oppressive and contrary to basic ideas of justice. Bishops sought to defend the High Commission in this regard by countering that the common law was worse, because litigants had to attend at Westminster.[51] But this only showed their ignorance. In civil cases,[52] everything at Westminster was done by attorneys and counsel; there was

---

[49] For an example see J. H. Baker, 'Personal Actions in the High Court of Battle Abbey 1450–1602' (1992) 51 CLJ 508–29; reprinted in *Collected Papers*, i. 442–65. Most of the adult male population of Battle must have been plaintiffs or defendants in the court at one time or another.

[50] Walter, 'Law-Mindedness' (n. 48 above) at p. 166.

[51] Baker, *Magna Carta*, p. 136.

[52] Criminal cases did not normally reach the central courts at all but were dealt with at assizes and quarter sessions or (if minor) by local magistrates. Bail was widely available except in the most serious cases.

no essential need for a lay presence there. No one who could afford a lawyer was forced to take time off work, or to lose his employment, unless he became entangled in courts of equity or religion. But who *could* afford a lawyer? The principal obstacle to accessible justice is cost. And here we find one of the most remarkable contrasts with the present day. Although there was no shortage of popular complaints about fees,[53] and there were doubtless hidden costs, official court fees were generally modest. In local courts, they were extremely modest: a shilling might finance a simple case from beginning to end.[54] Lawyers were not normally involved, and the non-professional attorneys received only a few pence for their trouble.[55] Yet even in the central courts the costs were usually manageable. Each step taken in legal proceedings required a fee to the appropriate clerk, but only a few pence or shillings at a time. A King's Bench *latitat*, which was used to commence most actions there, cost five shillings and a penny,[56]

---

[53] Thomas Lupton's dialogue between Siuqila (Aliquis backwards) and Omen (Nemo backwards) has the former complain, 'Our courts are so costly . . . that poor men cannot (nor many wise men dare not) begin or prosecute the law': *Siuqila Too Good to Be True* (1580), p. 117. Siuqila suggested that a suit might cost as much as £100, but this is not borne out by English evidence.

[54] Plaintiffs in the Battle Abbey court usually recovered costs of 10d. or 11d.: Baker, *Collected Papers*, i. 456.

[55] In the Manchester court leet in 1562 they were not allowed to charge more than 2d.: *Court Leet Records of the Manor of Manchester in the Sixteenth Century*, ed. J. Harland (Chetham Soc., 1864), pp. 95–6.

[56] The fee had increased from 3s. 5d. since the time of Henry VIII: BL MS. Lansdowne 44, fo. 9v (1585). One writer (next note) blamed the judges, 'who have appropriated unto themselves fees out of the process'.

which was comparatively expensive: twice as much as a Chancery subpoena. Most other writs cost about sixpence,[57] though the sheriff might have to be paid two shillings for returning them, and somewhat more for either expedition[58] or delay.[59] The clerks' fees for entering pleadings and judgments ranged from a shilling for a brief entry to multiples of ten shillings for whole rolls.[60] Costs were routinely awarded, even in heavy cases, at around £10 to £20.[61] For instance, in the much reported case of *Butler* v. *Baker* (1587–95), which was argued on points of law arising after trial in ten separate terms, the taxed costs were only £7. 19s.[62] *Slade's Case* was argued on three occasions in Serjeants' Inn and the Exchequer Chamber by

---

[57] R. Robinson, 'A brief and reformed collection of the several fees and charges usually defrayed or paid into divers courts and offices' (1597) BL MS. Harley 6806, fos. 116v–17. A contemporary table of fees in JHB MS. 109 includes 5s. 1d. for a *latitat* and 6d. for a *capias*.

[58] BL MS. Harley 6806 (previous note), at fo. 118v. If a debtor was in custody, the sheriff was entitled to a shilling in the pound: *Sulyard's Case* (1597) BL MS. Harley 4552, fo. 133v. But the sheriff was answerable for the whole debt if the debtor escaped: Ch. 3, n. 67.

[59] The attorney Roger Dowdeswell noted in 1593 that 'the sheriff may be bribed beforehand to feign some great business to delay the return of the venire facias': JHB MS. 865, fo. 9.

[60] Robinson (n. 57 above) said the prothonotaries charged 12d. for common pleadings, 2s. for a plea pleaded by a serjeant, 2s. for a judgment, and 10s. for a whole roll. The fees listed in JHB MS. 109 (c. 1600) include 12d. for common pleadings, 2s. for an ejectment, and 3s. 4d. for a declaration in an action on the case.

[61] Defence costs were much lower since the defendant did not have to pay for any writs. In *Buttes* v. *Averd* (1590) KB 27/1312, m. 48, a clerk of one of the under-clerks of the King's Bench sued to recover 32s. 4d. laid out in defending four King's Bench actions.

[62] *Butler* v. *Baker* (1587–95) KB 27/1303, m. 368; 3 Co. Rep. 25.

Edward Coke (the attorney-general) and Lawrence Tanfield for the plaintiff, and yet the taxed costs were only £10.[63] Such figures are equivalent to around £2,000 to £4,000 in today's money. They were, therefore, lower than present-day High Court costs, which typically range from about £5,000 to £100,000, and in heavy cases more. Libel cases afford the most striking contrast. The cost of a libel action nowadays can soar up to £1 million, several thousand times more than high-profile defamation cases under Elizabeth I, even though the issues are essentially the same. In the prominent libel case of *Boughton* v. *Bishop of Coventry* (1583), the costs were only £15,[64] though occasional awards can be found which are inexplicably low or high.[65] Simple debt cases were far less expensive. They cost typically about £2 and were well within the reach of ordinary people.[66] The few surviving bills of costs confirm the plea-roll evidence that

---

[63] *Slade* v. *Morley* (1595–1602) KB 27/1336, m. 305; 4 Co. Rep. 91. The figure was nevertheless high in proportion to the damages (£16).

[64] KB 27/1412, m. 717. Cf. *Bulkeley v. Wood* (1589–91) KB 27/1311, m. 381 (reported in 4 Co. Rep. 14) in which the costs were £22. 1s. In another slander case Sir Richard Bulkeley recovered £10 damages but £20 costs: *Bulkeley* v. *Gwyn* (1591) KB 27/1316, m. 640.

[65] E.g. *Earl of Leicester* v. *Heydon* (1571) Plowd. 400; the earl was represented by Fleetwood, Plowden and Manwood, and the costs were only £4. In *Lord Abergavenny* v. *Waller* (1577) KB 27/1260, m. 497 (defamation), a mere £2 was awarded. Yet the enormous sum of £66 was awarded in the property case of *Weltden* v. *Elkington* (1578) CP 40/1344, m. 1226; Plowd. 516.

[66] In *Ayshe* v. *Alford* (1599) CP 40/1620, m. 106, an attorney sued for £8. 8s. fees and costs in respect of four actions of debt, though he did not indicate how far they had proceeded; in three of them his term-fees of 40d. exceeded the outlay.

low figures were usual.[67] Even allowing for unknown hidden costs, they are evidence that litigation at the highest level was, by the standards of today, inexpensive.

No doubt even such low fees were beyond the means of the truly indigent. But paupers could, by the discretion of the court, have 'process and counsel of charity': that is, they could have writs and legal services without paying fees at all.[68] Little is known of these suits *in forma pauperis*, which rarely leave a trace in the plea rolls[69] or the law reports.[70] Poor plaintiffs were expected to use the Court of Requests if possible,[71] and the

---

[67] Bills of costs are more frequently found after 1605, when it became a legal requirement to present them to clients: 3 Jac. I, c. 17. Two Common Pleas examples from 1590 are in Folger Shakespeare Library, Washington, MS. L. d.974, 975. They include 3s. 4d. for the attorney's term-fee; 4d. for a rule of court; 11s. 4d. for a copy declaration of 17 folios; 6d. to record the defendant's appearance; 2s. 4d. to the gaoler; and 4d. for a copy of the jurors' names.

[68] YB Trin. 15 Edw. IV, fo. 26, pl. 2; 11 Hen. VII, c. 12; 23 Hen. VIII, c. 15. For the duty of counsel to assist the indigent without fee see N. Ramsay, 'The Fees They Earned: The Incomes of William Staunford and Other Tudor Lawyers' in *English Legal History and Its Sources*, ed. D. Ibbetson, N. Jones and N. Ramsay (Cambridge, 2019), pp. 139–58, at 157–8.

[69] E.g. *Austin* v. *Twyne* (1595) KB 27/1334, m. 348d, is marked 'in forma pauperis' in the margin.

[70] E.g. *Hughes* v. *Whetley* (1599) BL MS. Add. 25201, fo. 160v (tr.: 'I was appointed of counsel with the plaintiff *in forma pauperis*'); in the record, KB 27/1355, m. 201d, Hughes is not described as a pauper (he recovered £10 damages and £3. 10s. costs); *Anon.* (1599) BL MS. Harley 1575, fo. 53v (tr.: 'Williams sjt moved for various poor men'). As to Chancery see *Anon.* (1603) Cary 24. Note also Star Cha. Rep. 28, 106, 111, 126.

[71] *Sir Anthony Cooke's Case* (cited in 1601) LI MS. Maynard 66, fo. 154v (suits *in forma pauperis* allowed in the Common Pleas only in real actions, which were not within the jurisdiction of the Requests); *Anon.* (1612) 98 Selden Soc. 398, no. 191, *per* Lord Ellesmere LC. As to the Requests and equity courts see

very poorest classes were unlikely to have cases suitable for the central royal courts anyway; the nascent system of poor relief, managed by the local magistracy, did not come with justiciable rights. What is known, however, is that yeomen, husbandmen and lesser tradesmen were regular litigants at Westminster, and we sometimes find even servants and labourers suing for debts in the Common Pleas. In Hilary term 1563 alone, 293 actions were brought by yeomen and 57 by husbandmen, or their personal representatives; many more were brought by tradesmen, including a few with such lowly callings as chapman, drover, hackney-man, labourer, pedder, serving-man and trougher.[72] One of the defendants that term was Matilda Hamlyn, executrix of a Devonshire yeoman.[73] It may be supposed from the small sums of money claimed in other cases – often the bare minimum of forty shillings – that there were many other litigants of low status whose descriptions are not given. Christopher Brooks estimated that three-quarters of all litigants in the superior courts were below the rank of gentleman.[74] Even humbler people were engaged constantly in lesser local courts.[75]

A. Prossnitz, 'A Comprehensive Procedural Mechanism for the Poor: Reconceptualizing the Right to In Forma Pauperis in Early Modern England' (2020) 114 *Northwestern University Law Review*, 1673–1722.

[72] CP 40/1207, 1208, as indexed by Vance Mead on the Anglo-American Legal Tradition website. Social categories are blurred: e.g. one of the husbandman plaintiffs was *alias* of Clifford's Inn, gentleman (CP 40/1207, m. 380).

[73] CP 40/1207, m. 466 (suit for £100). On m. 71, John Hamlyn sues a husbandman for trespass to his house in Devon.

[74] Brooks, *Pettyfoggers and Vipers*, pp. 59–60 (70–80 per cent).

[75] See, e.g., Baker, *Collected Papers*, i. 442–65; C. Harrison, 'Manor Courts and the Governance of Tudor England' in *Communities and Courts in*

The relatively low cost of going to law, by today's standards, seems not to have been attributable either to factual simplicity or to comparatively low stakes. Litigation about real property often involved substantial assets and complex issues concerning family settlements, mortgages and the construction of letters patent. It is true that there was little corporate litigation, most of the big corporations having been dissolved by Henry VIII, though the monasteries and their former privileges – and the terms of the patents whereby they were granted out – still raised endless questions for the courts. The new trading companies were not yet much in evidence in the common-law courts.[76] Nevertheless, commercial cases between individual merchants might involve bills of exchange, marine insurance, charterparties or elaborate accounts, and there was sometimes an international element.[77] A case of 1581 reported by Coke concerned one of a series of partnership and factoring arrangements, including transactions in North Africa with goods worth over £5,000

Britain 1150–1900, ed. C. Brooks and M. Lobban (1997), pp. 43–59; Brooks, *Pettyfoggers and Vipers*, ch. 3 and pp. 96–101.

[76] An example is *Societas Mercatorum ad detegenda Nova Commercia* v. *Ferneley* (1594) KB 27/1330, m. 1104d (*assumpsit* to pay for twenty barrels of train oil). The plaintiffs were the Muscovy Company, as renamed in their charter of 1566; the train oil came from whaling.

[77] E.g. *Hermann Langerman* v. *Filippo Corsini* (1574) KB 27/1251, m. 20 (debt for £1,500 by a steelyard merchant for breach of a charterparty for a voyage to Livorno); *Marino De Gozzi* v. *Hans Blomert* (1599) BL MS. Add. 25201, fo. 159v; MS. Add. 35947, fo. 203 (a bankrupt owing £6,000). Many commercial disputes were dealt with informally or by specialist tribunals: see e.g. G. Rossi, *Insurance in Elizabethan England* (Cambridge, 2016).

(well over £1 million today in real terms, or £3.8 billion if one follows the 'economic share' index).[78] We do not know what the costs were, because no verdict or judgment is entered on the roll, but there is no reason to suppose that they would have been out of line with those in other cases.[79]

The Legal Profession

The modest level of court fees was matched by lawyers' fees, which likewise contrast markedly with those of today. This is especially remarkable, considering that the law had long been a calling of social importance. Popham CJ said in 1594 that 'in most parts of England there are more gentlemen's houses, and those of continuance, raised and advanced by that profession alone than by all the other professions that can be spoken of'.[80] He was referring to the Bar. But there were many kinds of lawyer, ranging from the lord chancellor or lord keeper of the great seal,[81] the judges and the law officers down to the humblest attorneys.

---

[78] *Dawbny v. Gore* (1581) Co. Nbk, BL MS. Harley 6687B, fo. 306v; KB 27/1277, m. 330; KB 27/1281, m. 66. For the complex dealings behind this case, involving the Jewish merchant Isaac Cabessa, see T. S. Willan, *Studies in Elizabethan and Foreign Trade* (Manchester, 1959), pp. 127–30.

[79] Cases in the Chancery and the Star Chamber could be very complex and more expensive. For the ramifications of an involved Star Chamber case arising from liabilities exceeding £1,000 see E. Kadens, 'New Light on *Twyne's Case*' (2020) 94 *American Bankruptcy Law Journal* 1–84. Coke reported the case at length: *Att.-Gen. v. Twyne* (1602) 3 Co. Rep. 82.

[80] Speech to the new serjeants at law, Poph. 43–5, at 44.

[81] Sir Nicholas Bacon LK procured a statute in 1563 confirming that the offices were the same: 5 Eliz. I, c. 18. The only Elizabethan chancellors were Sir Thomas Bromley (1579–87) and Sir Christopher Hatton

There were 200 or so attorneys active in 1558, all of them sole practitioners.[82] They had low overheads and were not the big earners which City solicitors have become, unless they were fortunate enough to obtain one of the major clerkships of the central courts[83] or some other lucrative administrative position. Though already claiming to be gentlemen ex officio, socially they were typically closer to the country yeoman or middling townsman.[84] They practised from their town-houses in the country, and in term-time would stay in one of the inns of chancery at low cost, taking their meals in commons there. Every attorney claimed a fixed fee of forty pence a term per client for his engagements in any of the central courts, and the same for attending the assizes, however much business was involved.[85] In recognition of inflation, this was twice the medieval fixed fee of twenty pence,[86] but it was

---

(1587–91), a court favourite who (though a member of the Inner Temple) seems not to have been a barrister.

[82] For the number see Brooks, *Pettyfoggers and Vipers*, p. 29; J. Baker, *The Men of Court 1440–1550* (2012), i. 20 n. 62.

[83] Richard Brownlowe, chief prothonotary of the Common Pleas 1590–1638, was said to be worth £7,000 a year by the time of his death: Baker, *Collected Papers*, ii. 682, 788, 791.

[84] Baker, *Men of Court* (n. 82 above), i. 37–40; Brooks, *Pettyfoggers and Vipers*, pp. 274–5. The average attorney earned around £40 to £100 per annum: Brooks, op. cit. 234–5.

[85] E.g. *Peter v. Barbye* (1596) KB 27/1337, m. 315 (Common Pleas attorney retained as a solicitor in the King's Bench in 1590 at 40d. a term); *Ayshe v. Alford* (1599) CP 40/1620, mm. 105, 106 (multiples of 40d. claimed by a Common Pleas attorney for soliciting suits in the Chancery, King's Bench and Star Chamber, and attendance at the assizes).

[86] YB Mich. 31 Hen. VI, fo. 8, pl. 1, at fo. 9; *OHLE*, vi. 123. An attorney who charged 20d. a term in 1532 was charging 40d. by 1540: *Ayer v. Stonard*

still under £100 in today's money, and it seems to have covered all the work required in attending the client, gathering evidence, suing out process, instructing counsel, and presence in court, regardless of the time actually spent, though a charge could be made for preparing documents. There were no billable hourly rates. At least, nothing of that kind is found in bills of costs until a century later. The Elizabethan attorney was certainly not purring in plush luxury.

A sixfold increase in litigation since the beginning of the sixteenth century,[87] coupled with the growing importance of the conciliar and revenue courts, gave rise to a fourfold increase in the number of attorneys during Elizabeth's reign,[88] and a contemporaneous increase in the number of barristers,[89] with a perceived lowering of professional standards in consequence.[90] There was a general belief that the multiplication of lawyers was contributing to the rise in litigation, especially unnecessary litigation. According to Holinshed,

(1543) KB 27/1126, m. 113 (retainer of 1532); *Ayer v. Bussey* (1542) CP 40/ 1114, m. 653 (the same John Ayer). The new rate was invariable throughout Elizabeth's reign.

[87] Brooks, *Pettyfoggers and Vipers*, p. 53 and ibid., ch. 4.

[88] Brooks, *Pettyfoggers and Vipers*, p. 113, counted 313 in the Common Pleas in 1580 and around 800 in 1606. There were also 236 King's Bench attorneys in 1606, many of them clerks and under-clerks in the chief clerk's office. The total therefore reached 1,000.

[89] Baker, *Collected Papers*, i. 63.

[90] See E. Hake, *A Touchestone of the Present Time* (1574), sig. B4v: 'the name of an attorney in the Common Place is nowadays grown into contempt, whether in respect of the multitude of them, which is great, . . . or whether in respect of their loose and lewd dealings, which are manifold, or whether in both those respects, I know not'.

until the 1580s one would not have heard more than two or three civil cases at the assizes, 'whereas now a hundred and more ... are very often perceived, and some of them for a cause arising of sixpence or twelvepence: which declareth that men are grown to be far more contentious than they have been in time past'.[91] In 1585 the chief justices were ordered to report to Lord Burghley on the number of attorneys in each shire, since their superfluous number had led to a proliferation of suits for 'very small and frivolous causes'.[92] That problem was partly solved in 1601, by forbidding the recovery of costs in trivial cases.[93] But all attempts to restrain the number of attorneys and improve their qualifications proved fruitless.[94]

The tide of litigation also swept in a new species of lawyer or paralegal: the common solicitor. Soliciting causes was an activity supposedly restricted to attorneys and barristers, or permanent employees, since assisting in litigation without a legal qualification or a contract of service amounted to the criminal offence of maintenance.[95] But the increase in contentious business had given rise to a penumbral class of legal assistants who had not been sworn and admitted as attorneys, let alone called to the bar. Edward Hake, an attorney, described

---

[91] R. Holinshed, 'The Description of England' in *Chronicles* (1587), p. 156. The figures were doubtless exaggerated. For a more comprehensive analysis of the possible causes see 4 Co. Inst. 76.

[92] BL MS. Lansdowne 46, fo. 90.

[93] *Proc. Parl.*, iii. 344, 410, 434; 43 Eliz. I, c. 6.

[94] Bills to this effect were presented in the Commons in 1581, 1589 and 1601: *Proc. Parl.*, i. 535–6, 537, 540; Brooks, *Pettyfoggers and Vipers*, p. 138; below, at n. 98.

[95] J. H. Baker, 'Solicitors and the Law of Maintenance 1590–1640' (1973) 31 *CLJ* 56–80; *Collected Papers*, i. 75–103.

them in 1574 as 'an huge rabble of petty-practisers or rather pettifoggers dispersed into every corner of the realm'.[96] The higher authorities were equally vituperative. In 1596 Egerton LK denounced solicitors in the Star Chamber as 'caterpillars of the common wealth', and promised to 'abolish and extirpate' them. Five years later, in the queen's presence, he told the Lords that the queen earnestly wished a law to be made against 'pettifoggers and vipers of the common wealth, prowling and common solicitors that set dissension between man and man'.[97] A bill 'to restrain the multitude of common solicitors' was duly read; it provided that 'no person whatsoever shall solicit, other than those which will do the same without fee or reward', saving that barristers and attorneys could solicit in all courts. It did not reach the statute-book.[98] In the event, extirpation was not thought practicable or sensible. The solution, found early in the next reign, was control rather than abolition, by making solicitors officers of the Court of Chancery. The best the courts could do for the time being was to try to stop them recovering their fees.[99]

---

[96] E. Hake, *A Touchestone of the Present Time* (1574), sig. B4v. Coke complained about conveyances drawn by men unlearned, and wills 'intricately, absurdly and repugnantly set down by parsons, scriveners and such other imperites': *Le Second Part des Reportes* (1602), preface, sig. ¶v.

[97] Hawarde 45–6; *Proc. Parl.*, iii. 305 (30 Oct. 1601). Hayward Townshend MP, a newly called barrister, used the expression 'prowling solicitors' in the same Parliament: ibid. 334.

[98] *Proc. Parl.*, iii. 361 ('also proviso that no mechanical person shall be made an attorney, viz. broker, scrivener, miller, smith etc.').

[99] *Germyn v. Rolle* (1593) CP 40/1514, m. 744; reversed in (1596) KB 27/ 1331, m. 365; Baker, *Collected Papers*, i. 90–1. This was an action for £19.

Since these Elizabethan pettifoggers prowled in the shadows, it is impossible to guess how many there actually were. Although the perception behind the official antagonism was that they fomented unnecessary litigation, there is no clear evidence that they added to its cost.[100]

Learned counsel – barristers, benchers and serjeants[101] – were more expensive than the inferior kind of lawyer, but even so, following medieval tradition, they usually received a fixed fee of a gold angel (ten shillings) for any court appearance or conference. If the standard fee was considered non-negotiable, it might explain the revival of the Classical notion that, as members of a liberal profession, barristers did not serve for lucre; the fee was merely a non-contractual honorarium.[102] In reality, though, counsel would not be expected to appear or offer advice without an angelic prompting in advance. Counsel were typically drawn

18s. 5d. for a solicitor's charges. There was an even longer declaration by the same solicitor, for charges incurred since 1579 amounting to £79. os. 4d., in *Germyn* v. *Ellyott* (1591) CP 40/1491, m. 1159 (7 membranes); this action was discontinued.

[100] John Germyn (previous note) claimed a term-fee or 'salary' of 40d., the same as an attorney.

[101] For the meaning of these categories see *IELH* (5th edn), pp. 167–75. In *Johnson* v. *Smith* (1584) BL MS. Harley 4562, fo. 32, Coke argued that an attorney could properly give counsel as a 'professor del ley', without committing maintenance; but this was disputed and there is no decision.

[102] It was said in 1586 that a gentleman would be 'more easy in fees ... than ten advocates of base and ungentle stock': J. Ferne, *The Blazon of Gentrie* (1586), p. 93. The honorarium notion has not been definitely traced before 1615: Baker, *Collected Papers*, i. 67. It endured until 1991.

from the lesser landed classes and were better educated than the attorneys. At the higher levels they were men of impressive talent. Whether or not they attended university first, they were graduates of the prestigious and expanding university in the inns of court, a great school of common law, far more vibrant and influential than the smaller law faculties at Oxford and Cambridge, which taught only Roman law and produced few graduates or publications of any juristic significance. In the 1570s and 1580s there were around 800 members of the inns of court keeping term,[103] of whom over 120 were barristers and about 50 were benchers.[104] There was a similar number in the eight satellite inns of chancery,[105] making the legal university not much smaller than the entire University of Cambridge at that time.[106] Some idea of the total size may

---

[103] In 1574 there were 759 residents in term-time: SP 12/95/91; *Calendar of Inner Temple Records*, i. 468–9. Returns sent to Lord Burghley in 1577 show around 200 in each inn, though the return for Gray's Inn is missing: BL MS. Lansdowne 106, fos. 92, 96, 97v. Gray's Inn was the largest in 1574 with 220 resident members, and in 1585 was said to have 274: BL MS. Lansdowne 47, fo. 113.

[104] Ibid. In 1602 Coke said that there were about twenty readers (or benchers) and sixty barristers in each house: 3 Co. Rep., preface. His figure of 160–180 'young gentlemen' in each house is comparable with that for 1574.

[105] For these inns see J. Baker, *The Inns of Chancery 1340–1640* (2017). The number of residents ranged from 40 (Thavies Inn) to 140 (Staple Inn): 1577 return (n. 103 above); BL MS. Lansdowne 47, fos. 118, 120–121; *The Admissions Registers of Barnard's Inn*, ed. C. W. Brooks (12 Selden Soc. Suppl. Series, 1995), pp. 161–7.

[106] There were 1,950 students at Cambridge in 1597: Burghley Papers, BL MS. Lansdowne 84, fo. 227.

be deduced from the fact that at the end of the reign there were about 200 admissions a year at the inns of court alone.[107] In term-time the more serious students were all interacting as members of a residential law school, with moots of various kinds on a daily basis, and in the two learning vacations (Lent and Summer) three or four weeks of lectures and discussions, often with the judges present. Learning and controversy flourished in this 'third university of England' before its slow decline in the seventeenth and eighteenth centuries. An Elizabethan aura pervades the inns to this day. It is a visible presence in Gray's Inn, where portraits of Elizabeth I, Lord Burghley and Sir Francis Walsingham watch over the benchers on the high table.[108] Across the road, the frontage of Staple Inn (1586) remains a prominent Holborn landmark, and its little hall (a replica of the 1584 building destroyed by incendiary bombs) sits between a court and a garden retaining the atmosphere of an Elizabethan inn of chancery. The Middle Temple is equally conscious of its Elizabethan heritage. The great hall was completed in 1574, and was frequently used in the following decades for committees of the House of Commons. In 1578 it was graced by an impromptu visit from the queen herself, the first known royal visit to any of the inns of court.[109] The ceremonial cupboard

---

[107] There were 2,008 admissions between 1590 and 1599, and 2,283 between 1600 and 1609: W. R. Prest, *The Inns of Court 1590–1640* (1972), p. 11.

[108] Gray's Inn hall was rebuilt in 1557–60: W. Dugdale, *Origines Juridiciales* (3rd edn, 1680), p. 272. It was virtually destroyed in the Blitz but thereafter restored to its original appearance.

[109] BL MS. Add. 16169, fos. 15v–16; translated in 133 *LQR* 535–7. Unfortunately, a second-rate lecture was in progress before a depleted

in the hall there, traditionally believed to have been rescued from Sir Francis Drake's *Golden Hind*,[110] and the Inn's Molyneux globes from the 1590s, are enduring symbols of the spirit of exploration and discovery which characterised the age.

audience, and all were so taken aback by the queen's appearance that they were struck dumb.

[110] Drake was admitted to the Inner Temple (1582), though his exploits were not universally admired there: J. Baker, *An Inner Temple Miscellany* (2004), pp. 213–14.

2

The Elizabethan Common Law

At the same time as geography, science, literature and theology were being transformed, the common law was enjoying a creative period of its own. To Edward Coke it was the perfection of human reason, a religion as much as a science. As he urged his readers in 1602, 'next to thy duty and piety to God ... and thy honour to thy parents, yield due reverence and obedience to the common laws of England; for of all laws (I speak of human) these are the most equal and most certain, of greatest antiquity, and least delay, and most beneficial and easy to be observed'.[1] Antiquity did not, of course, mean that the law was static. Coke was devoted to the late-medieval law reports (the year books), but during Elizabeth's reign the cases in which he had immersed himself as a student in the 1570s were becoming remote from the real life of the law and required a kind of intellectual translation by the reader and a deft use of analogy.[2] If the law books of the later sixteenth century seem more accessible to the present-day lawyer than their fifteenth-century precursors, that is mainly a consequence of the procedural changes mentioned in

---

[1] 'To the Learned Reader', *Le Second Part des Reportes* (1602), sig. ¶iiij verso.
[2] For Coke's technique in reinterpreting precedents see S. E. Thorne, *Essays in English Legal History* (1985), pp. 223–38.

34

Chapter 1. They were more accessible to the law student of 1600 as well.

It was an important characteristic of the common law that it could change, and it sometimes did so with rapidity, branching out in new directions. But it was always a result of reasoned argument, one step at a time. That is what Coke and his contemporaries had in mind when they asserted that the basis of the common law was immemorial.[3] This claim was not, as old-fashioned historians were wont to suppose, the absurd delusion of an uninformed myth-maker. Coke knew far more history than most of his contemporaries. He was referring to the system, not the details. The origins of English law were truly lost in remote antiquity, but it was always being improved, for 'out of the old fields must spring and grow the new corn'.[4] Moderate change was not a break with the past but a necessary consequence of the process of refinement and reflection which brought the law ever closer to perfection. The Elizabethan common law proved fully capable of transformative leaps, as when the copyholder was brought within its protection, when perpetuity clauses in family settlements were struck down as obnoxious, or when wager of law by debtors was effectively laid to rest.[5] Such innovations were

---

[3] See e.g. *Le Huictieme Part des Reports* (1611), sig. §§4 ('the grounds of our common laws were beyond the memory or register of any beginning'); Baker, *Magna Carta*, pp. 223–6, 349–50.

[4] *Les Reports de Edward Coke* [part 1] (1600), sig. C.iiij, paraphrasing Chaucer. For Coke's approach to legal history see I. Williams, 'The Tudor Genesis of Edward Coke's Immemorial Common Law' (2012) 43 *Sixteenth-Century Journal* 103–23; Baker, *Magna Carta*, pp. 349–50, 443–6.

[5] Below, at nn. 77, 87–91, 104.

never opposed on the ground that legal doctrine was set in stone. That kind of inflexibility had gone with the Medes and Persians. The fundamental premises of the law were another matter.[6]

Law and Procedure

One respect in which reported arguments still resembled those of the medieval period is that they continued the tradition of addressing questions of form as well as substance. This seems strange to our more informal culture, though it was engrained in the legal mind of the Tudor period. For one thing, strict adherence to the old forms of writs, process and pleading was thought to be a requirement of the statutes of due process. You could not make a move if you were offside. However, the arguments as to form did not arise from an obsession with formality for its own sake. They were predicated on the logic of the nisi prius system. The judges at Westminster, where legal argument occurred, were not trying the case and could not take notice of any facts other than those admitted by both parties or found on oath by a jury. What facts they knew were therefore ascertained solely by construing the pleadings in which the factual dispute was framed or the special verdict (if there was one) in which additional facts were summarised; and both were couched in formalised Latin. If the issue for the jury was wrongly joined, perhaps because of a slip in language, then the facts found by the jury would be irrelevant and the court would be prevented from

---

[6] See the judicial interchange of 1591 noted in *IELH* (5th edn), p. 368 n. 111.

addressing the substance. For example, in a case of 1586, an action of account was brought against someone as bailiff of a shop, having the care and administration of all the wares within; the defendant pleaded that he was only an apprentice and not bailiff of the wares, and that he had put all the takings into the 'shop box'. The jury found for the plaintiff. Yet he failed to obtain judgment, because the pleadings had not reached an issue. The defendant had only denied that he was bailiff of the wares, which was not alleged, and had not pleaded as to the shop.[7] Such a mistake was not fatal because there could be a fresh trial with better pleadings or the plaintiff could bring a fresh action. Parliament had enacted in 1576 that no judgment following the verdict of a jury should be stayed by reason of any default in form, including false Latin, or for want of any writ.[8] But this was construed with some strictness. It did not help the plaintiff of 1586, since the defect there was one of substance.[9] Nor did it save a plaintiff who had

---

[7] *Gomersall v. Gomersall* (1586) KB 27/1293, m. 345; Co. Nbk, BL MS. Harley 6687D, fo. 18; Godb. 55; 2 Leon. 194.

[8] An Act for Reformation of Jeofails, 18 Eliz. I, c. 14. Formal objections before trial were restrained by 27 Eliz. I, c. 5. In the debate on this statute, Fleetwood complained of the trifling and vain pleading 'now used', and said he had known £100 of land lost by 'cunning pleading': *Proc. Parl.*, ii. 116.

[9] The plaintiff abandoned that part of his claim. A clerical error in the verdict as to another part of the claim was held to be cured by the statute, and auditors were appointed. But the case was so complex that, in the end, it went to arbitration: KB 27/1298, m. 251. Two years later, the King's Bench rejected a motion by Coke for a verdict to be amended for a clerical mistake, 'for then all verdicts may be prayed to be amended': *Mornington v. Try* (1588) Cro. Eliz. 111.

brought the wrong kind of writ;[10] but there again the plaintiff was free to start again with a better one.[11]

Coke made his name as a junior barrister taking technical points, of which he was a consummate master; but in later years he regretted what he saw as a decline since the time of Edward III.[12] On the better view, it was not good practice anyway, as a lord chancellor indicated in his exhortation to the new serjeants called in 1580: 'In all your pleadings seek not advantages to trip one of you the other by covin, or niceness in form of pleading, but have respect to the substance of the matter; set forth your causes simply and plainly; and, as you are of one profession, so lovingly and brotherly warn one another of anything mistaken or misconceived in pleading.'[13] It was a counsel of perfection rather than the daily reality. But, in practice, a considerable relaxation was coming about through the rise of actions on the case,[14] which were less formal than the older actions, and also the recognition that

[10] E.g. *Walcott* v. *Apowell* (1588) 5 Co. Rep. 36; 3 Leon. 206. See also *Barham* v. *Dennys* (1600) BL MS. Lansdowne 1065, fo. 66, *per* Anderson CJ (tr.: 'If it were not for the mischief that every clerk would invent a new form according to his own fancy, I would allow this form . . . but here there is an old form of writ in the Register, which ought to be followed').

[11] This happened in *Lord Cromwell* v. *Dennye* (1578) 4 Co. Rep. 12. Here the plaintiff misrecited the statute on which the action was brought (misreading *mensonges*, lies, as messages).

[12] Co. Litt. 303.

[13] Chancery Decree and Order Book, C33/61, fo. 189v, *per* Bromley LC. Similar remarks were made by Sir Nicholas Bacon LK in 1559: J. H. Baker, *The Order of Serjeants at Law* (1984), at p. 304.

[14] *Onley* v. *Earl of Kent* (1576) Co. Nbk, BL MS. Harley 6687D, fo. 918v, *per* Dyer CJ (tr.: 'No such prescribed form is requisite in actions on the case as in other writs'). Cf. *Slade's Case* (1597) B. & M. 460, 461, *per* Dodderidge.

special verdicts did not have to be as precise as pleadings because they were deemed to be spoken by laymen. At the same time, arguments as to the substantive law were becoming predominant. They were made in the same way as now, identifying the relevant principles, citing authorities to support them, considering possible extensions by analogy and distinguishing the precedents relied on by the other side. Something should now be said of the substance of the law.

Personal Liberty

Constitutional law was a concept yet to be named, and public law in a broader sense did not feature prominently in the books and lectures of the Elizabethan common lawyers. That does not mean that they were unfamiliar with what we have come to call human rights and the rule of law.[15] There was a sense of pride in English liberty under the common law. Slavery was unknown to English law, and it was said around 1570 – when someone was whipped for claiming to own a slave brought from Russia – that the moment anyone set foot in the realm, he was free.[16] The air of England was too pure for slaves to breathe.[17] Villeinage, a lesser form of unfree status, had disappeared without the need for abolition. The inns of court had long taught that it was odious, being 'absolutely contrary to liberty'; and liberty, it was said in Henry VIII's time, 'is one

---

[15] See further 'Public Law' in Ch. 4.

[16] *Cartwright's Case*, probably in the Star Chamber: Baker, *Magna Carta*, p. 35 n. 193.

[17] This was said in 1640 to have been the resolution in *Cartwright's Case*, but the words may have been a later paraphrase.

of the things which the law most favours'.[18] Socially meaningless but personally demeaning, villein status had been widely discontinued, either by disuse or because the lord's claims had been extinguished by agreement and by legal devices involving fictions. The last solvent villeins were manumitted in the 1570s,[19] though perhaps the current taste for genealogy will lead to the discovery of some stray survivors.

Women also were free, though not yet in every respect equal. The Church excluded women from ordination and from the universities, and there were no women in the inns of court. They could not serve in Parliament or on juries, or vote in parliamentary elections. On the other hand, they could own property in the same way as men,[20] could engage in trade and make contracts, and could sue and be sued in the courts, though once they married – which was a strong social and moral expectation[21] – they lost most of their legal autonomy

---

[18] Quotation in Baker, *Collected Papers*, ii. 884, from a moot in Gray's Inn.

[19] Baker, *Collected Papers*, ii. 885. Sir Thomas Smith wrote that there were so few villeins left that it was 'not almost worth the speaking': *De Republica Anglorum* (1583), p. 108.

[20] Their rights of inheritance were more restricted, in that a woman with a brother could not inherit real property. This was a disability partly shared with younger brothers. Women without brothers actually fared better than multiple younger brothers, since all sisters inherited as co-heirs. Sometimes land was settled in 'tail male' so as to exclude female heirs altogether; but entails could be broken when landowners wished to rearrange the succession.

[21] A town court in 1584 forbade single women to exercise trades, since it was 'to the great hurt of the poor inhabitants having wives and children, as also in abusing themselves with young men and others, having not any man to control them': *Court Leet Records of the Manor of Manchester in*

until they were widowed.[22] Family law was a matter for the ecclesiastical courts; but the Church's legal regime did not dissolve marriages, look after children or provide much relief for deserted or abused wives.[23] The received (male) view, which owed as much to the Bible as to the law, was that the husband was the wife's 'lord, keeper, head and sovereign'.[24]

Aliens, likewise, were free and entitled to the protection of the common law, provided they were lawfully present in the country. Entering and remaining in the country was not a right but a privilege controlled by the government. The Jews had been expelled in 1290, but Jewish merchants and others were admitted under letters of safe conduct. Gypsies and Jesuits were strictly banned by statute,[25] and other more limited group-expulsions were effected under the prerogative. In 1594 all unemployed Irish labourers were ordered to be sent back to Ireland;[26] in 1597 the Privy Council ordered black immigrant workers to be shipped back to Spain, on the ground that they

the Sixteenth Century, ed. J. Harland (Chetham Soc., Manchester, 1864), p. 157.

[22] As to widows, and lawsuits with female parties, see below, n. 146.

[23] For the rarity of alimony awards see R. H. Helmholz, Oxford History of the Laws of England, vol. i (Oxford, 2004), pp. 558–60. A bill to permit divorce on grounds of adultery was presented in the Commons in 1585 but lost without trace: Proc. Parl., ii. 91; cf. IELH (5th edn), p. 534.

[24] W. Shakespeare, The Taming of the Shrew (written c. 1590), act 5, scene 2.

[25] Gypsies: 1 & 2 Phil. & Mar., c. 4; 5 Eliz. I, c. 20 ('false and subtle company of vagabonds called Egyptians'). Jesuits and 'seminary priests': 27 Eliz. I, c. 2. The former were barred because of habitual criminality, the latter because of their missions to seduce the people from their obedience and depose the queen.

[26] TRP, iii. 134. Besides being vagabonds, some were reputed to have fought against the queen's forces in the north of Ireland.

were reducing the employment opportunities for Englishmen;[27] and in 1598 the Hanse merchants were expelled from London, in retaliation for the expulsion of London merchants from Germany.[28] But foreigners who were allowed to remain, whatever their race or nationality, were subject to and protected by the same law as the English. Although there were waves of popular resentment against immigrant workers, the concerted harassment of aliens was treated by the Star Chamber as sedition.[29] And to guard against xenophobic prejudice if they found themselves in court, aliens were entitled to a half-alien jury.[30] The only serious legal disability was that aliens could not invest in land. In affirming that this ban extended to leasehold investments (as opposed to personal residences or business premises), Popham CJ remarked in 1598 that, if it were not so, 'aliens could take leases of the greater part of the principal houses in the principal cities of England . . . and alienate them to other aliens, which would be perilous and to the great disadvantage of natural subjects'.[31]

---

[27] Baker, *Magna Carta*, p. 112. Again in 1601, a 'great number of niggers and blackamoors' were ordered to be sent back to Spain, being recent immigrants and 'mostly infidels': *Calendar of the Manuscript at Hatfield House*, xi. 569. Many black immigrants did settle, were baptised, and were treated as equals: see M. Kaufmann, *The Black Tudors* (2019).

[28] *Calendar of State Papers (Domestic) 1588–1601*, p. 13.

[29] *Att.-Gen.* v. *Short* (1593) Star Cha. Rep. 63, no. 493 (threatening Flemings and Frenchmen who were perceived to be depriving poor Englishmen of their livelihoods).

[30] *IELH* (5th edn), p. 501. Any foreigners would do. Dr Julius Caesar's slander action against the Florentine merchant Filippo Corsini was tried partly by Flemish jurors: BL MS. Lansdowne 1078, fo. 15 (1593).

[31] *Croft's Case* (1587) Co. Nbk, BL MS. Harley 6686A, fo. 304.

Religion was not yet free, and the Elizabethan attempt to find a middle way met with fierce resistance from both flanks. Some Roman Catholic opponents of the Elizabethan settlement became involved with treason after Pius V's bull of 1570, which purported to free them from their allegiance to the queen, and underground activities would lead directly to the Gunpowder Plot of 1604–5. Non-violent papists suffered from superficial religious profiling as a result, though judges and lawyers drew a clear distinction between unenlightened 'superstition' and plotting to overthrow the queen and the state.[32] Even a Roman Catholic archbishop from Ireland, imprisoned in the Tower for 'religion', could expect a fair trial in England on a serious sexual charge.[33] Parliament stiffened the treason laws in response to the new fears for the queen's life, and several Roman Catholics suffered the grievous consequences of association with dark forces. But there was a virtual cessation of burnings for heresy after the revolting scenes of Mary I's day. No Roman Catholic went to the stake after the break with Rome; the four deplorable executions in the time of Elizabeth I were all for Arianism. Private thoughts, as opposed to overt actions, were indeed now free.[34] Opposition to the religious settlement from the

---

[32] Baker, *Magna Carta*, pp. 126–33.

[33] *R. v. Creagh* (1577) LI MS. Misc. 488, p. 36. Richard Creagh, archbishop of Armagh, was accused of raping a girl of seven or eight who waited on him in prison. After a two-hour trial in the King's Bench, when the evidence appeared to be perjured, he was acquitted.

[34] Baker, *Magna Carta*, pp. 260, 365. Cf. W. West, *Second Part of Symbolaeographie* (1594), sig. H.vii ('In our law, thought is free from offence').

Puritan end of the spectrum was channelled into legal argument rather than treasonous plots. The so-called 'Puritan' lawyers – most of whom were in fact liberal Anglicans – were prominent in the reinvention of Magna Carta in the 1580s as a weapon of defence against the Elizabethan High Commission, which was thought to be straying too far beyond its original purpose towards authoritarianism.[35]

It was already an important constitutional axiom that the monarch could not alter the law. Though far from being a new idea, it became common currency and found broader applications after the Middle Temple reading by the Puritan barrister James Morice in 1578.[36] It meant that the queen could not levy taxes or take goods from her subjects without an Act of Parliament,[37] and Morice held more controversially that she could not grant a monopoly in a common trade or make any occupation 'altogether private unto a few'.[38] Three years later, Robert Snagge, a fellow Puritan member of the Commons and of the Middle Temple, gave the first known reading wholly on chapter 29 of Magna Carta.[39] For him, the main target was the coercive jurisdiction of the High

---

[35] Baker, *Magna Carta*, pp. 251–61, 270–5. The arguments enjoyed some success. Lord Treasurer Burghley agreed that the procedure for compelling people to incriminate themselves on oath (the hated oath *ex officio*) was 'too much savouring of the Romish Inquisition': ibid. 260 n. 57.

[36] Ibid., ch. 7.

[37] Morice's reading, BL MS. Add. 36080, fo. 256. Cf., in the same vein, his treatise on the oath *ex officio*: HLS MS. 120, at fo. 131.

[38] Ibid., fo. 251v. See further *Darcy* v. *Allen* (1602–3) 11 Co. Rep. 84; Baker, *Magna Carta*, pp. 311–23 (in which c. 29 was cited).

[39] Baker, *Magna Carta*, pp. 251–5.

Commission. But the new learning was not the exclusive property of these mildly subversive politicians. John Popham, another Middle Templar, argued as attorney-general in 1582 that, as a result of chapter 29, 'every subject born and begotten in the realm' had the privilege of inheriting the laws of the realm, an inheritance 'from which no subject ought to be barred'.[40] This set English law apart from the Civil Law, which was supposed to give the will of the prince the force of law.[41] It emboldened lawyers – not just the Puritan wing but also law officers of the Crown such as Popham and Coke, and even the judges – to draw the conclusion that the queen and her ministers could not, without statutory authority, grant commissions or set up any new form of tribunal or authority which impinged upon the common law by meddling with liberty or real property.[42] The principle met with some resistance, but it paved the way for the eventual extirpation of all such prerogative jurisdictions in 1641. And it prevented the Privy Council from introducing new penal laws by proclamation:[43] the power to legislate could be derived only from Parliament. Moreover, leaving aside certain powers which were regarded

---

[40] Ibid. 468.
[41] See the eulogy of c. 29 by William Fleetwood, another Middle Templar: Baker, *Magna Carta*, p. 246. In *Darcy v. Allen* (1602) Anthony Dyot of the Inner Temple said that the rule of Civil Law, *Voluntas regis est regula legis*, 'is not a rule of our law, where the king conducts himself according to the law': LI MS. Maynard 66, fo. 246 (tr.).
[42] The governing authority for this was *Sir John atte Lee's Case* (1368) 42 Lib. Ass. 5, which was frequently cited.
[43] See Ch. 2, at nn. 21–2; Baker, *Magna Carta*, pp. 151–4.

as absolute and non-justiciable – such as declaring war, conducting military operations,[44] making treaties, appointing ministers and judges, or summoning and dissolving Parliament[45] – the courts could both demarcate and review the exercise of the royal prerogative.[46] There was no suggestion that the courts could review the use of absolute prerogative power, when exercised within its limits, but they could set and define the limits.

The principal machinery for giving effect to the fundamental principles of constitutional monarchy was the writ of habeas corpus, which, in its newfound role, was an Elizabethan invention.[47] The first major precedent was set under Catlin CJ in 1565, following a dispute with the archbishop of York over a recusant imprisoned by the Council in

---

[44] This was, inter alia, the justification for martial law: Smith, *De Republica*, p. 44. In *The Earl of Essex's Case* (1600) Co. Nbk, BL MS. Harley 6686B, fo. 423v, it was held that the queen's informal instructions to a military commander overrode the terms of his commission under the great seal, because, in respect of the absolute prerogative, the ruler's will had the force of law. But the court did review the earl's conduct, and held that it was ultra vires his instructions.

[45] *Dyer's Notebooks*, pp. lv, 27. In 1566 the judges ruled that the queen could prohibit the discussion of matters of state because she had the power of prorogation and dissolution; but this was not accepted by the Commons and there were angry scenes in the House: ibid. 125. In 1593 an adjournment for three weeks was effected by Puckering LK without a commission: LI MS. Maynard 63(1), fo. 5.

[46] For the distinction between ordinary and absolute prerogatives see Baker *Magna Carta*, pp. 144–7, 183, 322–3. In *Darcy v. Allen* (1602) LI MS. Maynard 66, fo. 260, Fleming Sol.-Gen. said that the absolute prerogative was transcendent and indisputable.

[47] *Dyer's Notebooks*, pp. lxxvii–lxxxiii; Baker, *Magna Carta*, pp. 159–63.

the North.[48] Some other early beneficiaries of the procedure were Roman Catholic recusants and Puritans in trouble with the high commissioners,[49] and one of these cases established the privilege against self-incrimination.[50] As early as 1572, Edmund Anderson of the Inner Temple (later chief justice of the Common Pleas) made the link between habeas corpus and chapter 29 of Magna Carta,[51] a fruitful if unhistorical connection which would be developed by Coke as attorney-general.[52] The new remedy not only enabled judicial oversight of the High Commission, the Councils in the North and in the Marches, and the Court of Requests[53] but also gave the courts for the first time a means of reviewing governmental and quasi-judicial activities affecting personal liberty, including

---

[48] *Lambert's Case* (1565) KB 29/199, m. 31; Baker, *Magna Carta*, p. 159. Catlin CJ had been collecting precedents: R. Crompton, *L'Authoritie et Jurisdiction des Courts* (1594), fo. 79 (committal by Wolsey in 1518); Alnwick Castle MS. 475, fo. 95 (committals by Wolsey in 1521 and by Dr Stokesley in 1522).

[49] The first attempt to use it to liberate a prisoner of the High Commission led to conflict, when the commissioners re-arrested the person concerned: *Mytton's Case* (1565) KB 29/199, m. 31 (the same roll as Lambert's case); Baker, *Magna Carta*, pp. 159–60. Mytton had been imprisoned for hearing mass.

[50] *Lee's Case* (1568) ibid. 160; *Dyer's Notebooks*, p. 143. Lee, suspected of hearing mass, had refused to answer incriminating questions under oath.

[51] *Marshall's Case* (1572) BL MS. Hargrave 8, fo. 163; CUL MS. Hh.2.9, fo. 61; HLS MS. 1192, fo. 25.

[52] Especially in his memorandum of 1604, prompted by the high-handed behaviour of Lord Zouche as president of the Council in the Marches: Co. Nbk, BL MS. Harley 6686B, fos. 600–4v; Baker, *Magna Carta*, pp. 346–7, 500–10.

[53] Baker, *Magna Carta*, pp. 135–7, 155–70, 207–8, 270–311.

all penal and fiscal impositions which depended on imprisonment as a sanction. In the 1580s and 1590s Magna Carta was on everyone's lips, and the potential of chapter 29 was soon recognised by the judges as well – including the most conservative of them.[54] There were at least eight citations in the Common Pleas in the years around 1600.[55] According to a bencher of the Middle Temple in 1587, it was 'the most honourable, most reasonable, most indifferent law that any nation in the world hath, or that can be devised'.[56] Even the queen's chief minister of state, Lord Burghley – a student of law in his youth – was heard to enthuse in the Star Chamber about the precious heritage of Magna Carta, which 'being so hardly got, we ought not so easily to suffer . . . to be lost'.[57]

The judges were emboldened by the new trend to make a collective protest in 1591 about the abuse of imprisonment by haughty councillors who regarded their own word as law. It was then established that habeas corpus would lie to

---

[54] *Barham* v. *Dennis* (1599) Baker, *Magna Carta*, pp. 289–90, *per* Walmsley J; *Bate's Case* (1601) below, n. 59, *per* Walmsley J.

[55] Besides the two in the previous note, see *Paramour* v. *Verrall* (1597–1600) Baker, *Magna Carta*, pp. 489–94 (local custom); *Stepneth* v. *Lloyd* (1598) HLS MS. 105(4), fo. 29 (Requests); *Deane's Case* (1599) BL MS. Hargrave 7B, fo. 186 (London custom); *Anon.* (1599) HLS MS. 1004, fo. 44v (Requests); *Anon.* (1600) BL MS. Lansdowne 1065, fo. 12v (Requests); *Baker* v. *Rogers* (1601) Baker, *Magna Carta*, p. 292 n. 95 (High Commission).

[56] R. Crompton, *A Short Declaration of the Ende of Traytors and False Conspirators against the State* (1587), sig. E4v. See also Baker, *Magna Carta*, pp. 260–75.

[57] Baker, *Magna Carta*, pp. 268, 520. (He was not, however, contemplating review of the central government.) Cf. Glanville J's reference to Magna Carta in 1599 as 'so sacredly established': ibid. 290.

release any person imprisoned on the order of a minister or councillor unless – and this was a politically necessary reservation – the committal was sanctioned by the Council or by the queen in person.[58] Walmsley J, who had signed the memorial in 1591, denied even those two exceptions in a case of 1601 which has only recently come to light.[59] John Bate, a merchant who was later to feature in a well-known case of 1606,[60] had been imprisoned by the Privy Council for pulling out of a venture by the East India Company, and he sought release in the Common Pleas, where he had conveniently made himself a litigant. Walmsley J, presiding in the absence of Anderson CJ, said that the judges were sworn to administer justice equally to rich and poor and were 'not to obey a superior power which commanded a thing contrary to law', not even the queen in Council, for the law in Magna Carta bound the queen herself. The effect of chapter 29 was that 'a subject's person is always privileged against the king, so that the king cannot imprison his person without due process and course of the law', save on suspicion of treason or felony (and then with the possibility of deliverance by jury). The Council might be the 'queen's mouth', but it could not

---

[58] 1 And. 297; Baker, *Magna Carta*, pp. 166–8, 495–9. The initial complaint, addressed to Hatton LC and Lord Burghley, was signed in autograph by all the judges on 9 June 1591: Burghley papers, BL MS. Lansdowne 68 (87).

[59] *Bate's Case* (1601) LI MS. Maynard 66, fo. 143; differently reported in BL MS. Lansdowne 1058, fos. 13v–14; MS. Add. 9844, fos. 22v–23v (quotations tr. from both). For the background see PC 2/26, fos. 40, 150, 167.

[60] The case of impositions: *Bate's Case* (1606) Lane 22; Baker, *Magna Carta*, pp. 328–31.

command anything contrary to law. He urged his colleagues to be resolute and not timorous. But they were more cautiously inclined. They agreed with him that the Privy Council had acted unlawfully. The Council, they said, could imprison in a matter of public concern (a 'state matter'), but the present case was not a state matter since the company was founded for private profit. They nevertheless managed to sidestep the constitutional question because they all agreed that Bate had made himself a Common Pleas litigant disingenuously in order to qualify for privilege,[61] and for that reason alone they refused bail.[62] The issue was thus avoided, and the bolder view advanced by Walmsley J did not finally prevail until 1628. Another bold interpretation of chapter 29, championed by Coke as attorney-general, was that it gave the King's Bench a means of overseeing the Court of Chancery; but this led to an impasse.[63]

In these cases, we see the beginnings of a new legal creed, increasingly associated with Magna Carta, that all those in

---

[61] Until Coke became CJCP, the Common Pleas only granted habeas corpus in cases of privilege (i.e. for litigants and attorneys in the court): Baker, *Magna Carta*, pp. 157, 354. Bate's advisers obviously regarded the Common Pleas as more likely to give relief than the King's Bench, which did have the necessary jurisdiction.

[62] According to the Maynard MS., the case was re-argued when Anderson CJ was present, and '(tr.) he said strongly that he was of the opinion of the other justices and wise men of England that he should not be bailed' (presumably referring to the reservation in the memorial of 1591). This provoked Walmsley J to 'persist as above in maintaining the authority and fidelity of a good judge'.

[63] *Throckmorton* v. *Finch* (1597) Co. Nbk, BL MS. Harley 6686A, fos. 222v–227; Baker, *Magna Carta*, pp. 284–9, 410–22.

authority under the Crown were subject to the law and accountable in the courts for their actions. No doubt this had long been the position in theory, but there had not previously been effective remedies. Even under Elizabeth, court favourites still wielded much extralegal power, and some of them affected an arrogant disregard for the law; but the judges were becoming more confident in defying them.[64] When, in 1583, a bench of eleven Cambridgeshire magistrates, led by Lord North, mistakenly had a woman cut-purse executed for stealing 10d., they were so soundly and repeatedly berated by Anderson CJ at the next assizes that North complained to Lord Burghley of a 'pageant' which had made the magistrates 'more hateful to the people'.[65] North's letter is most often quoted for his censure of Anderson CJ as 'the hottest man I did ever see sit in judgment'; but the chief justice was righteously indignant that those with the power to pass sentence of death had acted with such shameful carelessness. It should be seen rather as an instance of the judges' determination to impose the rule of law upon individuals of high rank who paid little heed to it.[66] The mistake by the Cambridgeshire justices was morally tantamount to manslaughter; but they could not be punished for what they had

---

[64] Note the early clash of cultures between the court and the courts in *Scrogges v. Coleshill* (1560) *Dyer's Notebooks*, pp. lxxvii, 34, 54, 55.

[65] BL MS. Harley 6693, fo. 61v. Stealing less than 12d. was petty larceny and not capital. It is hard to believe that none of the eleven JPs then sitting knew the difference.

[66] North accepted that a private rebuke would have been deserved but argued that 'the judges had nothing to do with this matter, and their handling the case in this sort shewed small discretion in them. This pageant, my good lord, sticketh so fast in mine and my fellows' hearts as, to deal plainly with your good lordship, we do not brook them . . . .'

done judicially, and so a public rebuke was the most effective remedy. Where there was no such immunity, as in the case of extrajudicial cruelty or mistreatment by magistrates and ministerial officers, heavy punishments were imposed by the Star Chamber. In 1577 a justice of the peace was fined £200 and dismissed from office for dragging a local landowner from his horse and pinioning him on his back for several hours before putting him in the stocks;[67] in 1588 the sheriffs of London were ordered to be imprisoned and heavily fined, and to pay £600 compensation to two gentlewomen they had caused to be whipped as prostitutes, besides craving the women's forgiveness in three public places;[68] and in 1602 Sir Henry Winston JP, ancestor of Sir Winston Churchill, was fined £500 for beating a poor man, knocking out two of his teeth, and having him evicted from his house.[69] Property was likewise protected against abuses of authority. For example, in 1582 a magistrate was fined and imprisoned by the Star Chamber for riotously entering a house to search for murderers when he had no cause,[70] and in 1595 a sheriff was heavily fined for causing a riot by forcibly entering a house with twenty-six men to execute a warrant, breaking six locks without asking for the

[67] *Buttle* v. *Harcourt* (1577) BL MS. Harley 2143, fo. 33; Baker, *Magna Carta*, 173; Star Cha. Rep. 67, no. 518. Buttle was lord of two manors in Stanton Harcourt and in dispute with the defendant. Harcourt died a few months later from the Oxford gaol fever (Ch. 1, n. 14).

[68] *Att.-Gen.* v. *Skynner and Catcher* (1588); Baker, *Magna Carta*, pp. 266–9; abridged in Star Cha. Rep. 89, no. 682. The sheriffs' behaviour was said to be against Magna Carta, c. 29.

[69] *Winston's Case* (1602) LI MS. Maynard 82, fo. 16 (reversing). These were common-law offences but aggravated by his being a magistrate.

[70] *Vaughan* v. *Tyre* (1582) Star Cha. Rep. 17, no. 123.

keys and handing over some of the goods that he seized to one of his own men.[71] The King's Bench held that it was lawful to bar one's door against a sheriff's officer seeking to execute civil process, referring to the old saying that everyone's house is his castle and fortress.[72] And, on the same ground, they ruled that the ecclesiastical high commissioners could not authorise their pursuivants to break into a house or arrest someone at night.[73] These examples show that, although the process of establishing legal protection against misuses of authority met with obstacles, infringements of liberty and security were now reaching the courts and the punishments were creating precedents. It was an important moment in the history of the rule of law.

Land Law

Turning to private law, it is hardly surprising to find that, in the Elizabethan period, it was still dominated by questions of

---

[71] *Att.-Gen.* v. *Willoughby* (1594) BL MS. Hargrave 26, fo. 44v (fine of 1,000 marks); apparently the same as Star Cha. Rep. 124, no. 922 (fine of 3,000 marks, 1595). Thomas Willoughby (sheriff of Kent 1590–1) was also accused of accepting a bribe to return a favourable jury.

[72] *Hayward* v. *Bettysworth* (1591) Co. Nbk, BL MS. Harley 6686A, fo. 292; *Semayne* v. *Gresham* (1602, re-argued in 1604) 5 Co. Rep. 91; Cro. Eliz. 908; Moo. 668; 1 Brownl. 50; Yelv. 28; KB 27/1371, m. 650 (no judgment entered). *Semayne's Case* was cited in *Fearn* v. *Tate Gallery* [2019] EWHC 246 (Ch) at 38, though (as Mann J observed) it was not helpful in the context of privacy.

[73] *Smith's Case* (1600) Co. Nbk, BL MS. Harley 6686B, fo. 375v; Baker, *Magna Carta*, p. 291. This is doubtless the same as *South* v. *Whetwith*, BL MS. Hargrave 17, fo. 188, in which Anderson CJ said '(tr.) in no case may a man's house be broken unless it is for treason or felony'.

real property. Every person of substance tried to acquire as much land as possible and to control its devolution in perpetuity. It was the principal form of investment, except for entrepreneurs in the merchant world. Land law was therefore by far the most important subject the law student had to tackle, beginning with his pocket copy of Littleton's *Tenures*.[74] Remedies for the protection of landed interests had been simplified. The perplexing array of medieval procedures, with the arcane learning built around them, had largely given way early in the reign to the more straightforward action of ejectment: straightforward, that is, if one makes allowance for the subterfuge that underlay it. Ejectment was in form an action in tort, designed to protect leasehold tenants; but a decision of 1499 to allow recovery of possession as well as damages was seen to give the leaseholder a more effective remedy than the freeholder. In the 1550s it dawned on lawyers that freeholders could make nominal leases for the purpose of trying the title in ejectment, and this became the practice for the next three hundred years, improved in the following century by the recruitment of fictitious parties to obviate physical ejections.[75] The reach of ejectment was not even limited to leaseholders and freeholders. Until Elizabethan times, owners of copyhold land – which constituted 'a great part of the

---

[74] This student book, written by Sir Thomas Littleton (d. 1481), had by 1600 gone through more editions than the English translations of the Bible.

[75] *OHLE*, vi. 724; J. H. Baker, *The Law's Two Bodies* (Oxford, 2001), pp. 51–2 n. 71. It was very much a King's Bench development, accounting for 8 per cent of its workload by 1606 (as against 1 per cent in the Common Pleas): Brooks, *Pettyfoggers and Vipers*, p. 69.

realm'[76] – had no protection outside the manorial courts; but since copyholders were held able to make leases protected by ejectment, they could by that means gain possession of their holdings in the King's Bench.[77]

Procedure aside, property law seemed to be becoming more and more complicated. Landholding had been much disturbed by the distribution of enormous quantities of land from the dissolved monasteries, including their manors and tithes,[78] and disputes were increasing as succeeding generations sought to unravel the consequences of the scramble for grants. Coke considered that the dispersal of monastic land had been a major cause of the overall increase in litigation.[79] It was also from the early years of Elizabeth I that the trust of land began its modern life. In the form of 'uses', trusts had already been commonplace in medieval times as a way of enabling land to be left by will; but uses of the old kind had been turned into legal estates by the Statute of Uses 1536,[80] and since 1540 landowners had been able to leave land by will without recourse to uses.[81] Trusts were nevertheless not completely extirpated, and they

---

[76] *Hobart* v. *Hammond* (1600) 4 Co. Rep. 27 (tr.). It had begun as 'tenure in villeinage'.

[77] *IELH* (5th edn), p. 327. This was at first disputed: *Anon.* (1572) Co. Nbk, BL MS. Harley 6687B, fo. 54. Cf. *Wells* v. *Partridge* (1596) Cro. Eliz. 469.

[78] Tithes belonged to the rector of a church, but appropriated monastic rectories came into lay hands after the Dissolution as 'lay rectories'.

[79] 4 Co. Inst. 76. The problems are mentioned in the statute 35 Eliz. I, c. 3.

[80] 27 Hen. VIII, c. 10. The purpose was to prevent the avoidance of feudal dues, which did not attach on the death of a beneficiary under a use.

[81] Statute of Wills, 32 Hen. VIII, c. 1.

were found to have a number of valuable new functions for conveyancing purposes.[82]

The hottest contentions in property law arose from perpetuity clauses, which were attempts by landowners to tie the devolution of their landed property until the ends of time, or at least until their name and blood expired. It might seem bizarre that any living person should have such power over the remote future, but the possibility had begun with the statute *De Donis Conditionalibus* 1285. As interpreted in the later medieval period, this had begotten the entail, a 'juridical monster' (as Milsom called it) which defied the common law by enabling land to be limited to a person's descendants indefinitely, with 'remainders over'[83] in case the issue died out. To alleviate the consequences of this, a means of barring the entail had been devised in the fifteenth century, using a fictitious lawsuit with a judgment by consent (known as a 'common recovery'), and it was perfected in Elizabeth's reign by the agonised decision – contrary to legal logic – that a recovery would also bar any remainders.[84] But the perpetual entail was the legal philosophers' stone, constantly

---

[82] *Duchess of Suffolk* v. *Herenden* (1560) B. & M. 142; *Sir Moyle Finch's Case* (1600) 4 Co. Inst. 86; N. G. Jones, 'Trusts in England after the Statute of Uses: A View from the 16th Century' in *Itinera Fiduciae*, ed. R. H. Helmholz and R. Zimmermann (Berlin, 1988), pp. 173–205.

[83] *IELH* (5th edn), pp. 300–3. A remainder was an estate created to take effect upon the end of the estate first granted.

[84] *Capel's Case (Hunt v. Gateley)* (1592) 1 Co. Rep. 61. This commenced in 1581, and in 1583 the judges had tried to persuade the parties to settle (Ch. 1, n. 33).

sought after by those instructed to immortalise landed dynasties.

The Statutes of Uses (1536) and Wills (1540), designed to augment Henry VIII's revenue, had incidentally brought in a new legislative magic which seemed to offer a means of frustrating common recoveries. It was not until the last decade of Elizabeth I's reign that their side-effects began to vex the courts, as descendants fell out over the consequences of earlier experiments in conveyancing. The immediate problems affected only the elite, with their elaborate family settlements and the means to endure protracted litigation; but wider social problems were foreseen, and the judges were coming to view with grave concern the prospect of perpetuities being raised from the dead.

The principal invention of the perpetuists was a clause purporting to remove from a family settlement anyone who so much as began an attempt to break it, so that (before any common recovery could be completed) the title would pass to the person next in line as if the person so offending were dead or had never been mentioned at all. Such perpetuity clauses were not only novel but often unnecessarily verbose and convoluted,[85] perhaps drawn out to a tedious length in order to perplex the reader and thereby deter challenges. They would not work at common law, but if they were contained in a use or a will they were arguably given

---

[85] Coke counted over 1,000 words in one proviso: 6 Co. Rep. 43. He also disliked powers of revocation in settlements ('new inventions and fooleries'): *Earl of Shrewsbury's Case* (1597) Co. Nbk, BL MS. Harley 6686A, fo. 188; (1598) MS. Harley 6686B, fo. 316*bis*.

legal effect by the broad wording of the Henrician legislation. Before 1536 uses had taken effect by tying the consciences of the trustees without affecting the legal title, and so any form of conscionable arrangement was valid. Uses were 'not directed by the rules of the common law but by the will of the owner of the lands; for the use is in his hands as clay is in the hands of the potter, which he in whose hands it is may put into whatever form he pleaseth'.[86] But the Statute of Uses turned them into legal estates, knocking out the trustees: ergo, legal devices could now be created by means of a use without conforming to the common-law doctrine of estates. It was a strange kind of sorcery, but it was what the statute seemed to say.

The attack on this seductive logic commenced in earnest in *Chudleigh's Case* (1594),[87] argued with much eloquence and learning by Coke and Bacon before a receptive judiciary. When the assembled judges discussed it in the Exchequer Chamber, they spoke vehemently against the possible adverse effects of the statute. According to Popham CJ:[88]

> Uses are at this day more perilous and mischievous to the common weal than ever they were before the passing of the said statute. Whereas many men have erected their houses and families in name and blood by such conveyances, thinking to eternise them and their posterity by such perpetuities, in truth after two or three descents it had been

---

[86] *Brent's Case* (1575) B. & M. 157, 158, *per* Manwood J.

[87] *Dillon* v. *Freine* (1594) KB 27/1308, m. 65; 1 Co. Rep. 113; B. & M. 169. See further Ch. 3, at nn. 92–4.

[88] CUL MS. Hh.2.1, fo. 105 (tr.); B. & M. 174. Anderson CJ made a similar speech: 1 And. at 338–42. There is an eloquent and cogent treatise to the same effect, dated 1 Jan. 1602, in BL MS. Lansdowne 216, fos. 54–64.

(and would be) the utter subversion of such families who have so provided for their posterity, and the utter decay thereof in time to come.

Two evil social consequences were mentioned. One was that the landowner was deprived of the means of providing for his younger children and for the advancement of his daughters in marriage, and was 'as a man locked up and *quasi* tied to a post'. The second was that eldest sons were assured of their inheritance, however badly they behaved:

> This manner of conveyance breaks asunder the law of nature and rends in sunder the very entrails of nature, so that when the disobedient and sensual son thinks to himself that his father cannot dispose of his land at his good pleasure, but must leave the heritage to him willy-nilly, by this way of thinking in his unripe and immature years – being seduced by those vices and passions which for the greater part infest youth – he becomes undutiful in demeanour against his parents, in manner and conversation dissolute, and in the end subject and made as prey to all brokers and usurers, and wrongfully subverted and ruined, to the overthrow of the family and impregnable grief to his parents and friends.

There was also the uncertainty caused by endless legal wrangling. Francis Bacon chose the Statute of Uses as the text for his Gray's Inn reading of 1600,[89] avowedly to try to ease some of the confusion. It was, he said,

---

[89] BL MS. Harley 6688, fo. 13; MS. Stowe 424, fo. 133; inaccurately printed in *The Learned Reading of Francis Bacon upon the Statute of Uses* (1642), p. 1. In the printed edition, 'neither is this' became 'whether this is'.

> a law whereupon the inheritances of this realm are tossed
> at this day like a ship upon the sea, in such sort that it is
> hard to say which barque will sink and which will get to the
> haven, that is to say, what assurances will stand good and
> what will not; neither is this any lack or default in the pilots
> (the grave and learned judges), but the tides and currents of
> received errors, and unwarranted and abusive experience,
> have been so strong, as they were not able to keep a right
> course according to the law.

He went on to rejoice that a straight course was settled in 1594, and the strong implication was that his own argument had succeeded where others had failed to hit the mark.[90] In truth, the outcome was not as decisive as Bacon would have it, but it was the beginning of the end.

In 1595, in *Germyn* v. *Arscott*,[91] more rhetoric and scripture were deployed to undo the supposed side-effects of the Statute of Wills 1540, which empowered every landowner to dispose of his land 'at his free will and pleasure', notwithstanding any law to the contrary.[92] As in the case of uses, some thought that this free will and pleasure extended to the types of estate which could be created by will, replacing the established rules of the common law with the fluid individual predilections

---

[90] Bacon's success was recognised by his appointment as the first queen's counsel extraordinary: below, n. 161. He hinted in his argument that Coke, his leader, had emphasised the wrong points.

[91] *Germyn* v. *Arscott* (1595) B. & M. 177. Cf., to the same effect, *Cholmeley* v. *Humble* (1595) ibid. 178; *Corbett* v. *Corbett* (1600) ibid. 175; 1 Co. Rep. 77; *Mildmay* v. *Mildmay* (1601) LI MS. Maynard 66, fo. 165.

[92] 32 Hen. VIII, c. 1. If the land was held by knight-service, one-third had to be allowed to descend so that the king would have rights of wardship and livery.

of the lay mind.[93] This was anathema to Coke. He lambasted this view of the statute, and those who misused it:[94]

> Devises of land being permitted by statute against the good liking of the common law, many undigested wills concerning land so abound, and give more trouble to the estate of the justice of this realm with perplexed questions, through the ignorance or carelessness of those who pen them, than any other kind of matter does. Moreover, men at this day attempt by their last wills to establish perpetuities for their posterities, against the provision and providence of God: and thus, pretending to leave a blessing, they leave a curse.

Owen J likened perpetuities to the tower of Babel:

> Those who make perpetuities make them as strong as a tower which will reach to heaven, and which will continue as the days of heaven ... And Babel, by interpretation, signifies confusion. Likewise, those who construct perpetuities bring confusion to their posterities. And commonly those who pen these perpetuities commit great absurdities, repugnancies and contradictions in them, as in our case at bar.

Anderson CJ agreed that 'all the absurdities, contrarieties, repugnancies and inconveniences which could be devised or imagined to be in a will are brought together in this will'.[95] But obscurity was not the only problem. Beaumont J, turning to the

---

[93] *Scholastica's Case* (1571) Plowd. 403; *Dyer's Notebooks*, pp. 198, 235.
[94] Co. Nbk, BL MS. Harley 6686A, fos. 123v–8, at fo. 127v (tr.).
[95] LI MS. Misc. 491, fo. 99 (tr.).

Classics, compared perpetuities to the monster Hydra, which as often as Hercules cut off one head sprouted three others: 'likewise someone who endeavours to reform one inconvenience between a hundred inconveniences which these perpetuities bring in, so long as they remain, greater inconveniences will follow, and therefore it is necessary to extirpate them by the roots, and by the rules of the law to overthrow them utterly'.[96] Anderson CJ developed the argument in apocalyptic terms:[97]

> If this devise should be allowed, then by the same reasons [as in *Chudleigh's Case*] all the land in England might be tied up with these perpetuities. If that should happen, no termor or occupier would be sure of his term or interest,[98] and from thence it would follow that there would be no bargaining or contracting between man and man for land. And the mischief would not stop there, but by these means the land itself would in a short time lie fresh and untilled for want of occupiers ... Therefore, the mischiefs being so great, the law ought to have providence and foresight to prevent such things before they come about.

Some thought this a little far-fetched;[99] but it was obvious that, if entails could not be broken, more and more land

---

[96] Ibid. (tr.). The allusion is to *Genesis*, 11:4.

[97] BL MS. Hargrave 7A, at fo. 144 (tr.); same report in LI MS. Misc. 491, fo. 100.

[98] A tenant in tail could grant leases only for a maximum of twenty-one years, and this power was subject to several statutory qualifications: 32 Hen. VIII, c. 28. Lessees were therefore at risk of being evicted by the issue in tail.

[99] In *Mildmay* v. *Mildmay* (1601) LI MS. Maynard 66, fo. 165, Warburton JCP described the argument as 'frivolous'.

would become permanently entailed. This was problematic not merely for would-be purchasers or tenants but also for the owners of settled land themselves, since as tenants in tail they were unable to make desirable adjustments to their landholdings, to set up their daughters and younger children, to raise money by mortgage, or to obtain a proper income from leasing. The judges were therefore determined to quash perpetuity clauses, whatever the statutes said. If the statutory wording was applied literally, without regard to the social consequences, its effects would go far beyond the original revenue purposes of the legislation, and Parliament could hardly have intended that. The proper construction of the statutes was therefore to conform them to the common law, as had been done (in a different context) in *Shelley's Case* (1581).[100] By this means the pernicious magic could be snuffed out, and the control of land restored to the living.[101] There will be more to say about this bold approach to legislative interpretation in Chapter 3.

The Law of Contract

Contract cases were numerically the largest category in the Elizabethan plea rolls because of the timeless predominance of

---

[100] B. & M. 163. This was the first major case argued by Coke and it sealed his reputation, thanks in part to a report of his own argument which he circulated widely in manuscript.

[101] The King's Bench were more hesitant than the Common Pleas: *Sherington* v. *Mynors* (1596–9) KB 27/1336, m. 602; Moo. 543; apparently reversed in *Mildmay's Case* (1605) KB 27/1365, m. 439; 6 Co. Rep. 40. The matter was finally settled in *Mary Portington's Case* (1613) 10 Co. Rep. 37.

debt, though debt actions rarely raised questions of substantive law. The remedies for debt were available to rich and poor alike, in the real rather than the Ritz Hotel sense. But the old action of debt was bedevilled by a survival from Anglo-Saxon times called wager of law, which meant that an unprincipled debtor could swear his way out of debt without a trial of the facts. There was an arguable justification for this, given that the parties themselves were barred from giving evidence, and the only relevant written evidence was likely to be a plaintiff tradesman's book. Wager of law had admittedly become tainted with dishonour,[102] but it was still in regular use. Creditors therefore needed a better remedy than the action of debt. They found it in the action called *assumpsit*. This had been in use for over a century to enforce promises, treating a breach of promise as an honorary tort; but it was the Elizabethans who worked out the governing principles. The main principle was that an informal promise or contract – that is, one not evidenced by a deed under seal – was enforceable only if it was supported by good consideration, a doctrine formulated in the 1560s. Consideration brought together the notion of *quid pro quo* (a benefit to the promisor), which was the hallmark of a bargain, and the detriment to the plaintiff which was requisite for an action in tort.[103] In 1561 it was held that a binding contract could also arise from mutual promises, since

---

[102] It was said in 1601 that a gentleman would rather pay an undue claim than lose credit by waging law: *Proc. Parl.*, iii. 419–20. See also D. Ibbetson, 'Sixteenth Century Contract Law' (n. 104 below), at 313 n. 100.

[103] J. Baker, 'Origins of the "Doctrine" of Consideration 1535–1585' (1977) reprinted in *Collected Papers*, iii. 1176–1201; D. Ibbetson, 'Consideration and the Theory of Contract in the 16th Century Common Law' in

each could be consideration for the other, thus establishing a consensual concept of contract. And at the end of the reign it was finally settled – dismissing the doubts of Walmsley J and other Common Pleas judges – that debts could be recovered in *assumpsit*. The debtor's failure to pay was a continuous breach of the implied promise of payment inherent in every debt.[104] This last decision put paid to wager of law for most purposes[105] because it was not available in *assumpsit*, though it did not kill off actions of debt, which were still used to enforce debts acknowledged under seal (bonds).[106] The triumph of *assumpsit* enabled the formulation of a unified law of contract, transcending the forms of action, and before long a law of restitution as well. *Assumpsit* also facilitated the enforcement of bills of exchange against the drawer, notwithstanding the lack of contractual privity as later understood.[107]

Towards a General Law of Contract, ed. J. Barton (Berlin, 1990), pp. 67–124.

[104] *Slade's Case* (1597–1602) B. & M. 460; J. H. Baker, 'New Light on Slade's Case' (1971) reprinted in *Collected Papers*, iii. 1129–75; D. J. Ibbetson, 'Sixteenth Century Contract Law: Slade's Case in Context' (1984) 4 *Oxford Journal of Legal Studies* 295–317.

[105] Even in the King's Bench, actions of debt were being brought and barred by wager of law as late as 1602. Remarkably, there were fourteen examples in the term following the judgment in *Slade's Case*: KB 27/1376, 1378. But wager of law soon became rare: *IELH* (5th edn), pp. 81, 371.

[106] Brooks, *Pettyfoggers and Vipers*, pp. 67, 69, 88–9. Actions of debt actually increased in the Elizabethan period, while the proportion of actions on the case remained steady (2 per cent in the Common Pleas, 19 per cent in the King's Bench). But the debt actions were predominantly brought on bonds. Wager of law was not allowed against a deed, and *assumpsit* was not available to enforce a deed.

[107] Baker, *Collected Papers*, iii. 1248–51.

The Law of Torts

Tort is as timeless as debt, but negligence actions are conspicuous by their virtual absence in the Elizabethan period. We cannot be too confident about interpreting the surface appearances, because an action for direct injury to the person – even if accidental – would properly have been framed as battery 'with force and arms'. But we can be fairly sure that if negligence actions had been common, they would have left more indirect evidence. Accident litigation was simply not frequent,[108] and the few reported cases of negligence arose from breaches of contract. Trespass actions were common enough, but most of them were for trespass to land and were essentially about property interests of various kinds. The action of trover and conversion, for converting goods, was essentially about movable property. The law as to wrongs against the person was at the time dominated by defamation. At the beginning of the reign, slander actions were more numerous even than *assumpsit*; indeed, they were deemed too common. Although the judges generally welcomed amplifications of their jurisdiction, they were embarrassed by such unmeritorious litigation and devoted themselves to finding ways of stemming the flow.[109] Trivial disputes over words were best left to the Church courts, which had an extensive slander jurisdiction but awarded penance rather than sums of money. In the King's Bench, nuisance and various forms of fraud followed next in terms of frequency. But the catalogue of torts was not closed, and there are some glimmerings of

---

[108] See further Ch. 4, at n. 46. [109] *IELH* (5th edn), pp. 470–2.

new torts which were to become important in later centuries, such as passing-off and the infringement of trademarks.

The first action for infringing a trademark, brought in 1584, provides a good example of the way in which the common law could move almost imperceptibly in new directions.[110] The action met with the opposition which lawyers are engaged to provide, and with the judicial qualms which properly greet all innovation. It is not certain that there was a judgment. Yet the question was not whether to open the floodgates by introducing a new law of intellectual property – a concept which had not then occurred to anyone – but the more focused question of how far the action on the case for deceit could be stretched to deal with an obvious wrong. Whether people were free to use symbols in the way they could use their own names, even if they were already in use by competitors, had simply not been tested before; but it seemed obviously wrong to do so deceitfully.

Criminal Law

The criminal law comes last in the survey because it was not much the concern of practising lawyers. Counsel were not allowed to represent defendants on trial for murder or felony and were not in practice engaged for the prosecution either. It was left to the judges to try to ensure justice while ploughing

---

[110] *Stamford's (or Samford's) Case* (1584) B. & M. 673. This has attracted the interest of modern trademark scholars as a legal starting point: see e.g. K. M. Stolte, 'How Early Did Anglo-American Trademark Law Begin?' (1997) 8 *Fordham Intellectual Property Journal* 505–44.

through heavy assize calendars. Although lives were at stake, the criminal process was still seen more as an administrative exercise in emptying the gaols, with the assistance of local people, than as a forensic exercise in the investigation of evidence. There was no police force, and the pursuit of offenders was a matter for the community. Local residents were elected annually as constables, unpaid but with duties governed by law. The preparation of prosecutions for trial was a matter for the justices of the peace. They collected evidence in the form of written depositions, which were laid before grand juries composed of local people. If a grand jury thought the evidence sufficient, the accused was tried by a different jury of twelve; if not, he was discharged. Trials were short, even in capital cases, and most decisions were left to the jurors with scant guidance from the judge.

It was regarded as one of the cornerstones of the English constitution, seemingly confirmed by Magna Carta,[111] that issues between the Crown and the subject – in civil as well as criminal cases[112] – were entrusted to juries of neighbours, whose decisions were final.[113] This relieved the judges from much of the responsibility for the outcome. If

---

[111] This notion was popularised by William Lambarde, *Eirenarcha* (1581), p. 436; Baker, *Magna Carta*, p. 38. But it was orthodox learning that the jury originated before the Norman Conquest.

[112] The Crown's property rights had to be ascertained by inquisition. Lambarde said this showed the 'melodious harmony' of the constitution, and that it was 'a prerogative peculiar to the English nation': Lambarde, *Charges*, p. 188 (addressing an inquisition post mortem in 1600).

[113] Lambarde, *Ephemeris*, pp. 104–8. On the other hand, Lambarde cautioned against the 'feigned equity' of juries who knowingly acquitted the guilty: ibid. 120. Juries could be punished by the Star Chamber for

legal questions arose at all in a criminal trial, it was only because the judge or a friend of the court pointed them out; and there are few law reports of such cases. When judges themselves were unlearned, as might be the case at quarter sessions, blatant errors could occur.[114] But there could also be differences between one assize judge and another, or even between the two benches at Westminster,[115] and it was clearly unsatisfactory that a criminal's life should turn on which judge happened to try him, with no appeal. For instance, stealing lead from a church roof was held to be felony at York in 1560 but not felony at Stafford in 1588.[116] The judges themselves were concerned about such divergences, and were beginning to achieve some uniformity through the practice of reserving cases from the assizes for discussion back in town.[117] In a prominent instance of 1584, arising from a burglary at Anderson CJ's house (Arbury Court) in Warwickshire, the definition of breaking and

---

doing so against the evidence: e.g. Star Cha. Rep. 19–20. But their verdict stood.

[114] Note the fatal mistake in 1583, above, at n. 65. Anderson CJ's indignant reaction suggests that it was unusual.

[115] E.g. the King's Bench held unanimously that in felony cases the Crown could not challenge jurors without cause, whereas the Common Pleas unanimously held the opposite: *Anon.* (1591) Moo. 595, cited sub nom. *Savage v. Brooks.*

[116] Baker, *Collected Papers*, ii. 1011–12. The question was whether it was real property, like the church itself. On either view, it might be felony if the lead was left on the ground long enough to become a chattel.

[117] See 109 Selden Soc. xcii–xciii. The paucity of such cases in the law reports may indicate that the practice was not as 'routine' as there suggested, save in treason cases.

entering was clarified in judicial assemblies at Serjeants' Inn before the trial. The judges held that breaking a glass window-pane and inserting hooks to pull out carpets amounted to breaking and entering:[118] a decision still in the textbooks when the writer was a student.[119]

Generally speaking, the criminal law was kept simple and undeveloped because it was designed to be understood by common jurors. Sentencing was also simple, in that murder and all felonies (other than petty larceny) carried a fixed capital sentence. Nevertheless, the majority of those sentenced to death were not executed. Most prayed the benefit of clergy, if available.[120] A common question in practice was whether a convict was entitled to escape by that route, and this could involve difficult questions of statutory construction. Judges might also use their discretion to find fatal slips in the indictment if they thought the evidence weak,[121] and they could recommend reprieves and pardons

---

[118] Clench's reports, BL MS. Harley 4556, fos. 154 (discussed at dinner, Mich. 1583), 155v (Hil. 1584); 1 And. 114 (Hil. 1584); Sav. 59; BL MS. Hargrave 88, fos. 117, 117 (Pas., Trin. 1584); LI MS. Maynard 66, fo. 35v; 3 Co. Inst. 64. Anderson CJ did not recuse himself.

[119] *Kenny's Outlines of Criminal Law*, 18th edn by J. W. C. Turner (Cambridge, 1962), p. 248.

[120] For this weird survival see *IELH* (5th edn), pp. 554-7. A number of sixteenth-century statutes removed 'clergy' from particularly heinous offences, beginning with murder (Ch. 3, n. 118) and in 1576 adding rape (18 Eliz. I, c. 7).

[121] An explicit example is *R. v. Longe* (1596) Cro. Eliz. 489. Extrajudicial factors may have underlain other quashings on pernickety technical grounds: e.g. *R. v. Lenthal* (1589) ibid. 137 (convicted murderer discharged because Hereford not stated to be in Herefordshire). Flaws in indictments were common, but generally ignored.

in suitable cases.[122] It was not only meritorious defendants who were saved by technical errors. One convicted murderer was discharged solely because the indictment had laid the murder on 31 June, an error which cost the clerk of assize a fine of £40 in the Star Chamber for failing to point it out until it was too late:[123] which was a little hard, since the trial judge cannot have been paying much attention either. Reprieves could be a source of corruption when courtiers became involved.[124] On the other hand, pardoning could be harnessed to the public interest in facilitating the country's seafaring exploits and colonial projects. Even venturing across the Atlantic was, for some offenders, marginally preferable to the gallows. Official mercy was, nevertheless, unpredictable; and this in part explains why acquittal rates were higher than now.

There was little or no common law concerning misdemeanours – not even as much as a coherent list – though a wide range of statutory offences was punishable by local magistrates.[125] As many as two-thirds of all offenders

---

[122] Kesselring, *Mercy and Authority*, pp. 93–5. For the origins of routine judicial reports after every circuit recommending pardons to adjust punishments, see ibid. 79–81. Professor Kesselring calculated that, during Elizabeth's reign, 1,730 defendants escaped death by this means. Some contemporaries thought the judges too merciful: ibid. 163.

[123] *Lewis's Case* (1599) Moo. 555; CUL MS. Dd.8.48, p. 67; MS. Gg.2.5, fo. 276v.

[124] Serjeant Fleetwood complained to Burghley in 1585 about courtiers trading in reprieves, claiming that ten days' respite (enough to seek a pardon) could be obtained for £20: BL MS. Lansdowne 44, fo. 113. The bribe presumably went to the sheriff.

[125] For a survey based on the Essex quarter sessions see Emmison, *Elizabethan Life: Disorder*.

presented by constables at Kent quarter sessions in the first half of 1602 were charged with statutory offences created during the sixteenth century.[126] Most forms of behaviour considered reprehensible were punishable by fine, whipping, stocking (in the pillory) or a short period of imprisonment. It was a rough and ready form of local justice, though any flagrant abuse of the magistrates' powers could result in punishment by the Star Chamber and an award of compensation.[127] Imprisonment was not used as widely as today, though Parliament was introducing more and more fixed custodial sentences, usually for three months, six months or a year.[128] In 1598 the assembled judges ruled that magistrates could punish serious misdemeanours not only with fines and imprisonment but with 'any other open punishment and shame which does not involve life and limb'.[129] Public shaming was less burdensome to the local authorities than imprisonment, and it was considered to be effective as both a deterrent and a punishment. Cases of theft were sometimes dealt with in this way, off the record, rather than by indictment for felony, when the evidence was thought too thin to place before a jury. A recently discovered justice's memorandum book, now in the author's possession, contains

---

[126] Kesselring, *Mercy and Authority*, p. 23, based on data in L. Knafla, *Kent at Law, 1602*, vol. i (1994).

[127] See above, at nn. 67, 69, 70; below, Ch. 5, n. 28.

[128] There were forty-four such enactments under Elizabeth, five of them prescribing a life sentence: Kesselring, *Mercy and Authority*, pp. 29–31.

[129] Co. Nbk, BL MS. Harley 6686A, fo. 305. By 'shame' was usually meant the stocks or pillory, occasionally the wearing of 'papers' (labels describing the offence).

several examples of such informal justice, all absent from the quarter sessions records. For instance, in 1602 an unmarried couple who were wandering about robbing people, and living in sin, were merely fined 40s. (the money being distributed to the poor) and the woman was put in the stocks; had they been convicted of robbery they would have been hanged.

Much of the magistrates' petty jurisdiction was concerned with the enforcement of social policy, and in particular the war on idleness, which was seen as the root of most crime. Soon after becoming a justice of the peace for Norfolk in 1586, Coke wrote that 'there are three causes of theft at this day, namely (1) idleness, or its brother, unlawful pastimes, . . . which is greatly nourished in alehouses and inns; (2) gorgeous apparel; (3) want of an occupation or trade, for those whose parents do not educate them in any good knowledge cannot work'. [130]

Popular entertainments such as wakes (rustic raves) were considered especially dangerous, not merely because of the disorders to which ale-drinking commonly led, and the profaning of the Sabbath, but because of the risk of spreading fatal infection during epidemics.[131] Large gatherings were, however, worryingly difficult to police. When a fair was held in

---

[130] BL MS. Harley 6687A, fo. 7 (tr.), paraphrasing a passage in Thomas More's *Utopia*. There is more in the same vein in the charges to grand juries in Lambarde's *Ephemeris*. See further Ch. 3, at nn. 104, 105.

[131] E.g. Emmison, *Elizabethan Life: Disorder*, pp. 228–31; Anthony Kynnersley JP's memorandum book (JHB MS. 2496), fos. 57, 59–61 (1603). The frequent outbreaks of plague in towns killed many thousands, and there were ad hoc isolation regulations for those who had visited infected regions such as London. Infected persons due to attend the courts at St Albans in 1593 were to carry red rods a yard long to facilitate distancing: *TRP*, iii. 130.

Uttoxeter in 1603, following an outbreak of plague elsewhere, wardens were appointed to watch every street end, each with a scribe and messenger and victuals brought to them 'that they should not stir from their posts'; there were also to be 'three whippers at the town's charge appointed to ... whip away rogues, vagabonds and beggars'. These regulations were not statutory, but were 'consented unto and agreed upon ... by the constables and inhabitants'.[132] There was some resentment at the restrictions. But in 1596, when an action of false imprisonment was brought against a mayor for confining someone from a plague-ridden house who refused to isolate himself in accordance with an emergency local ordinance, Anderson CJ said he had deserved the imprisonment, and really deserved to be imprisoned again for bringing the action.[133] Towns could not create new custodial offences; but the common law was accommodating when necessity required it.

While county magistrates were chiefly concerned with public order and behaviour, a plethora of regulatory offences were prosecuted in the central courts by information, usually under legislation which gave the informer half the penalty.[134] This was another inexpensive system of law

---

[132] Kynnersley's memorandum book, JHB MS. 2496, fo. 57v. There were no statutory powers before 1603: 1 Jac. I, c. 31, s. 7.

[133] *The Mayor of Coventry's Case* (1596) BL MS. Add. 25211, fo. 129v. Anderson CJ then recalled a case on circuit in Devon where a plague victim with visible sores was executed for murder after he caused the death of his sister and all her children by going to her house and embracing her.

[134] D. R. Lidington, 'Parliament and the Enforcement of the Penal Statutes' (1989) 8 *Parliamentary History* 309–28; Kesselring, *Mercy and Authority*,

enforcement; but it generated a horde of prying entrepreneurs who made a career of informing for profit. Unsurprisingly, common informers (or 'promoters') were an unpopular breed of people, and measures had to be taken to protect them from public protests.[135] Despite their usefulness, Thomas Egerton Sol.-Gen. was moved to attack them in Parliament as caterpillars and blood-suckers of the commonwealth:[136] they were, it seems, as bad as solicitors.[137]

More imaginative developments of the criminal law were undertaken by the Star Chamber, which could invent misdemeanours without recourse to legislation. The court could be severe – while not allowed to deprive a wrongdoer of life or limb, it took the view that limbs did not include ears and nostrils[138] – but it had yet to acquire the bad reputation which has stuck to it since the time of Charles I. It was a court which stood up for the ordinary person oppressed by abuses of authority[139] or

pp. 43–4; D. C. Smith, *Sir Edward Coke and the Reformation of the Laws* (Cambridge, 2014), pp. 51–3.

[135] *TRP*, ii. 288, referring to 'great routs' and physical attacks on 'informers upon penal laws and statutes, commonly called promoters'.

[136] *Proc. Parl.*, ii. 120. William Fleetwood said the use of informations had served only to increase the private gain of 'the worst sort of men': ibid. i. 201. Proposals for reform were considered in 1571: SP 12/20, fos. 46-50v. Modest reforms came in 1576 and 1589: ibid., ii. 482, 487, 488; 18 Eliz. I, c. 5; 31 Eliz., c. 5. See further Baker, *Magna Carta*, p. 199.

[137] Cf. Egerton's similar remarks about solicitors, Ch. 1, n. 97.

[138] Ears could be either tacked to the pillory or cut off. For slitting nostrils see e.g. Star Cha. Rep., nos. 288, 647, 828.

[139] This was considered to be one of its main purposes: see Smith, *De Republica*, pp. 95-7. Note e.g. the case of the sheriffs of London, above, n. 68.

local bullying.[140] It punished forgery, perjury, embracery, riot and other abuses of legal process, and sniffed out frauds and more subtle mischiefs which the regular common law did not reach.[141] For instance, in 1596 it imposed a sentence of imprisonment, augmented with fines, whipping and the pillory, for inveigling gullible young inns of court students into bogus investment schemes.[142] Its power to overawe and frighten was generally deployed in the interests of justice, and it was the Star Chamber which declared that 'it were better to acquit twenty that are guilty than condemn one innocent'.[143] Nevertheless, the danger of entrusting criminal jurisdiction to a body of courtiers, judges and bishops who proceeded summarily, without juries, and without any possibility of appeal,[144] was already perceived.[145]

---

[140] For notorious riots in connection with property disputes see J. Baker in *Landmark Cases in Criminal Law*, ed. P. Handler, H. Mares and I. Williams (Oxford, 2017), at pp. 51–4; Star Cha. Rep. 17, no. 121, and p. 75, no. 580 (Drayton Basset, Staffs, 1578); Lambarde, *Charges*, pp. 158–61 (Malling, Kent, 1592).

[141] E.g. enticing young people into unsuitable marriages: Star Cha. Rep., 21–2; W. Hudson, *Treatise on the Star Chamber* [1621], ed. F. Hargrave (1787), pp. 110–11.

[142] *Att.-Gen.* v. *East and How* (1596) BL MS. Hargrave 26, fo. 60; abridged in Star Cha. Rep. 48, no. 369 (dated 30 Eliz.); cf. similar cases ibid. 47–8, 132.

[143] Hawarde 320 (1607).

[144] The Star Chamber held its own decrees to be irreversible, even when wrong: *Att.-Gen.* v. *Whitecroft* (1597) BL MS. Hargrave 26, fo. 65 (but they recommended a pardon).

[145] Lambarde, *Ephemeris*, p. 106. Lambarde also objected to summary jurisdiction being conferred on magistrates.

Law, Society and Government

The language and principal features of the law were embedded in the consciousness of a large part of the Elizabethan population. This was not merely because many of the male gentry attended the inns of court and chancery. As was noticed earlier, numerous husbandmen and minor tradesmen were litigants in the central as well as the local courts. Women, too, were not infrequent plaintiffs, especially when liberated by widowhood.[146] The law of the land was the common property of everyone, and its benefits were accessible to anyone with a little education or knowledge of the world. For the poorer classes, contact with the law would largely have meant the criminal and ecclesiastical courts. For the middling sort, it was a matter of recovering or avoiding debts, or dealing with the consequences of debt. For landowners, it involved frequent contact with lawyers to deal with sales and purchases, leases, mortgages and family settlements. Few owners of property stayed out of the law courts for long, since buying land often meant buying potential lawsuits, risks as well as opportunities. Even with the procedural reforms brought about by the action of ejectment, many questions of real property seem to have been won or lost on technicalities.

---

[146] In Hilary term 1563, 167 actions were brought by widows and 5 by other single women: CP 40/1207, 1208 (see Ch. 1, n. 72). These figures exclude actions by women as personal representatives, which were common, and several hundred actions brought by married women jointly with their husbands. See also M. L. Cioni, *Women and Law in Elizabethan England with Particular Reference to the Court of Chancery* (Cambridge PhD dissertation, 1975); T. Stretton, *Women Waging Law in Elizabethan England* (Cambridge, 2009).

This feature jumps out at anyone reading the Elizabethan law reports. Litigation could resemble a game: not exactly a game of chance, but a game in which a formal mistake or an arcane piece of learning could be fatal or at least costly.

Despite this drawback, the Elizabethan age was devoted to the idea of the rule of law, even if that precise expression was not yet in use.[147] Government according to law was at the heart of constitutional monarchy.[148] James Morice argued at the beginning of his reading on the royal prerogative in 1578 that the English kind of monarchy was preferable both to aristocracy (which was plagued by faction) and to democracy ('the government of the inconstant rude and ignorant multitude').[149] The prerogatives belonging to the queen were not a mark of absolute monarchy since they were not unlimited but were allowed and defined by the common law. In England, said Morice, the prince ruled 'not by his licentious will and immoderate affections, but by the law, that is, by the prudent rules and precepts of reason agreed upon and made the covenant of the commonwealth'; in consequence of this, the people lived safely, and quietly enjoyed their property. In other words, there was a national 'covenant' – or, as we

---

[147] Note 'the rule of reason and law' (1598) used in a similar sense, Ch. 3, at n. 81. The medieval phrase 'due process of law' had some of the same connotations.

[148] See further above, at nn. 37–42; and 'Public Law' in Ch. 4.

[149] BL MS. Egerton 3376, fo. 4; MS. Add. 36080, fo. 230v. Robert Bell (also of the Middle Temple) had made the same distinction as Speaker in 1576: *Proc. Parl.*, i. 468. They were doubtless influenced by Jean Bodin's *Les Six Livres de la Republique* (Paris, 1576). Note also Charles Merbury, *A Briefe Discourse of Royal Monarchie, as of the Best Common Weale* (1581), pp. 9, 11–12.

should say, a constitution – under which the law bound the monarch as well as the people. The law was not dictated by the queen; it was a common inheritance, expounded and applied by the queen's judges, and the queen could change it only with the advice and consent of the great council of the realm. Parliament was revered, at any rate by those with a voice or a vote. Though not in constant session, it was considered, or at least expected, to be both a safeguard of the people's liberties and a model of reasoned deliberation. Sir Thomas Smith, in the 1560s, praised the 'marvellous good order' in the House of Commons, where debates might be vigorous but were usually conducted without altercation or disrespect.[150] Perhaps the reality did not always conform to this idealistic description; but there was a general acceptance of the ideal.

The Reign of Elizabeth I

What, finally, of Elizabeth herself, and her reign in general? Hers being a constitutional monarchy of the kind described by Morice, she did not seek to sit in judgment or change the law by decree, but she was not completely isolated from the making of law or from its operation. Unable to make law herself, without Parliament, she could certainly stop law being made. She exercised freely the prerogative of refusing her assent to bills in Parliament,[151] dissolving Parliament, or

---

[150] Smith, *De Republica*, p. 40. He was himself an MP.

[151] She vetoed seventy bills (about 14 per cent of the total) during her reign, but only ten of them for general political reasons: C. Haigh, *Elizabeth I* (2nd edn, 1998), pp. 126–7.

declining to summon parliaments at all, and was not above locking up members of Parliament – usually under benign house arrest – if they overstepped the mark in debate.[152] Liberty of speech, as Egerton LK haughtily informed Coke when he claimed it as Speaker, was no more than to say 'aye or nay', not to speak whatever came into their brains. Coke was rebuked by the queen in person for allowing Morice to present a bill seeking a clarification of Magna Carta, and Morice himself was 'sharply chidden'. She had not called the Parliament to make new laws, she said, let alone to make innovations in the state, and since she had the power to summon and dissolve it, she could direct what it discussed.[153]

The queen was personally involved in the choice of judges, serjeants and law officers; but her appointments were made on professional merit and gave general satisfaction. She did not expect subservience. Unlike James I, Elizabeth never summoned the judges to explain – submissively, on their knees – why they had decided cases unfavourably to the prerogative. She sometimes offered strong guidance, as when she apparently intimated that grand juries were in future not to be charged to enquire into ecclesiastical abuses.[154] She was inclined to impose martial law in times of crisis, albeit this was usually

---

[152] Some of the judges confirmed extrajudicially in 1566 that members might be imprisoned at the queen's pleasure for 'arrogant and presumptuous' speeches: *Dyer's Notebooks*, p. 126.

[153] *Proc. Parl.*, iii. 68 (1593); Baker, *Magna Carta*, p. 273. Four members were imprisoned for daring to propose that the Crown be entailed.

[154] She had been annoyed at the indictment of an ecclesiastical judge in Norwich: Baker, *Magna Carta*, p. 138.

averted on better advice.[155] And she sometimes intervened
in private suits, not to direct a specific result but to make
the judges aware of her close interest and to chivvy them
into a speedier resolution.[156] When the first stage of
Chudleigh's Case was argued in 1586, some privy councillors advised her that she stood to lose many privileges and
prerogatives, and that many titles depended on the same
difficulty, whereupon 'she thought it best not to disturb
the sleeping dog' and told the lord chancellor and
Secretary Walsingham to secure an agreement between
the parties.[157] The parties duly complied, but that did not
prevent the same entail from becoming the subject of the
leading case in 1594.[158] An even more striking example
occurred in 1598, when the queen apparently wrote to the
judges desiring them to bring a speedy end to a case
commenced eighteen years earlier, with all 'honourable
favour' to the plaintiff 'that in justice and equity may be',

---

[155] Ibid. 430; Kesselring, *Mercy and Authority*, p. 40. The judges thought it
better to stretch the law of constructive treason than to execute people
without trial.

[156] E.g. in the cases of Elizabeth Mynne (1572), Henry Shelley (1581), Robert
Brett (1596), Richard Atkinson (1596), Thomas Throckmorton (1597)
and the countess of Derby (concerning the Isle of Man, 1598). See Baker,
Magna Carta, pp. 286, 303; Dyer 313; *Harvye* v. *Facye* (1596) BL MS.
Harley 1059, fo. 4v (Brett's case); 4 Co. Inst. 284 (Isle of Man); and also
Dyer 236, pl. 24 (1564).

[157] *Chudleigh* v. *Dyer* (1586) Bodleian Library MS. Rawlinson C.85, fo. 180
('el pensa bien de ne muer le chien dormant'); KB 27/1292, m. 714
(discontinued).

[158] *Dillon* v. *Freine* (1594) above, n. 87. This was brought by a feoffee of John
Chudleigh (the real plaintiff of 1586), who had died in 1589, and
concerned lands in a different county.

and to afford him relief so far as they could 'without breach of the course of our justice'.[159] Such an intervention may strike us as shocking; but the letter was drafted by someone else for her signature, and may not even have been sent. The judges took a further three years anyway. Sometimes the queen was critical of lawyers who put legal nicety before equity, and in 1586 she accused them of being 'so fine – you regard so much the words, syllables, and letters [of the law] more than the true sense and meaning indeed – that oftentimes you make the same to seem absurd'.[160] She was doubtless not alone in that opinion. But the Bar were free to argue against the Crown in the courts, and if a barrister proved too good at it, the remedy was not to punish or silence him but to neutralise him by taking him into the royal service. The rank of queen's counsel was introduced in 1594 as just such a measure, to stop Francis Bacon using his talents on the wrong side.[161]

Elizabeth liked to represent herself, and with some truth, as a supporter of justice and law. On appointing Coke as attorney-general in 1594 she said to him:[162]

---

[159] SP 12/268, fo. 157 (draft); 12/273, fo. 129 (draft, referring to the former letter as having been sent). It referred to *Lord Cromwell* v. *Androwes*, which began in 1580, and also to *Lord Cromwell* v. *All Souls College, Oxford*, which began in 1590.

[160] *Proc. Parl.*, ii. 379. She was explaining why she would not have Mary, queen of Scots, tried according to the common law.

[161] BL MS. Harley 1697, fo. 43; MS. Harley 6745, fos. 59, 98v; MS. Hargrave 50, fo. 97v; Baker, *Collected Papers*, i. 124–5. Bacon had been importunately seeking preferment, but Elizabeth was not willing to make him Sol.-Gen. He was not given a patent as KC until 1604.

[162] Co. Nbk, BL MS. Harley 6686A, fo. 80v. Cf. her remarks when he became Sol.-Gen. in 1592 (ibid., fo. 29): 'I charge thee first to carry thyself

> I charge thee that my subjects receive at thy hands that
> which to them appertaineth according to law and justice,
> for a better prince hereafter you may have when I have
> gone but never any that have a more fervent desire to
> execute justice and do right to all, and see that my subjects
> have justice with expedition, and with as small charge as
> conveniently may be.

They were not empty words. Coke wrote them down to be remembered, and he did not forget them. He remained attorney-general for the rest of the reign, and yet, without fear of dismissal, he regularly took action to frustrate abuses of the royal prerogative by courtiers and profiteers,[163] and to curb excesses of prerogative jurisdiction. This was a new constitutional climate, for which the queen and her wise first minister, Lord Burghley, must be given much of the credit. Burghley was a new type of councillor, educated in humanistic learning at Cambridge and called to the bar by Gray's Inn. It has been said that 'his long tenure of office stands out as a crucial moment in the process by which English dynastic monarchy slowly changed into the embryonic nation state of the next century'.[164]

uprightly and justly, using neither my prerogative or name, nor thy place wherein I have set thee, to the wrong or injury of any of my subjects. God forbid (quoth she) that any prerogative should be used to wound mine own conscience.' She gave similar charges to Egerton: Baker, *Magna Carta*, p. 149. See also 3 Co. Inst. 79.

[163] E.g. by means of monopolies, purveyance and patents of concealment: Baker, *Magna Carta*, pp. 200, 324, 338–9. See his letter to Burghley complaining of extortions and oppressions, 29 Aug. 1597: BL MS. Lansdowne 84, fo. 145.

[164] W. MacCaffry in *ODNB*.

The queen's subjects – other than the Roman
Catholic underground, who did not regard themselves as
her subjects – seem generally to have approved of her
reign. Lawyers certainly did. Not long before her death,
Coke wrote, 'Bless God for Queen Elizabeth', for constantly telling her justices not to refrain from doing right
by reason of any writs or letters under the great or privy
seal, and for upholding chapter 29 of Magna Carta.[165]
Edward Hake, the following year, said that her reign had
been 'one of the most blessed patterns of just government
in the world', since she had never acted contrary to law.[166]
These passages went beyond dutiful sycophancy and identified in the queen's person all that was thought praise-
worthy in a country blessed with a newfound confidence
in its own superiority. To the eyes of lawyers like William
Lambarde, the Continent of Europe was to be pitied as
a backward part of the globe, much of it under totalitarian
rule in Church as well as state, a harbour for terrorists and
potential enemies, characterised by drunkenness and
obnoxious behaviour.[167] French visitors to legal London
might fairly be pardoned for not understanding the

---

[165] E. Coke, *Le Second Part des Reportes* (1602), preface, sig. ¶v; Baker,
Magna Carta, p. 149. The same point had been made by Serjeant Wray as
early as 1571: *Proc. Parl.*, i. 199.

[166] Hake, *Epieikeia*, p. 84.

[167] See e.g. the remarks to grand juries in Lambarde, *Ephemeris*, pp. 129–30
(1596), 144 (1600). Lambarde also excoriated the Scots, while he thought
the Irish ungovernable, idle, thievish and – for the most part literally –
beyond the pale. To be fair, he did not think much of the lower classes in
England either.

English lawyers' version of French,[168] and yet for a French jurist to criticise Littleton's *Tenures* as 'confused, absurd and awkward' was not merely ignorant but (in Coke's view) obviously malevolent.[169] Nowadays such opinions might be dismissed as rampant nationalism. At the time, they were coloured more by the Papal Curia's virulent hostility towards the queen than by simple xenophobia. However, notwithstanding Miss Hamlyn's injunctions, this is not the place to evaluate them. They are noted as part of the Elizabethan *res gestae*, as historical facts in themselves.

The demi-paradise which Shakespeare's audiences recognised in the later years of Gloriana's reign was not only the seat of Mars.[170] While naval prowess made England seemingly impregnable and a potential world power, and the City of London was becoming a prosperous international trading centre, it was the rule of law which was thought – by lawyers, anyway – to make her great. As Coke reflected in 1602:[171]

---

[168] J. H. Baker, *Manual of Law French* (2nd edn, Aldershot 1990), pp. 4–5, quoting G. Delamothe (1592). Sir John Fortescue, a century earlier, thought that it was the vulgar French who could not speak the language properly.

[169] F. Hotman, *De Feudis Commentatio* (Cologne, 1573), p. 661, s.v. *feodum* (tr.) (referring to Littleton's definition of fee simple). Coke criticised this in his reading on uses (1592) BL MS. Hargrave 33, fo. 134, and later (with more bitterness) in the prefaces to 10 Co. Rep. (1614) and Co. Litt. (1629).

[170] W. Shakespeare, *Richard II* (written *c.* 1595), act 2, scene 1.

[171] *Le Second Part des Reportes* (1602), sig. ¶iiij verso. Cf. to the same effect W. Lambarde, *Ephemeris*, pp. 79, 83; and two speeches by Christopher Yelverton (1589, 1597) noted in C. W. Brooks, *Law, Politics and Society in Early Modern Britain* (Cambridge, 2008), pp. 62–3; Hake, *Epieikeia*, pp. 78–9.

> If the beauty of other countries be faded and wasted with bloody wars, thank God for the admirable peace wherein this realm hath long flourished under the due administration of these laws [the common laws of England]: if thou readest of the tyranny of other nations, wherein powerful will and pleasure stands for law and reason ... praise God for the justice of thy gracious sovereign, who (to the world's admiration) governeth her people by God's goodness in peace and prosperity by these laws.

The radiance of Good Queen Bess would shimmer ever more brightly in retrospect as foreign understandings of monarchy threatened to destroy the old order in the next reign. By the troubled 1620s, Coke thought that she deserved to be remembered as Elizabeth the Great.[172] To this day, in Gray's Inn, the old queen's 'pious, glorious and immortal memory' is toasted when the loving cup is passed on Grand Days. It may seem an affectation, but it recalls an ancient memory of what was once seen as a golden age.

---

[172] He was objecting to the error of calling her Elizabeth Tudor, 'Tudor' being a Welsh forename: 4 Co. Inst. 239. See also 8 Co. Rep. 77 ('a wise, learned and most excellent princess, and the phoenix of her sex'); Co. Litt., proemium ('she was the Queen of Queens').

3

An Age of Common Law
and an Age of Statute?

The main object of these lectures is to draw a comparison between the law of the first Elizabethan age and that of the present. It is hardly practicable for present purposes to bridge the two by surveying the intervening legal history; but a question which merits an intermediate detour is whether the master key to understanding the differences between the law of the two periods might be the increasing dominance of legislation.

The case is familiar enough,[1] and might be made broadly as follows. Elizabeth I's reign lay in the middle, perhaps at the zenith, of the Age of Common Law. The common law was then revered as a body of accumulated wisdom, brought ever closer to perfection by centuries of argument and refinement. Its basic principles were attributed to timeless natural reason, perceived through study, practical experience and precedent. Legislation was a necessary gloss upon this unwritten common law, sometimes intended to

---

[1] For more nuanced versions of it see G. W. Keeton, 'The Twilight of the Common Law' in *The Passing of Parliament* (1952), pp. 1–12; G. Calabresi, 'Choking on Statutes' in *A Common Law for an Age of Statutes* (Cambridge, MA, 1982), ch. 1; J. Beatson, 'Has the Common Law a Future?' (1997) 56 CLJ 291, 298–302. See also Burrows, *Thinking about Statutes*, p. 1 ('Statutes are swallowing up our common law').

restore and rescue it from recent perversions, sometimes to supplement it, but rarely to replace it. And it was essentially less perfect in nature. In the reign of Elizabeth II, by contrast, we are well into the Age of Statute. The common law is now merely a residue lurking in the interstices of a huge mass of statutes, statutory instruments and directives. Most of the law in force descends on the courts from Parliament, augmented in recent times by a good deal of written law flowing into the country from overseas, with no border control. All of it results from political decisions at various levels, and it can be changed only by politicians. Judges cannot try to make the underlying policies more reasonable, or even mutually consistent, without infringing democracy, but must confine themselves to interpreting the texts with which they are presented from outside the common-law system.

This bald contrast between the two ages has an obvious over-simplicity about it. Yet there has, on any reckoning, been a broad shift from case-law to a superabundance of legislation and delegated legislation made by politicians. The purpose of this excursion will be to investigate how far this really is the principal difference between the law today and the law of the Tudor period.

Legislative Continuity

Parliament has in many respects been transformed since 1603. It is now a Parliament of the United Kingdom, with a universal adult electoral franchise; it can discuss whatever it wishes; and it is in almost continuous session. Yet the Parliament which sits at Westminster today is in law a continuation of the English Parliament which sat at Westminster in 1559, and for centuries before that. From the historian's viewpoint, this continuous identity is a fiction which only silly lawyers could possibly believe in. But from the lawyer's viewpoint those remote bodies truly are the same Parliament, because any of their legislative acts which remain unrepealed are statutes possessing the same force in England as those passed today and are susceptible to alteration or repeal only by today's Parliament or tomorrow's. For instance, part of the Act of Supremacy 1559 is still in force,[2] as are several other Elizabethan statutes, including that to which two universities owe their corporate status.[3] As a purely legal proposition, the organic sameness of all these parliaments is perfectly sensible and real.

An obvious symbol of this continuity, likewise imbued with fiction, is the state opening of Parliament. There we see, sitting upon the woolsack immediately before the throne, a select group of judges. In fact, all the 120 or more High Court judges and lords justices of appeal will have been summoned by writ to 'treat and give their advice' upon the 'arduous and urgent affairs' for which the Parliament was summoned, obedience to which they are in no wise to omit. Most of them will have been advised informally at the same time that they are in no wise to obey: there are insufficient woolsacks, and too many trials and appeals in progress elsewhere. Those who do attend lend colour and dignity to the

---

[2] 1 Eliz. I, c. 1, s. 8.
[3] The Oxford and Cambridge Act 1571; Letters Patent Act 1571; Simony Act 1589.

occasion, but their advice is no longer sought, however arduous the affairs. It was last sought in 1898, and that was on an appeal, not on proposed legislation.[4] Asking their advice on changing the law would now be seen as offending the principle of the separation of powers, a principle which ten years ago led – some think needlessly – to the abolition of the appellate jurisdiction of the House of Lords.[5]

When Queen Elizabeth I attended her first Parliament, on 25 January 1559, the proceedings looked in essence the same. The queen sat crowned in state, with the lord keeper standing at the foot of the throne. The peers (all hereditary – as they still were, apart from the law lords, in 1952), the bishops and all the judges were there in their scarlet robes, and crowded in at the bar were the Commons, led by the Speaker – in those days always a senior barrister.[6] The presence of the judges, however, still had some purpose. It is true that their role as triers of petitions from Gascony and the lands beyond the seas had been relegated to the fictional part of the ceremony. But they did still, occasionally, put in bills of their own devising.[7] More importantly, some of them (especially the chief justices) were active on Lords' committees

---

[4] *Allen v. Flood* [1898] AC 1.

[5] Constitutional Reform Act 2005 (c. 4), ss. 23 and 40, and Sch. 9. This came into force in 2009.

[6] The Speaker in 1559, Sir Thomas Gargrave, was a barrister but had spent much of his career in Yorkshire. He was criticised for his lack of eloquence and for addressing the Commons as if in an alehouse: J. Baker, *The Men of Court 1440–1550* (2012), i. 727–8. All his successors under Elizabeth I were benchers of their inns.

[7] E.g. Manwood CB in 1584 devised bills concerning trials and demurrers: *Proc. Parl.*, ii. 66.

perusing and amending bills.[8] Their advice might also be sought on electoral law and matters of procedure,[9] and on legal questions currently under consideration.[10] Even so, a quarter of a millennium had passed since a judge could claim to know authoritatively what an Act of Parliament meant because he had helped to make it.[11] Lawmaking by 1559 was a separate process from declaring what the law was.

Tudor Concerns about Legislation

Even if the Elizabethan period was an age of common law, it was an age already painfully aware of what seemed to be an ever-increasing torrent of legislation. Although most of it was accepted as necessary,[12] the volume alone was coming to be seen as a problem. The proliferation of new statutes, often overlapping each other, their piecemeal and often short-term character, their convoluted draftsmanship, the clash of

---

[8] For Dyer CJ's involvement see *Dyer's Notebooks*, p. lv.

[9] E.g. *Dyer's Notebooks*, p. 50 (on proxies, 1559); *Thomas Fitzwilliam's Case* (1593) Co. Nbk, MS. Harley 6686A, fo. 49v; *Proc. Parl.*, iii. 86–92, 159–62 (on whether an outlaw could be an MP); 1 And. 294 (on prorogation, 1593); MS. Harley 6686A, fo. 213 (on the need for the queen's presence in person or by commission, and the distinction between prorogation and continuance, 1597). Cf. Coke's later view that judges ought not to give any opinion on matters touching Parliament, since they were governed by the law of Parliament and not the common law: 4 Co. Inst. 15.

[10] E.g. in 1586 Anderson CJ, Manwood CB and Gawdy J were directed to attend the Lords to discuss the trial of Mary, queen of Scots: *Proc. Parl.*, ii. 369.

[11] *Aumeye's Case* (1305) YB 33–5 Edw. I (Rolls Series), p. 82, *per* Bereford J.

[12] See *Att.-Gen.* v. *Twyne* (1602) 3 Co. Rep. 82 (quoting Aristotle).

statutes apparently dealing differently with the same subject-matter, the lapse of temporary statutes, the revival of repealed statutes, and the ambiguity of some apparent repeals, all led to considerable dissatisfaction with the corpus of legislation at this period. Statutes were also becoming longer and longer, some of them lengthened by provisos added to the original bills. This tendency towards prolixity perturbed the lawyer members of Parliament throughout the reign. William Fleetwood advised the Commons in 1563 that 'overcharging of a bill with larger words than was convenient, and more provisos than to the purpose, [was] oft the overthrow of that which was truly meant'.[13] He later complained that 'all our bills are long bills, full of *tautologia* and *cakaphonia*, penned in barbarous English ... I have been these thirty years of this Parliament and never saw bills so illiterately drawn, and therefore we have such hacking and hewing of them.'[14]

In 1563 the lord keeper, Sir Nicholas Bacon, charged the House of Commons 'to examine whether there be too many laws for any one thing, which breedeth so many doubts that the subject is some time to seek how to observe them and the counsellor how to give advice concerning them'.[15] Two years later he devised a scheme for consolidating the statutes then in force under alphabetical headings, omitting all repealed or duplicated matter, and he nominated the best

---

[13] *Proc. Parl.*, i. 217. Francis Bacon, likewise, warned in 1601 that 'if you will put in so many provisos as be desired, you will make so great a window out of the law that we shall put the law out at the window': ibid., iii. 451.

[14] *Proc. Parl.*, ii. 110, 124 (1585). He added, 'I remember once a bill of the subsidy had like to have been overthrown, it was so long.'

[15] *Proc. Parl.*, i. 83.

eighty lawyers of the day to serve as twenty committees of four members each to prepare the various titles.[16] Nothing came of this grand scheme, which suffered from what Winfield called the 'curious fatality of impotence' which haunted all such projects.[17] The proposed consolidation of the statute-book was taken up by Bacon's son during the Parliament of 1593. Francis Bacon complained that the statutes were now 'so many in number that neither the common people can half practise them nor the lawyer sufficiently understand them'.[18] But he enjoyed no more success with reforming them than his father had. Judges and practitioners had to manage for the time being with the privately edited collections of statutes in force, such as William Rastell's, which did at least rearrange them alphabetically.

The Elizabethans were not to know that their complaints would pale into insignificance compared with the experience four centuries later. By present standards, their problems were modest. Parliament was not in continuous session, and the 13 parliaments of Elizabeth I produced only 273 public Acts. This represents an average of six statutes a year for the whole reign, and a third of them were concerned either with particular places or with the regulation of particular branches of trade or commerce. The average so far for the reign of Elizabeth II, with Parliament functioning almost continuously, is sixty-seven a year. Although in the last thirty years the rate has fallen to

---

[16] SP 12/105, fo. 208 (29 Dec. 1575); *Calendar of State Papers (Domestic) 1547–80*, p. 507.

[17] P. H. Winfield, *Chief Sources of English Legal History* (Cambridge, MA, 1925), p. 91. See also G. R. Elton, *Parliament 1559–81* (1986), pp. 79–80.

[18] *Proc. Parl.*, iii. 75. On this, at least, Coke agreed with him: *Le Quart Part des Reportes* (1604), sig. B3.

forty-one a year,[19] the number of pages per annum has increased. It should also be borne in mind that in Elizabeth I's reign there was virtually no delegated legislation in the modern sense.[20] There were, it is true, sheaves of proclamations emanating from the Privy Council;[21] but, since these were issued under the royal prerogative rather than a 'parent' statute, they could not alter the law.[22] Lord Keeper Egerton and Francis Bacon caused a stir in 1597 when they announced that the Privy Council was minded to start legislating by proclamation. That was seen as unconstitutional, but it was an issue left over till the following reign, when it was resolved in favour of parliamentary supremacy.[23]

Legislation was considered an inferior form of law, coming from outside the reasoned and coherent learning of the

---

[19] The decrease began during the Labour administration of Mr Blair in 1999, falling to twenty-four statutes in 2005. Taking the reign as a whole, however, there is no correlation between the number of statutes and the political complexion of the government. The maximum seems to have been the ninety-eight statutes passed in 1964 under Mr Wilson's Labour government. The lowest number was twenty-three in 2012 under a coalition government.

[20] The most significant exceptions were the legislation produced for Wales by the Privy Council under the authority of the Laws in Wales Act 1543 (34 & 35 Hen. VIII, c. 26), and the bye-laws made by commissioners of sewers (below, n. 108).

[21] See F. A. Youngs, *The Proclamations of the Tudor Queens* (Cambridge, 1976).

[22] Baker, *Magna Carta*, pp. 151–4. Henry VIII's retreat on this point was still remembered: *Proc. Parl.*, i. 207; ii. 113.

[23] *Att.-Gen.* v. *Parker and Others* (1597) Hawarde 78–9; *Case of Proclamations* (1610) 12 Co. Rep. 74; Baker, *Magna Carta*, pp. 151–4, 390–6.

common law. Francis Bacon said that there were 'more doubts that arise upon our statutes, which are a text law, than upon the common law, which is no text law'.[24] Especially dangerous were the occasional statutes which cast aside core principles of the common law. Coke, who had been Speaker of the Commons in 1593, wrote ten years later that it was 'a maxim of policy, and a trial by experience,' that the alteration of any fundamental point of the common law was dangerous, 'for that which hath been refined and perfected by the wisest men in former succession of ages, and proved and approved by continual experience to be good and profitable for the common wealth, cannot without great hazard and danger be altered or changed'.[25] Like Bacon, he was scathing about obscure draftsmanship. The greatest questions in law, he wrote in 1602, arose not upon the rules of the common law but on the interpretation of 'Acts of Parliament overladen with provisos and additions, and many times on a sudden penned or corrected by men of none or very little judgment in law'. The remedy, he said, was that 'if Acts of Parliament were after the old fashion penned, and by such only as perfectly knew what the common law was . . . then should very few questions in law arise, and the learned should not so often and so much perplex their heads to make atonement and peace by construction of law between insensible and disagreeing words, sentences and provisos, as they now do'.[26] It is evident from the law reports that the courts were confronted with an ever-growing number of statutory

---

[24] *Life and Letters of Francis Bacon*, vi (J. Spedding ed., 1872), p. 67.
[25] *Le Quart Part des Reportes* (1604), sig. B2v.
[26] E. Coke, *Le Second Part des Reportes* (1602), sig. ¶v verso. He made the like complaint about conveyances drawn by the unlearned (Ch. 1, n. 96).

questions. Over a third of the cases in Coke's notebooks from the time of Elizabeth dealt with matters of statutory interpretation.

Interpretation of Statutes and the Common Law

The reported cases from Coke's time remind us that the judiciary was not hermetically isolated from legislation. Although judges did not make statutes, it was their role to interpret and apply them, and in carrying out this function they would follow 'the rule and reason of the common law'.[27] This was justified on the ground that the common law was antecedent to any statute, and it could therefore be supposed that statutes were consciously made in the context of pre-existing law.[28] It was a fallacy to suppose that, once a matter was dealt with by statute, the common law was irrelevant, 'for without knowledge of the ancient law they shall neither know the statute nor expound it well, but shall (as it were) follow their noses and grope at it in the dark'.[29] Since the 'makers' were *functi officio* once a parliament

---

[27] *Harbert's Case* (1584) 3 Co. Rep. 11, 13 (tr.: 'judges and sages of the law have always expounded general statutes according to the rule of the common law, which is built on the perfection of reason . . .'); *Milborn's Case* (1587) 7 Co. Rep. 6 (tr.: 'It is a good exposition of a statute to expound it according to the reason of the common law'); *Fermor's Case* (1602) 3 Rep. 77, 78; Baker, *Magna Carta*, p. 364 n. 148, *per* Warburton J (1607) (tr.: 'a statute is to be expounded according to the rules of the common law'). Cf. Plowd. 10v, 88v (1550s).

[28] See *Stowell* v. *Lord Zouche* (1565) Plowd. 353, 363, *per* Browne J (tr.: 'the way to understand the sense is to consider the common law, which is older than all positive laws'); cited in Hake, *Epieikeia*, p. 91.

[29] Fleetwood, *Discourse*, p. 141.

was dissolved, the task of interpretation necessarily devolved on the 'sages of the law' as 'oracles'.[30] The courts therefore had the last word on the meaning of statutes: for 'whereas judges have no voices in making of laws, in expounding of laws no man hath voice but they'.[31] This did not give rise to conflict in practice. Parliament did not find it necessary to override the judges by passing statutes of reinterpretation, as opposed to passing better statutes or (very occasionally) passing 'statutes of explanation' to clarify earlier statutes.[32] Coke as attorney-general was intrigued by the unique provision in the Treason Act 1350 that all cases of doubt concerning treason should be referred to Parliament and not decided by the judges; but he concluded, on the strength of case-law, that even this did not prevent equitable interpretation of the statute itself.[33] Judicial interpretation was not only necessary but legally authoritative, since it was part of the judges' office to give a consistent practical effect to statutes by declaring what they meant. Indeed, Coke claimed in 1602 that

---

[30] [?C. Hatton], *A Treatise concerning Statutes* [c. 1590] (1677 edn), pp. 29–30, concluding: 'the sages of the law . . . have the interpretation in their hands, and their authority no man taketh in hand to control: wherefore . . . we seek these interpretations as oracles from their mouths'.

[31] 'De Statutis' (1589) BL MS. Harley 5265, fo. 190.

[32] E.g. 34 & 35 Hen. VIII, c. 5 (explanation of the Statute of Wills); 31 Eliz. I, c. 11 (explanation of the Statute of Forcible Entry). Such statutes were supposed to be construed beneficially: *Case of the Dean and Chapter of Norwich* (1598) 3 Co. Rep. 73, 74 (referring to a statute of 1593 explaining the statute of 1539 for dissolving the monasteries).

[33] Co. Nbk, BL MS. Harley 6686A, fos. 55, 117, 249v-249A. The courts had, e.g., decided that accessories could be convicted of levying war even though they did not themselves perform the principal overt act.

one of the main reasons why law reports were needed was that they contained 'the true and genuine sense and construction of such statutes and Acts of Parliament as were from time to time made and enacted'.[34] It was the meaning which the judges read into statutes, rather than any other, which took effect as law.

To this end, the judges had developed principles of interpretation, and these principles were an integral part of the common law.[35] They depended on common-law reasoning and could be found in the law reports – especially in the later year books and Plowden's *Commentaries*. Treatises on statute-law first appeared in the Elizabethan period. Four are known, though none of them was printed until much later. The most familiar is that by William Fleetwood, which was printed in 1658 and again (anonymously) in 1942.[36] It was begun in the 1550s, and revised after the publication of the first part of Plowden in 1571. Five manuscripts are at present known.[37] Secondly, there is the chapter 'De Statutis' in the

---

[34] E. Coke, *Le Tierce Part des Reportes* (1602), sig. C.ij.

[35] *OHLE*, vi. 80; *Wimbish v. Tailbois* (1550) Plowd. 38v, 46v, *per* Saunders sjt (tr.: 'by the rules of the common law' a penal statute was not to be taken by equity); *Townesend's Case* (1553) Plowd. 111, 112v (tr.: 'the judgment of the common law' as to affirmative statutes).

[36] W. Fleetwood, *The Office of a Justice of Peace, Together with Instructions How and in What Manner Statutes Shall Be Expounded* (1658); [Anon.], *A Discourse upon the Exposicion & Understandinge of Statutes*, ed. S. E. Thorne (San Marino, CA, 1942) (which makes no reference to the 1658 edition or to most of the manuscripts).

[37] H. E. Huntington Library, San Marino, CA, MSS. EL 496, 2565 (whence the edition by S. E. Thorne in 1942); BL MS. Harley 5265, fos. 201–16v; MS. Hargrave 34, fos. 32–40v; London Metropolitan Archives, CLC/270, MS. 86, fos. 1–9v. The authorship, which Plucknett mistakenly attributed to Egerton, is discussed in Baker, *Magna Carta*, pp. 232–7. There is an earlier draft in BL

anonymous tract *De Legibus Angliae*, which is still unprinted.[38] This is dated 1587 internally and has some of the characteristics of Fleetwood's writing, though the coverage is different. The third is a small treatise printed in 1677 as the work of Sir Christopher Hatton, though the authorship is open to question. An internal reference to the earl of Leicester (d. 1588) as 'lately deceased' suggests a date of composition around 1590.[39] Finally, there is Edward Hake's *Epieikeia: A Dialogue on Equity*, printed in 1953.[40] This was mainly written in the 1590s and completed around 1603. The second part of Hake's dialogue, entitled 'The Equity of the Common Laws of England', includes a discourse on the equity of statutes. All these authors purported to distil a series of maxims from reported cases, most of which had not in terms laid down any principles at all. The principles were deduced retrospectively from the results.[41]

MS. Hargrave 409, fos. 376–402. Fleetwood said in 1585 that one version was stolen: *Proc. Parl.*, ii. 109 ('my book was picked from me').

[38] BL MS. Harley 5265, fos. 176–98, at 188–98. At fo. 190v the author listed some similar maxims from Roman law and concluded: 'We have in use almost of all the civilians' learning.'

[39] Printed as *A Treatise concerning Statutes* (1677). The reference to the earl of Leicester is on p. 19.

[40] E. Hake, *Epieikeia: A Dialogue on Equity in Three Parts*, ed. D. E. C. Yale (New Haven, CT, 1953). The passage on the equity of statutes is at pp. 85–93. Hake had been admitted as an attorney: *A Touchestone of the Present Time* (1574), sig. E4v.

[41] Other collections of cases on statutory interpretation, but with little or no analysis, were R. Crompton, 'Le Treshault Court de Parliament' in *L'Authoritie et Jurisdiction des Courts* (1594), fos. 1–28; and Co. Nbk, BL MS. Harley 6687D, fos. 804v–813v.

Legislative Intent and Equity

By the sixteenth century it was common learning that, in case of doubt, an attempt should be made to ascertain the intent of the 'makers' of a statute.[42] The original idea was that the judges and lawyers in the parliament which passed a statute could be consulted directly about its meaning; but, on that footing, it was difficult or impossible to ascertain their subjective meaning once they were gone.[43] A more fundamental difficulty was that the individuals concerned might all have had different views,[44] and the only reliable evidence as to the shared meaning of a group of people is the wording on which they have collectively agreed. That is why the courts traditionally did not look at parliamentary debates to throw light on Parliament's meaning, and why logically they should not do so.[45] The makers' intention was, in truth, a constructive or imaginary intention, divined by the judges through a process which was sometimes – following Aristotle – described as *epieikeia* or 'equity'. Plowden – again following

---

[42] See e.g. YB Pas. 4 Edw. IV, fo. 4, pl. 4 (discussed in Hake, *Epieikeia*, pp. 85–7); early Tudor cases in *OHLE*, vi. 77 n. 168, 79–80; Fleetwood, *Discourse*, p. 151 n. 143; Elizabethan cases in *Dyer's Notebook*, p. lx.

[43] Fleetwood, *Discourse*, pp. 151–2. Serjeant Broke said in 1519 that 'in the case of old statutes no one can know the intention of the makers': *OHLE*, vi. 79. Serjeant Saunders made the same point in 1553: ibid. 78.

[44] Fleetwood, *Discourse*, p. 151 ('So many heads as there were, so many wits; so many statute-makers, so many minds').

[45] See J. H. Baker, 'Statutory Interpretation and Parliamentary Intention' (1993) 52 *CLJ* 353–7 (a case-note criticising *Pepper* v. *Hart* [1992] UKHL 3); *Williams* v. *Central Bank of Nigeria* [2014] UKSC 10, at p. 37, para. 104, *per* Lord Neuberger.

Aristotle – suggested a technique: you should suppose the law-maker to be present, ask him your question about the meaning, and then give yourself the answer you imagine he would have given had he been present.[46] As with the 'officious bystander' test in the law of contract, this works only if the answer is so obvious that it goes without saying, as where there is an evident mistake. Where a statute was broadly worded, the fiction of parliamentary intention could give the judges considerable latitude in declaring what they thought it must have meant, and in filling obvious lacunae. However, if Parliament had declared its intention in a preamble, any such freedom was greatly reduced. Dyer CJ said that the preamble was 'a key to opening up the minds of the makers of the Act and the mischiefs which they intended to remedy'.[47] It also threatened to shut the door on creative interpretation.

In a judgment of 1584, still remembered today,[48] Manwood CB said that the correct approach to statutes was straightforward and non-technical:[49]

> ... he did not understand there to be any fixed principle for construction of statutes, be they penal or beneficial,

---

[46] *Eyston* v. *Studde* (1574) Plowd. 459, 467.

[47] *Stowell* v. *Lord Zouche* (1565) Plowd. 353, 369. See also Fleetwood, *Discourse*, pp. 114–17. Even the title might be a guide to the intent: *Stradling* v. *Morgan* (1560) Plowd. 199, 203v.

[48] See *R. v. Secretary of State for the Environment*, ex p. *Spath Holme Ltd* [2001] 2 AC 349, 397, *per* Lord Nicholls; *Re Northern Ireland Human Rights Commission's Application* [2018] UKSC 27, at p. 92, para. 207 (in a quotation).

[49] *R. v. Heydon* (1584) Co. Nbk, BL MS. Hargrave 6687B, fo. 333 (tr.); reworded and expanded in the printed version, 3 Co. Rep. 7 (1602).

> restrictive or enlarging of the common law, but only to
> consider the mischief which was before the statute, and the
> remedy which Parliament intended to provide, and
> thereupon to make a construction to repress the mischief
> and advance the remedy according to the intent of
> Parliament.

This has sometimes been called the 'mischief rule', and it was to enjoy a long life. Indeed, despite some opinions that it should be dismissed as obsolete,[50] it has been treated as current law during the present reign.[51] It was not even new in 1584, because focusing on the mischief – the problem which the statute was designed to solve – had been the approach of the readers in the inns of court since the fifteenth century.[52] The main subsidiary principle which Manwood CB was waving aside – and he was not the first to do so[53] – was the older doctrine that a penal or restrictive statute should be construed strictly, whereas a generally beneficial or 'enlarging' statute, such as one which improved the working of the common law, or made

---

[50] In 1969 the Law Commission said it represented a balance between executive, Parliament and public which was no longer acceptable: Law Com. 21, at pp. 19–20. Likewise Lord Hailsham: below, n. 112.

[51] It is still regarded as the governing principle in *Bennion on Statutory Interpretation* (7th edn by D. Bailey and others, 2017), pp. 29–40. It was applied in *Royal College of Nursing* v. *DHSS* [1980] UKHL 10; and cf. *The Presidential Assurance Co. Ltd* v. *Reshal St Hill* [2012] UKPC 33, at p. 23, *per* Lord Mance.

[52] See also *Hill* v. *Graunge* (1557) Plowd. 164, 178v, *per* Brooke CJ (tr.: 'statutes made to help the people out of a grievance (*griefe*), or relieve them from a mischief, have before now been amplified by equity').

[53] *OHLE*, vi. 78.

life better, should be taken equitably.[54] Professor Thorne considered this to have been 'an objective rule of primary importance'.[55] Yet it had been conceded more than once that even a penal statute could in some cases be extended by the equity.[56] The difficulty, as Hake pointed out, was that every statute was penal against someone and there was always a beneficiary. His solution was that the benefit which mattered for this purpose was a benefit to the majority.[57] But Manwood CB's approach was to lay aside these general maxims and treat every statute individually, in the light of the mischief which it addressed.

Although we no longer hear of equity as a living tool for the interpretation of statutes, the fiction of legislative intent has survived to the present day.[58] Yet in origin they

---

[54] This was said in 1493 to be a common principle: *OHLE*, vi. 78 n. 170. See also Fleetwood, *Discourse*, pp. 143–5; Hake, *Epieikeia*, pp. 88–91. The different distinction between negative and affirmative statutes may have derived from scriptural exegetics: Fleetwood, op. cit. 35–42, 117–22; 'De Statutis', BL MS. Harley 5265, fos. 191–2.

[55] Introduction to Fleetwood, *Discourse*, pp. 51–2. He made the ingenious claim that the constant refutations of the distinction demonstrated its strength.

[56] *Reniger* v. *Fogossa* (1550) Plowd. 1, 10, *per* Saunders sjt; *Partridge* v. *Straunge* (1553) ibid. 77v, 82. But Saunders and Whiddon sjts argued the contrary in *Wimbish* v. *Tailbois* (1550) Plowd. 38v, 46v, and the contrary was accepted by the court in *Partridge* v. *Straunge*, ibid. 86v.

[57] Hake, *Epieikeia*, pp. 89, 92 ('the matter which must guide the exposition of our positive statute laws must be a respect of benefiting the multitude'), 92–3; likewise [?Hatton], *A Treatise concerning Statutes*, pp. 23–4. The same point is made in *Platt's Case* (1550) Plowd. 35, 36v; *Wimbish* v. *Tailbois* (1550) ibid. 38, 59v.

[58] Burrows, *Thinking about Statutes*, pp. 13–21.

were the same thing,[59] as was the mischief rule. Manwood CB had himself indicated that considering the mischief was the best way of getting at the intent behind the remedy. The equitable approach was likewise predicated on being able to gather the sense and purpose behind words, which in themselves are lifeless printed characters on the page; and that meant discerning the objective of the statute as a whole, having regard to the problem it was designed to overcome. Equity could not work contrary to the express words, if they were clear and precise. Nor could it work when statutory provisions were utterly incomprehensible or self-contradictory. In such cases it was the practice to declare them 'void', in the weak sense of being ineffective rather than legally invalid. The author of the treatise attributed to Hatton regarded this as a 'great doubt', since no lesser court could correct errors by Parliament; but he concluded that 'when the matter is plain, every judge may esteem of it as it is, and, [the statute] being void, is not bound to allow it for good and forcible'.[60] It does not in theory impugn the validity of an Act of Parliament to say that it lacks any meaning which can be given sensible

---

[59] *Anon.* (1463) YB Mich. 3 Edw. IV, fo. 14, pl. 8, *per* Jenney sjt (tr.: 'within the equity, and therefore within the intent of this statute'); *Dod* v. *Chyttynden* (1502) B. & M. 113, 115 ('. . . within the statute by the equity, for he is within the intention of the makers'); *Partridge* v. *Straunge* (1553) Plowd. 77v, 82, *per* Saunders sjt (tr.: 'a penal statute shall be extended by the equity if the intent of the makers thereof may be perceived'), 82v.

[60] *A Treatise concerning Statutes*, pp. 20–1. The effect of repugnancy was discussed in *The Case of Alton Woods* (1600) 1 Co. Rep. 40, 47. See also I. Williams, 'Dr Bonham's Case and "Void" Statutes' (2006) 27 *Journal of Legal History* 111–28; Baker, *Magna Carta*, pp. 88–91. For a modern statute rendered ineffective by inherent impossibility see below, n. 154.

effect. It is just ineffective, in the same way that a statute which has not been brought into force is valid but ineffective.

Even today, it is inescapable logic that if two provisions in the same Act directly contradict each other, at least one of them must be disregarded. Moreover, statutes can only change the law, not the facts of life. Coke is reported to have said that Parliament could not make a woman a man, or an infant a man, though it could make an infant of full age.[61] Parliament has proved the first example to be questionable,[62] but the point remains good. Parliament still cannot alter a person's age or chromosomes; it can only enact that they do not determine adulthood or gender, in the ways that they used to, for legal purposes. And that was Coke's point. For the like reason, whatever political parties may claim, Parliament cannot create happiness or goodness, or produce wealth which is not there. It may purport to do so, but the words by themselves will be ineffective in the realms of fact. The more difficult question is how far the notion of ineffectiveness by reason of factual or linguistic absurdity can be extended to legal absurdity or incongruity. Coke thought that it could. For centuries his view was rejected as being inconsistent with parliamentary sovereignty, but some have recently come to treat it more sympathetically.[63]

---

[61] *Proc. Parl.*, iii. 236 (1597). Parliament did alter the age of majority from twenty-one to eighteen as from 1970, thereby making infants between those ages instantly of full age: Family Law Reform Act 1969 (c. 46), s. 1.

[62] Coke assumed – as most people did until recently – that 'man' and 'woman' were natural rather than legal concepts, though he recognised the existence of ambiguous cases (Co. Litt. 8). Parliament put paid to this assumption with the Gender Recognition Act 2004 (c. 7).

[63] This will be considered further in Ch. 4.

Equitable Interpretation in Elizabethan Practice

The Elizabethan treatises on statute-law gave much prominence to the concept of equitable interpretation. As Hake made clear, equity in this sense was a branch of the common law independent from the equity of the Chancery. But in gathering year-book cases to illustrate its application, the writers were displaying a degree of legerdemain, because the medieval judges had not often used the vocabulary of equity. It was just what they did. For the treatise-writers, however, the cases from an age of more concise and open-textured statutes – and a freer approach to their elucidation – were taken to furnish judicial authority for regarding a broad equitable approach to statutes as part of the common law. And there were enough recent references to equity, especially in Plowden's *Commentaries*, to show that the technique was still available to the courts.

A classic example was that of a gaoler's liability to the creditor when a debtor escaped from his custody. A statute of 1378 had provided that a writ of debt would lie against the warden of the Fleet prison if he suffered a debtor to leave the prison.[64] The reason was that the creditor lost his remedy against the debtor once he was out of custody, and it was the warden's responsibility to keep him in. But the draftsman had failed to lift his thoughts to the level of general principle. The courts therefore supplied the want. They held, first, that a bill of debt could be brought by the equity, even though the

---

[64] 1 Ric. II, c. 12.

statute specified a writ,[65] and also that it would lie for an involuntary escape, even though the statute said 'suffered'. Then, since it hardly made sense to limit to a single gaoler a measure so beneficial to judgment-creditors, the courts applied the underlying principle to all gaolers holding debtors in execution.[66] Never mind that this bore hard on sheriffs and other gaolers; it affected them only if they failed in their official duty, whereas the absence of a remedy could deprive blameless creditors of their debts. It was an extraordinary leap from the particular to the general, but the interpretation was too well established in the sixteenth century to be questioned by going back to the words of the statute. It led to some esoteric questions in the Elizabethan law reports. Did liability attach to the under-gaoler with actual custody of the debtor or to the head of the gaol?[67] Did the liability pass to a deceased gaoler's executors or to his heir?[68] And what if a sheriff took his prisoner to Westminster by an indirect route or let him out for the night on trust? In those cases it was contended that, even though the prisoner was duly delivered on the day, the debtor's liability had been irreversibly extinguished by

---

[65] YB Mich. 7 Hen. VI, fo. 5, pl. 9. This affected jurisdiction. Only the Common Pleas could proceed by writ of debt.

[66] J. Port, 'Statutes et Equities' (c. 1495) 102 Selden Soc. 115, pl. 62; *Platt's Case* (1550) Plowd. 35; *Note* (a. 1558) Bro. Abr., *Escape*, pl. 9; Hake, *Epieikeia*, p. 90; Co. Nbk, BL MS. Harley 6687D, fo. 813v. It is not mentioned in Fleetwood's *Discourse*.

[67] It was held that the under-marshal of the Marshalsea, rather than the marshal, was liable: *Gawdy's Case* (1568) Dyer 278; *Peacock's Case* (1597) BL MS. Lansdowne 1104, fo. 193v; MS. Add. 25198, fo. 252.

[68] *Anon.* (1568) Dyer 271 (not the heir); *Whitacres v. Onsley* (1573) ibid. 322 (executors).

a constructive escape and thereby happily transferred to the more solvent sheriff.[69] But the contention was rejected, and it was rejected on the strength of year-book authorities rather than upon principles of statutory construction. It was as if the principle had become common law; indeed, it might have been more straightforward had the judges held the statute merely to confirm a wider common-law principle.[70] But it was seen as an acceptable application of equity. Now, it is a safe conjecture that no court today would contemplate opening such a box of snakes by seeking to promote the broader policy behind legislation which was over-narrowly expressed. Judges do not forget the stinging rebuke which Lord Simonds delivered to Denning LJ for his 'naked usurpation of the legislative function under the thin guise of interpretation'.[71] More to the present point, one might hazard a guess that an Elizabethan court would have been equally reticent. Whatever the writers tried to build on the older authorities, resort could be had to equity only where a statute

---

[69] *Boyton* v. *Andrewes* (1589–92) 3 Co. Rep. 43; *Grylles* v. *Ridgway* (1594) KB 27/1323, m. 126; 3 Co. Rep. 52; CUL MS. Ff.5.26, fo. 128v (where Coke cites the statute of Ric. II).

[70] This is hinted at in *Platt's Case* (1550) Plowd. 35, 35v. There were numerous medieval cases recognising a gaoler's liability for an escape without resting it upon statute: see T. Ashe, *Promptuarie* (1614), fo. 121v, para. 7. In *Garnons* v. *Hereford* (1600) Co. Nbk, BL MS. Harley 6686B, fo. 414, it was held (anachronistically) that the common-law remedy was an action on the case and that the statute merely gave a new remedy in debt.

[71] *Magor and St Mellons Rural District Council* v. *Newport Borough Council* [1952] AC 189, 191. Cf. *Williams* v. *Central Bank of Nigeria* [2014] UKSC 10, at p. 29, *per* Lord Neuberger ('The fact that context and mischief are factors which must be taken into account does not mean that . . . the court can take a free-wheeling view of the intention of Parliament').

was vague or ambiguous or where there were unforeseen problems which the legislator had not contemplated or seen fit to provide for.[72] For instance, where Parliament imposed a penalty on parsons for non-residence in their parishes, it was reasonable to suppose that the penalty was not intended to be incurred by a parson who was prevented from residence by imprisonment.[73] Whether or not a statutory offence is one of strict liability is, of course, still a matter of looking for a tacit legislative intent.

The few cases in Coke's Elizabethan notebooks referring explicitly to the equity of a statute illustrate the narrowness of its scope.[74] In one of them, Monson J held a remainder in use to be within the equity of the Statute of Uses, though not explicitly mentioned, because the instances given in the statute were intended as examples rather than as an exhaustive definition.[75] And in 1585 a fifteenth-century statute concerning bonds taken by sheriffs was held to extend to oral promises, because a statute extending to a greater mischief would necessarily apply also to a lesser.[76] On the other hand, it was held that

---

[72] See *Bossevile v. Borough of Bridgewater* (1583) Co. Nbk, BL MS. Harley 6686A, fo. 115v, *per* Owen (tr.: 'where the words in an Act of Parliament are general or indefinite they may be extended with equity; but where they are restrained to a person, or a time, or a certain thing, they cannot be extended beyond the restraint').

[73] *Goodale v. Butler* (1598) 6 Co. Rep. 21.

[74] For cases in his printed reports, some from the next reign, see Thorne, introduction to Fleetwood, *Discourse*, pp. 64–5.

[75] *Vernon v. Vernon* (1573) Co. Nbk, BL MS. Harley 6687B, fo. 347v. Here there was an analogy with the Statute *De Donis*, which gave illustrations of different kinds of entail but was not treated as excluding others.

[76] *Denby v. Heathcott* (1585) Co. Nbk, BL MS. Harley 6687D, fo. 709, *per* Wray CJ.

the Statute of Wills 1540 could not be taken by the equity, both because it was a revenue statute which 'goes in abridgment of the common law and imposes a charge on the inheritance'[77] and because the Statute of Explanation 1543 revealed Parliament's own intention that its wording should be construed literally.[78] One of the broadest examples of equitable interpretation occurred in 1587, when it was held that the statutory liability of local residents to compensate victims of highway robbery did not extend to robberies at night, when respectable folk were abed, even though the statute (passed in 1285) made no mention of time; but this was attributed to the 'reason' of the common law rather than equity.[79]

A well-known example of flexible interpretation occurred in a celebrated case of 1598. It was held that a statutory power for commissioners of sewers to act 'according to their discretions' did not authorise them to act arbitrarily, as by assessing taxes in a disproportionately unfair manner, for 'their proceedings ought to be limited and bound within the rule of reason and law, inasmuch as discretion is a science ... and they are not to act according to their wills and private affections'.[80] This was Coke's gloss on a remark by Anderson

---

[77] *Wiseman's Case* (1583) Co. Nbk, BL MS. Harley 6687B, fo. 325v. This was a year before Manwood CB denied there was such a principle: above, n. 49.

[78] *Butler v. Baker* (1591) 3 Co. Rep. 25, 31; cited on this point with approval in *Saunton v. Merewether* (1599) Co. Nbk, MS. Harley 6686B, fo. 338v. The explanatory statute was 34 & 35 Hen. VIII, c. 5.

[79] *Milborn's Case* (1587) 7 Co. Rep. 6.

[80] *Wythers v. Rookes and Smythe* (1598) 5 Co. Rep. 99, 100 (tr.), sub nom. *Rooke's Case*; original text in Co. Nbk, BL MS. Harley 6686A, fo. 250v; record (whence the spelling) in CP 40/1577, m. 1807.

CJ, and he was probably not present when it was uttered. But all those who were in court were alive to its importance, and it has come down to us in several versions mentioning variously reason, equity and justice.[81] Its effect was to give the judges an overriding power to review discretionary decisions. The principle was rediscovered in the present Elizabethan age,[82] and Coke's report of 1598 is still remembered as its foundation.[83] Despite its importance, however, the decision involved equity only in a weak sense. It was merely a matter of giving a sensible interpretation to a single word, a word which had several connotations but was here to be associated with the judicial function rather than arbitrariness.[84]

The reason for the relative dearth of Elizabethan examples of equity was that the broad approach was rarely

---

[81] BL MS. Add. 25199, fo. 18 (tr.: 'discretion is knowledge of . . . what right is to be done in reason and justice'); CUL MS. Add. 8080, fo. 22v (tr.: 'their discretions ought to be guided and measured by the rule of law and reason'); HLS MS. 1004, fo. 22 (tr.: 'the word "discretion" shall not be expounded that they may do whatever they please, but rather that they shall be directed by equity and reason'). 'Reason' might now be called reasonableness.

[82] The turning point was slightly earlier: *Associated Provincial Picture Houses Ltd* v. *Wednesbury Corporation* [1948] 1 KB 223. But the landmark House of Lords decisions were *Ridge* v. *Baldwin* [1964] AC 40; *Padfield* v. *Minister of Agriculture, Fisheries and Food* [1968] AC 997; *Anisminic Ltd* v. *Foreign Compensation Commission* [1969] 2 AC 147.

[83] It was cited in *R.* v. *Tower Hamlets London Borough Council, ex p. Chetnik Developments Ltd* [1988] AC 858, 872, *per* Lord Bridge, quoting W. Wade, *Administrative Law* (5th edn, 1982), p. 355. See also *Sharp* v. *Wakefield* [1891] AC 173, 179, *per* Lord Halsbury LC; *Frome United Breweries Co.* v. *Bath Justices* [1926] AC 586, 605, *per* Lord Atkinson.

[84] *OHLE*, vi. 45.

applicable to the more intricate and precisely drawn statutes of the sixteenth century, with their lengthy preambles
designed to limit judicial free enterprise. In trying to
understand modern statutes, the judges were more likely
to rely on rules of grammar than principles of equity.[85] It
may have been true that, as Fleetwood told the House of
Commons in 1571, sometimes statutes were construed in
a way directly contrary to the words, and that 'some
statutes are winked at by non-observance, so that they
seem to be no laws'.[86] And it was arguable that, if the
judges did not sometimes depart from the wording in
order to give effect to the intention, Parliament would
have to pass 'infinite statutes, one upon another, which
a man could not read in his lifetime'.[87] Generally speaking,
however, the judges were not at liberty to presume an
intention contrary to the express wording of a statute:
A verbis legis non est recedendum.[88] Anderson CJ did not
even regard equity as universally applicable, for, as he
pointed out in 1594, the many cases on equitable interpretation did not establish any rule as to when statutes should

---

[85] Fleetwood, *Discourse*, is full of grammatical points. For his interest in
philology see Baker, *Magna Carta*, pp. 232–3. For Dyer CJ's use of
grammar see *Dyer's Notebooks*, p. lxi. See also 'De Statutis', BL MS.
Harley 5265, fos. 190v-191.

[86] *Proc. Parl.*, i. 236 ('The words of an Act of Parliament are not ever [i.e.
always] to be followed . . .').

[87] *Butler* v. *Baker* (1591) Co. Nbk, BL MS. Harley 6686, fo. 9 (tr.:), *per* Clench
J. This was omitted from the printed version in 3 Co. Rep. 25.

[88] *Edrich's Case* (1603) 5 Co. Rep. 118 (tr.: 'One must not depart from the
words of the statute'). Coke was here borrowing the language of Aristotle
and Aquinas.

be taken by the equity and when not.[89] Thirteenth-century statutes were another matter altogether. They had been woven into the common law and had acquired an encrustation of learning not to be found in their laconic words alone. And this enabled the judges to indulge in reinterpretation, or even 'winking'. There are two striking examples of this, one of restriction and one of extension.

In the cases on perpetuity clauses, mentioned in Chapter 2,[90] the judges in effect put paid to the apparent policy behind the statute *De Donis* 1285. The statute was intended to give effect to the intentions of donors who gave land upon condition that it should pass only to the donees' descendants and revert on failure of issue. It was probably not originally meant to extend beyond the issue of the first donees, or at most the third generation, and yet it was held to have created a new kind of property. The fee tail which derived from the statute was quite different in nature from the common-law fee simple. It enabled land to be tied inalienably to a person's descendants for centuries into the future. This awkward result had come about as a result of textual exegesis, applying legal reasoning to broad words which had not spelt out their consequences: since no one could inherit more than his ancestor had, any initial restriction on alienation necessarily descended with the entail to each successive heir in turn. This exegesis had developed over decades and centuries in the lectures and moots in the inns of court and arguments in Westminster Hall. But many came to regret the outcome, and lawyers in the fifteenth century devised the common recovery

---

[89] *Dillon v. Freine* (1594) 1 And. 309, 335. [90] Ch. 2, at nn. 87–91.

as a way of barring the entail and turning it into an alienable fee simple. After the Statute of Uses, as we have seen, conveyancers began to retaliate by inserting into family settlements conditions against barring the entail. It might be thought that, since such conditions were designed to protect the operation of a parliamentary statute against blatant evasion, they would have been regarded with some favour. But the Elizabethan judges reached the bold decision that entails were inherently barrable, and that conveyancing devices to prevent barring were ineffective.[91] In Coke's opinion, it was the birthright of every tenant in tail to bar the entail by recovery.[92] The reasoning behind this, as outlined in Chapter 2, was that the consequences of widespread perpetuities would be so dire that Parliament could not possibly have intended them. But the kind of unreasonableness which justifies bold interpretation has to be distinguished from the more political kind of unreasonableness which is not properly to be judged by judges. From today's point of view, the Elizabethan judges were here straying outside the permissible limits. They were deploying policy arguments, relating to the best use of land and the control of families by fathers, in order to deprive a statute – a statute which Parliament had more than once declined to repeal[93] – of much of its force. No doubt

---

[91] *IELH* (5th edn), pp. 300–3, 307.

[92] *Smith* v. *Thorpe* (1597) CUL MS. Ff.2.14, fo. 35; *Sir Hugh Cholmeley's Case* (1597) 2 Co. Rep. 50, 54.

[93] Even while *Chudleigh's Case* was pending, a bill for 'cutting off perpetuities' was discussed in Parliament but did not pass: *Proc. Parl.*, iii. 117–18 (1593). Serjeant Harris said in the debate that it was 'against the nature and gravity of our land to skip by way of transubstantiation'. *De*

Parliament in 1285 did not intend to create the 'juridical monster' which entails became. But that was not the point in 1594. The judges were not here merely applying equity, rediscovering an original intent more palatable than the late-medieval gloss. They were giving effect to changed under-standings of land-ownership. It verged on repeal.

When it suited them, the judges were equally capable of stretching an ancient statute far beyond the original intent. Magna Carta is the prime example. On the one hand, there was no compunction in treating its provisions as void or spent when they had outlived their time.[94] For instance, chapter 11 of Magna Carta 1225 prohibited the hearing of common pleas in the King's Bench, and yet the development of bill proce-dure in the fifteenth century had made this a dead-letter. Popham and Anderson CJJ justified this by saying that it was 'in judgment of the law excepted out of the general Act to the end that no subject shall be without remedy to recover that which by the law belongs to him'.[95] On the other hand, in the case of chapter 29, the presumed policy was extended and elaborated in ways which could never have been contem-plated in 1225. The wording was broad enough: 'No free

Donis is still in force today, though entails can no longer be created: Ch. 4, n. 39.

[94] E.g. *Ilderton's Case* (1581) *Dyer's Notebooks*, p. 392; BL MS. Lansdowne 1078, fo. 59 (tr.: 'It appears from Magna Carta, c. 7, that a woman shall not have dower of a castle; but the justices held the contrary'); judgment affirmed on a writ of error, KB 27/1279, m. 211. For earlier examples see Baker, *Magna Carta*, pp. 88–9.

[95] *Agard* v. *Cavendish* (1599) Co. Nbk, BL MS. Harley 6686B, fo. 373. It might have been better to say that the original mischief had gone, since the King's Bench was now (de facto) stationary in Westminster Hall.

person shall be taken or imprisoned, or disseised ... or out-lawed, or exiled, or in any way destroyed ... except by the lawful judgment of his peers or by the law of the land.' The draftsman who penned those stirring words had not thought of habeas corpus, mandamus, trial by jury, or even Parliament. But that did not matter. The magnification and expansive interpretation of chapter 29 was the apotheosis of the old common-law approach to statutes. And there was a special reason behind it. Even if Magna Carta was for the most part deemed to be merely confirmatory of the common law, its unique value lay in its power to place effective moral restraints on queen and Parliament. As Coke never tired of pointing out, it had been confirmed thirty-two times, by king after king.[96] This repeated royal acknowledgement served to define the limits of the queen's monarchical inheritance, which (like an entail) descended with the limitations irrevoc-ably embedded in it, guaranteeing irremovable liberties to her people. The story was to reach its climax in 1628 with the great debates in Parliament on the liberty of the subject, culminat-ing in the Petition of Right. But the groundwork was laid, not in the seventeenth century, as most older commentators would have it, but in the reign of Elizabeth I.[97]

Until the second half of the sixteenth century, Magna Carta had featured little in constitutional discourse. It was not mentioned in Sir John Fortescue's treatise on limited

---

[96] He had learned this from Serjeant Fleetwood: Baker, *Magna Carta*, pp. 264 n. 80, 350.

[97] For what follows see Baker, *Magna Carta*, especially chs. 7–8; 'Personal Liberty' in Ch. 2.

monarchy. It seems first to have been accepted judicially in
1532 that arbitrary imprisonment on the king's authority was
an infringement of chapter 29; but there was at that date no
effective remedy.[98] As has already been mentioned, the
remedy was found by Elizabeth's judges in the writ of habeas
corpus, and the authority for it was soon located in chapter 29.
The so-called Puritan lawyers in the Elizabethan House of
Commons then seized on the great charter as a means of
attacking the high-handed ecclesiastical High Commission.
If the queen could not lock people up without cause, no more
could she empower commissioners to do so, without clear
statutory authority. The same principle applied to excesses of
jurisdiction by all prerogative and conciliar courts, to the
unlawful imposition of fines, and to all improper forms of
taxation or regulation (such as monopolies) which depended
ultimately on the sanction of imprisonment. By the end of the
reign, Magna Carta was seen as the reason why – unlike the
sovereigns of most other countries – the kings of England
ruled by law and not by their absolute power.[99] Here, then,
was a statute which through interpretation – in this case,
Elizabethan interpretation – had come to have more far-
reaching consequences than the makers had imagined. The
point must, however, be repeated that this form of equity
could be applied only to broadly worded ancient statutes. It
was not the usual approach, nor even a possible approach, to
the more elaborately worded legislation of the sixteenth

---

[98] *Serjeant Browne's Case* (1532) Spelman's reports, 93 Selden Soc. 183;
OHLE, vi. 91; Baker, *Magna Carta*, pp. 100–1.

[99] Hake, *Epieikeia*, pp. 78–9; Baker, *Magna Carta*, p. 270; Ch. 2, n. 41.

century. For the most part, the judges approached statutes in the same way as today. Lord Denning's boldness would not have been the norm, and Lord Simonds's rebuke would have been understood to represent the orthodoxy.

The Advance of Legislation

In most of the respects discussed so far, the relationship between judges and statutes seems not to have changed materially since the sixteenth century. What, then, do we mean if we say that we have moved into an age of statute? The immediately obvious answer is that there are now six to ten times as many statutes passed every year, and a far greater quantity of statutory instruments. The proportion of English law which is unwritten, and derived solely from legal reasoning, is therefore correspondingly smaller – and daily diminishing. Yet this imbalance could easily mislead. Most of the legislation which now swells the statute books is regulatory, dealing with specific spheres of activity on which the common law is silent. It is added on to the common law without changing it. The increase in legislation does not therefore indicate a correlative decline in the scope of the common law. It merely diminishes its share of the whole corpus of English law. If we look at the statute book of Elizabeth I's reign, we find exactly the same phenomenon on a smaller scale. Only around one in eight statutes was concerned with private law, and none of these interfered with its basic principles, as opposed to procedural reform. The principal concerns were criminal law, religion, revenue and – most of all, numerically – economic regulation and the relief of the poor.[100] There was no limit to what might legally be attempted by legislation: Parliament, said Manwood CB, can do all things.[101] But it generally left the substantive common law well alone. The comparison based on numbers is therefore one of scale and balance rather than something more fundamental.

The quantity of legislation has grown steadily ever since the sixteenth century, when lawyers already thought it was getting out of hand. But there was a seemingly more fundamental shift in the nineteenth century. A new age of reform, facilitated by the widening of the franchise in 1832, was inspired by the notion that society could be reformed by legislation. The process of reform was tackled with unprecedented thoroughness. Parliamentary select committees and royal commissions investigated in minute detail the workings of the legal system and the nation's social problems, beginning with the condition of the poor, producing book-length public reports. The solutions included discretionary regulatory regimes which depended on public funding raised by taxation, and operated outside the ordinary law. This was far removed from anything judges were able to do. Judges were not equipped to conduct social experiments, and they were

---

[100] An approximate classification of the public statutes might be:
31 per cent, economic and social regulation; 16 per cent, government and religion; 13 per cent, criminal law; 12 per cent, private law and procedure; 10 per cent, revenue (two subsidies per session); 18 per cent, special statutes.

[101] *Englefield's Case* (1591) Moo. 303, 336, *per* Manwood CB ('Parliamentum omnia potest'); 4 Leo. 174, 176. For the Latin maxim (echoing the canonists' *Papa omnia potest*) see also Baker, *Magna Carta*, p. 529 (1607).

not empowered directly or indirectly to impose taxation. They were able to deal only with individual cases coming before them according to the evidence adduced by the parties in relation to their own concerns; the public, or the government, could not intervene. It was therefore not merely acceptable but constitutionally imperative for judges to leave reforms of that kind to Parliament and content themselves with expounding the letter of the statute-book.

Of the unprecedented scale of the nineteenth-century reforms there is no doubt. It has inspired every generation since. It is commonly said, when something is amiss, that 'there ought to be a law against it'; and that is often what follows. There may even have arisen a popular belief that statute is a better kind of law than unwritten case-law. It is law made by the elected representatives of the people and put into an authoritative written text which everyone may read. Once again, however, it is questionable whether there has been any fundamental change in this respect. The Tudors had exactly the same belief that society could be improved, and the economy beneficially controlled, by means of legislation.[102] It was the belief which drove the Elizabethan poor laws, which were born of much agonised debate over how to distinguish the deserving poor from the idle

---

[102] See P. Slack, 'Dearth and Social Policy in Early Modern England' (1992) 5 *Social History of Medicine* 1–17; P. Slack, *Poverty and Policy in Tudor and Stuart England* (1988); D. Dean, *Law-Making and Society in Elizabethan England* (Cambridge, 1996), ch. 5; M. K. McIntosh, 'Poverty, Charity and Coercion in Elizabethan England' (2005) 35 *Journal of Interdisciplinary History* 457–79. For the preceding half of the Tudor period see *OHLE*, vi. 34–9.

scroungers, vagrants and beggars: how to support the former through taxation,[103] and how to get the latter into work.[104] It drove measures to combat the increase of town populations and the erosion of agriculture, and the consequent growth of urban unemployment and poverty.[105] It was the belief which drove competition law and the measures against profiteering. In fact, it was the belief which drove all the economic and regulatory legislation which filled the Elizabethan statute-book, much of which was preceded by the consideration of different schemes, albeit without a public investigation by royal commission.[106] Extensive governmental powers, including (for some purposes) powers of taxation, were delegated to the justices of the peace, who remained the principal local

---

[103] 5 Eliz. I, c. 2; 14 Eliz. I, c. 5; 39 Eliz. I, c. 3; 43 Eliz. I, c. 2. Francis Bacon said in 1601 that there had been so many bills for relief of the poor that they amounted to 'a feast of charity': *Proc. Parl.*, iii. 441.

[104] 5 Eliz. I, c. 4 (unemployed tradesmen compellable to follow trades), c. 20 (counterfeit gypsies); 14 Eliz. I, c. 5 (vagabonds); 18 Eliz. I, c. 3; 39 Eliz. I, c. 4 (rogues, vagabonds and 'sturdy beggars'), c. 5 (work-houses and houses of correction), c. 17 (lewd and wandering persons pretending to be soldiers); 43 Eliz. I, c. 7. For proclamations against rogues, vagabonds and 'masterless men' see *TRP*, ii. 415, 438, 539; iii. 46, 83, 96, 134, 157. See also Ch. 2, n. 130.

[105] 5 Eliz. I, c. 2 (protection of tillage); *TRP*, ii. 310 (tillage and enclosures, 1569); 13 Eliz. I, c. 13; 31 Eliz. I, c. 7 (cottages not to be built in the country without at least four acres of ground); 35 Eliz. I, c. 6 (town-houses not to be divided or let to lodgers); 39 Eliz. I, c. 1 (for preventing decay of towns and houses of husbandry), c. 2 (against the conversion of arable land to pasture). The dividing of houses in London, which led to overcrowding, had been forbidden by proclamation in 1580: *TRP*, ii. 466.

[106] See e.g. the wide-ranging contents of Lord Burghley's papers, BL MSS. Lansdowne 1–122.

authorities until the Local Government Act 1888. The justices' quarter sessions behaved in this mode more like administrative tribunals than courts of law. And there was at least one other model for the later form of tribunal in the commissioners of sewers, who had discretionary powers of taxation, demolition and compulsory purchase, with fines for default, and (by a statute of 1571) the power to make bye-laws without the royal assent.[107] Such sweeping powers were controversial from the outset, and it was in this context that Anderson CJ in 1598 made his celebrated pronouncement that a discretionary power conferred by Parliament was subject to judicial review.[108]

The Immortality of Common Law

Allowing that the shift towards statute is primarily a change of scale, a more persuasive argument for a jurisprudential shift might be that the change in the proportion of statute-law has itself brought about a revolution in the way statutes are viewed. In the days of Coke, the common law could be seen as an imposing edifice which had taken centuries to construct, in different styles of architecture, and was no less prized because of its antiquity, though some apartments had occasionally to be closed off by Parliament so that more modern arrangements could be made.[109] Those arrangements might

---

[107] 23 Hen. VIII, c. 5; 13 Eliz. I, c. 9.
[108] Above, at nn. 81–2. Fleetwood had objected to using the word 'discretion' in statutes at all: *Proc. Parl.*, i. 223.
[109] The metaphor is adapted from Bl. Comm. iii. 268.

be permanent, but some were temporary. Either way, the old structure was always there, and if Parliament removed the chains and No Entry signs it would return to use. It is doubtful whether anyone views the common law this way anymore. There is still a common law, but when pieces are chipped off by Parliament they are thrown away, or placed in museums guarded by legal historians. Although it has regained some of its former vitality since 1950,[110] the common law is perceived differently. Instead of being constantly in place, ready to revive when statutes are repealed, it is diminished in scope every time it is altered by statute. Statute law is no longer seen as merely supplementary to the eternal common law[111] because, however short its own life, a statute can extinguish part of the common law for ever.

It is one thing to assert this changed perception as a fact, but it is another matter to prove it to be legally correct. It turns on how repeals are thought to work. Do they exterminate fatally, or only suspend? Coke held that when a repealing statute was repealed, the original statute was revived.[112] This was not universally accepted, and perhaps

---

[110] Lord Hailsham thought that, in the first half of the twentieth century, the common law was so exhausted that it almost 'ran out of steam': Hailsham, *Hamlyn Revisited*, p. 36. Cf. Scarman's comments, Ch. 4, n. 117.

[111] Hailsham, *Hamlyn Revisited*, p. 67, said that the mischief rule was 'based on a theory of statute law as merely corrective of or supplementary to the common law which no longer corresponds to fact'. However, in 1974 Scarman asserted that the English judge still regarded legislation as 'an exception to, a graft upon, or a correction of, the customary law in his hands': *English Law – The New Dimension*, p. 3.

[112] *Case at a Committee concerning Bishops* (1606) 12 Co. Rep. 7. He later said, 'This is true and cannot be denied' (2 Co. Inst. 685).

was not true of every repealing statute;[113] it was a matter of parliamentary intention. But it may have been a working presumption. The same presumption of revival applied to statutes altering the common law.[114] Coke said that a statute which 'restrained' the common law would be taken strictly, and that an affirmative statute would not 'restrain' the common law.[115] The language of restraint suggests control rather than permanent abrogation. Certainly, in the case of statutory experiments which were time-limited – the true Henry VIII clauses,[116] though now of late called sunset-clauses – it was assumed that the common law would return when the term expired. No doubt this was the legislative intention implicit in

---

[113] Cf. *Anon.* (1560/80) BL MS. Hargrave 322, fo. 106v (tr.: 'If a statute is repealed, and then the statute of repeal is repealed, and there are no words of revival in the statute, the law is at large, and both the first statute and the last are gone etc. Gerrard Att.-Gen.: Such is the statute of 2 Edw. VI, [c. 21], which willed that all positive laws and ordinances prohibiting priests to marry ... shall be void; but this statute was repealed by 1 Mar. [sess. 2, c. 2], and no words of reviving the positive laws.'

[114] See e.g. Co. Nbk, BL MS. Harley 6686A, fo. 76 (1594) (tr. 'I also cited the statute of 1 Edw. VI, c. 2, which is repealed by the statute of 1 Mar., c. 2, sess. 2, whereby [i.e. by the former] it was provided that all process shall be made out by ecclesiastical judges in the king's name ... which proves that these were formerly the bishops' courts; and so they now remain after the repeal of the said Act.' In *R* v. *Somervile* (1583) ibid. (6686B), fo. 582, it was held that the repeal in 1554 of a statute of 1541 brought back the common law; but the 1554 statute expressly said that the common law was to be restored.

[115] 2 Co. Inst. 455, 472.

[116] They were widely used in his time, but were even older. What is now called a Henry VIII clause was introduced under Queen Victoria.

their temporary character: but were not almost all statutes impermanent in comparison with common law?

A good example of a statute changing the common law temporarily was the 1512 statute which took away benefit of clergy from laymen convicted of murder. This was an experiment, 'to endure to the next Parliament'. It was fiercely condemned by the prelates and allowed to lapse, whereupon the common law returned. Murderers could again claim clergy until 1531, when the benefit was once more removed by a time-limited statute, though this time the statute was renewed and in 1540 made perpetual.[117] It seems probable that if the 1540 statute had been repealed by Parliament later in the sixteenth century, the common law would have come back in the same way as it had in 1515. But by the time the 1540 statute *was* eventually repealed (in 1863), benefit of clergy had been abolished and so the question could not arise.[118] However, when the statute of 1827 abolishing benefit of clergy was itself repealed in 1967,[119] benefit of clergy did not this time return. Had anyone felt that an explanation was needed, which no one did, it was to be found in another statute. The Interpretation Act 1889[120] (since re-enacted[121]) provided that

---

[117] 4 Hen. VIII, c. 2; 23 Hen. VIII, c. 1; 32 Hen. VIII, c. 3. Much confusion was caused by the amendment and partial repeal of this legislation under Edward VI, followed by the partial repeal of the amendments: see *R.* v. *Powlter* (1610) 11 Co. Rep. 29.

[118] 7 & 8 Geo. IV, c. 28.

[119] Criminal Law Act 1967 (c. 58), sch. 3. Since s. 1 of the statute abolished the distinction between felony and misdemeanour, a revival of benefit of clergy (which applied only to felonies) would have been nugatory anyway.

[120] Interpretation Act 1889 (52 & 53 Vict., c. 63), s. 38(2).

[121] Interpretation Act 1978 (c. 30), s. 16(1)(a).

where an Act repeals an enactment, the repeal does not, unless the contrary intention appears, revive anything not in force or existing at the time when the repeal takes effect. This intriguing enactment merits a closer inspection.

Statutory Extinguishment of Common Law

The word 'anything' in the Interpretation Act was a deliberate extension of the wording in a previous statute,[122] and it is generally assumed to extend to the common law as well as to repealed statutes,[123] unless a contrary intention appears. A contrary intention may (perhaps) be presumed where the rule of law in question is one of procedure or evidence rather than substance. For instance, the repeal in 1954 of parts of the Statute of Frauds 1677, which provided that actions could not be brought on certain categories of contract unless evidenced by a memorandum in writing, seemingly brought back the common law, so that such contracts could again be enforced without writing.[124] The general assumption, however, is that the

---

[122] Lord Brougham's Act 1850 (13 & 14 Vict., c. 21), s. 5, which dealt only with repeals of repealing statutes.

[123] A. L. Diamond, 'Repeal and Desuetude of Statutes' (1975) 28 *Current Legal Problems* 107–24, at 110–11; *Bennion on Statutory Interpretation* (7th edn, 2017), pp. 211–12, 668. Cf. *Craies on Legislation* (11th edn by D. Greenberg, 2017), pp. 683–4, which seems to state the contrary; but the only case cited was concerned with sub-subsections (c)–(e). The contrary position was also taken by Dr P. T. O'Neill in 1973: 36 MLR 642; 37 MLR 360.

[124] Law Reform (Enforcement of Contracts) Act 1954 (2 & 3 Eliz. II, c. 34). Diamond (previous note) explained this on the ground that the general rule does not apply to statutes which merely amend or suspend the

common law is no longer something 'in force or existing' when statute has replaced it. This has some odd results. One is that a considerable part of the law is now contained in repealed statutes, which rule us from their graves. Their work was done in a single day, but the effect lives on. For anyone who happens to know what the common law was – and the books of common law contain no expiry dates – it is necessary to consult statutes long since repealed, perhaps as long ago as the time of Queen Victoria, to find out what today's law is. If one were to think of the common law as subsisting in eternity, a great part of it is suppressed or kept in suspense by statutes which have been repealed. The explanation for this seemingly remarkable state of affairs is that no one does think – and apparently no one thought in 1889 – that the common law still has that kind of immortality. If it did, the common law would still be 'existing' after a statute has supplanted it, and therefore outside the terms of the Interpretation Act.

If this represents a change of thinking since the time of Elizabeth I, it is chiefly a consequence of the effluxion of time. In the Tudor period, although much of the common law had been sidelined by reforms, little of it had been permanently swept away. The old real actions, even trial by battle, were still part of the law and available for use, though largely dormant.[125] Most legislative adjustments were seen as fine-tuning or reinforcing

common law. A better explanation might be that the 1677 Act did not invalidate the contracts in question but only introduced an exclusionary rule of evidence which the 1954 Act abolished.

[125] Elaborate preparations for a trial by battle in a writ of right were made in *Lowe and Kyme* v. *Paramour* (1571) Dyer 301. But the case was settled before battle commenced.

the common law rather than replacing it. Today, however, it would be meaningless and absurd to assert that, were it not for some old statutes (which have long since been repealed), one was still entitled at common law to bring a writ of right, or an appeal of felony, and risk trial by battle. That body of law will never be brought back and has therefore ceased in any meaningful sense to 'exist'. The common law of procedure has gone forever, as has most of the law of real property. There is no meaningful sense in which such long-gone law still exists as the common law of England, though it is true that bits of it may still live on in exile as the common law of other nations beyond the seas.

The repeal provision in the Interpretation Act nevertheless raises several puzzles. One has already been mentioned: the present law can be ascertained only by knowing about, and looking at, repealed statutes. If someone commits a statutory offence, and then the statute is repealed, he is still liable to be convicted of the offence because the repeal is not a retrospective annulment.[126] That is an odd result, but the House of Lords has held it to be a consequence of the Interpretation Act.[127] The reasoning is opaque, and it might have been better to hold the relevant provision of the Interpretation Act void for self-contradiction.[128] It means

---

[126] *Bennion on Statutory Interpretation* (7th edn, 2017), p. 212, limits the principle to prosecutions started before the repeal, relying on s. 16(1)(e) (as to which, see n. 129 below).

[127] *R. v. West London Magistrates, ex p. Simeon* [1983] AC 234 (upholding a conviction under the Vagrancy Act 1824 which occurred three months after the statute repealing that Act came into effect).

[128] Section 16(1)(d) and (e) provides that a repeal does not affect 'any . . . penalty, forfeiture or punishment incurred [before the repeal] . . . or

that, although the original statute is no longer 'in force', it can still send someone to prison. This quality of operating after repeal is in contrast to the common law, which cannot operate after abolition. Stranger than this, juristically speaking, there can be legal vacuums. The explicit abolition of the rule in *Shelley's Case* (1581) in 1925[129] has never caused problems, because family settlements are no longer made in the form to which it referred. But Parliament did not put a different rule in its place, and, were it still important, the courts would be faced with a conundrum. Are they allowed independently to come to the same conclusion as the judges in *Shelley's Case*, without feeling bound by it as a rule, or are they expected to find a different rule, or should they treat each case as turning on the parties' intention and not try to formulate a rule at all? An odder example is the curt enactment of 1977 that 'Detinue is abolished'.[130] Even Parliament cannot alter the fact of detinue – that is, detaining other people's goods – and the

---

any . . . legal proceeding or remedy in respect of any *such* penalty . . . and any *such* penalty . . . may be imposed as if the repealing Act had not been passed.' The word 'such' shows that this refers only to a penalty or punishment 'incurred' before the repeal, and this does not naturally refer to an offence which has not yet been tried. On the other hand, the words 'may be imposed' can only refer to a penalty not yet 'incurred'.

[129] Law of Property Act 1925 (15 & 16 Geo. V, c. 20), s. 131. A more recent example is the rule in *Bain* v. *Fothergill*, abolished by the Law of Property (Miscellaneous Provisions) Act 1989 (c. 34), s. 3. In some Canadian provinces, the rules in *Purefoy* v. *Rogers*, *Whitby* v. *Mitchell* and *Saunders* v. *Vautier* have also been abrogated by statute, and in 2009 Ireland followed suit in respect of the first two.

[130] Torts (Interference with Goods) Act 1977 (c. 32), s. 2(1); *IELH* (5th edn), pp. 76, 426.

statute cannot have referred to the writ of detinue, which was abolished over a hundred years earlier. It presumably referred to the body of law derived from the old action of detinue; but that law was mostly embodied in the 1977 Act and therefore not really abolished. At least in that case the new position was set out, and the Act can be complied with merely by refraining to use the word 'detinue' anymore.

Let us now consider a more perplexing case. Suppose the Theft Act 1968 were to be repealed in a statute-law revision exercise. Would the common law of larceny, robbery and burglary return? Presumably not, since the 1968 Act expressly abolished those common-law offences by name and so the law which governed them no longer 'exists'.[131] But would theft then become lawful, for want of any law against it? No doubt the common law, like nature, abhors a vacuum. But the courts cannot create new offences, and if they tried to fill the vacuum they would be usurping the legislative function by refusing to give effect to two clear statutes, one abolishing the common-law offences and the other repealing the statute which replaced them. It is a far-fetched example, chosen to make the point; but, given the number of statutory provisions which are repealed nowadays, the question is not an idle one. It is already an issue in relation to statutes, such as the Fixed Term Parliaments Act 2011, which abolish or modify parts of the

---

[131] Theft Act 1968 (c. 60), s. 32(1) ('any offence at common law of larceny, robbery, burglary . . .'). Parliament rarely indicates expressly that it is abrogating the common law, though another example is the Animals Act 1971 (c. 22), s. 8. Where there is no express abolition, a common-law offence cannot be impliedly abolished by the creation of a statutory offence which overlaps with it: *R.* v. *Goldstein* [2005] UKHL 63.

royal prerogative. And it could arise in a more subtle way if legislation restating the common law, with or without modifications, were to be repealed. There is an example of this with a connection to Elizabethan law. The common-law judges developed a practice in Elizabethan times of refusing to allow the enforcement of a penal money-bond if the debtor paid the debt, with damages and costs. In 1705 this regime was placed on a statutory footing, with some alterations. Then, in 1948, the statute was repealed. It has been assumed by eminent modern authorities that there is still a common law of penalties, in parallel with equity, though this is seemingly at odds with the Interpretation Act.[132]

A more important case might be the Human Rights Act 1998, which has recently been threatened with repeal or modification. To the extent that it can be taken as a restatement, replacement and enlargement of the common law, a repeal should in theory put paid to its contents for good.[133] But can it be supposed that repeal of the Human Rights Act and of chapter 29 of Magna Carta[134] would bring back a long-forgotten prerogative power to imprison people and confiscate their property

[132] The effect of the repeal was not considered in *Cavendish Square Holding BV* v. *El Makdessi* [2015] UKSC 67. This point emerged in discussion with Dr P. Turner. See also *IELH* (5th edn), pp. 346–7.

[133] Whether a statutory regime replaces, freezes or merely supplements the common law depends on the supposed intention of Parliament: Burrows, *Thinking about Statutes*, pp. 58–67. Cf. *New Windsor Corporation* v. *Taylor* [1899] AC 41 (as to custom and statute); *Att.-Gen.* v. *De Keyser's Royal Hotel Ltd* [1920] AC 508 (as to royal prerogative and statute).

[134] The courts have assumed that Magna Carta, c. 29, has not been overtaken and impliedly repealed by the Human Rights Act. Indeed,

without due process? Presumably not. But, if not, then the repeal would be nugatory. It would still be necessary to find the current law in the repealed statutes, as reinterpreted over the centuries, or in the decisions which became entwined with them over the centuries when they were in force.

This is not the place to try to resolve such conundrums, which seem not to have bothered many people in practice before now. The historical lesson to be drawn from the Interpretation Acts – and the reason for this lengthy excursion – is that Parliament is now so powerful that it may obliterate parts of the common law in an instant. It is outright abrogation, not retirement or suspended animation. As a consequence of this, the common law is no longer seen as a comprehensive body of enduring jurisprudence covering all aspects of human relations, but rather as the patchwork of bits and pieces that are left after centuries of legislative cutting.[135] In that sense, as well as in the more obvious sense that we have many more statutes, we have indeed moved into an Age of Statute.

The Value of the Common-Law Method

The dominance of statute law is, for these reasons, complete; but it is only part of the picture. Dominance is not the same

there is a doctrine that c. 29 (unlike other parts of Magna Carta) cannot be impliedly repealed.

[135] It is otherwise comprehensive: *McLoughlin* v. *O'Brian* [1983] 1 AC 410, 429–30, *per* Lord Scarman ('The common law . . . covers everything which is not covered by statute. It knows no gaps; there can be no *casus omissus*'). Cf. Ch. 4, n. 46.

as superiority, and the supposed superiority of statute law has become less easy to accept than the general benevolence of its vast empire. There is still a school of thought that if common-law principles are put into statutory form, or codified, they become clearer and more accessible. But this is only likely to be so if the common law is already clear, and if it can be assumed that no further refinement will be necessary. Those criteria are seldom met. The comparative advantages of the common law were recently spelled out in the Hamlyn lecture given by Sir John Laws: 'The common law is gradual, but legislation is immediate ... Parliament's very sovereignty dooms its products to a transient, at least a precarious, existence. Whereas the courts hone and refine principles over time, the legislature creates new regimes at every turn ... Courts and Parliament both make new lamps, but the courts make new lamps from old.' [136] Coke's ghost would surely have nodded with approval. To Coke, the innate superiority of judge-made law, refined through many successions of ages, was obvious. But even Coke knew that the judges were not competent to erect most of the beneficial regimes introduced by Parliament, such as the poor law or the regulation of watercourses, since they encroached on the autonomy of the individual and required taxation. He accepted that legislation was not just a necessary evil but a potential for good as well as bad.[137] Indeed, he was prominent in preparing such legislation himself in the 1590s, and in enforcing it.

[136] Laws, *The Common Law Constitution*, p. 21.
[137] See *Att.-Gen.* v. *Twyne* (1602) above, n. 12.

Nobody could doubt the correctness of this distinction. But we are now four centuries on from Coke, and well over a century past the great days of Victorian law reform, which was carried out with immense care and skilful draftsmanship. A memory of that world lives on in the Law Commission, created in 1965 with a statutory responsibility 'to take and keep under review all the law ... with a view to its systematic development and reform, including in particular the codification of such law, the elimination of anomalies, the repeal of obsolete and unnecessary enactments, the reduction of the number of separate enactments and generally the simplification and modernisation of the law'. [138] Most written law, however, does not come from that studious source but from politicians. And Parliament has been transformed in character.

The House of Commons in Coke's time was packed with barristers and others who had at least read something of Littleton and Magna Carta in the inns of court. They did not belong to political parties, warring with each other to gain and cling on to their moment in power. Coke, the leading lawyer of his day, was proud to have been elected to Parliament in 1593 by 7,000 Norfolk electors without dissent.[139] No one now has the time to serve in the Commons except full-time politicians who have often done little else. Career politicians aspire to be ministers of state, and some ministers measure

---

[138] Law Commissions Act 1965 (c. 22), s. 3.
[139] Autobiographical note in BL MS. Harley 6687A, fos. 13v–14. It helped, of course, that he had already been nominated as the next Speaker and was unopposed.

their success as much by the quantity of legislation they pass as by whether it ultimately succeeds in its aims.[140] Unkind observers have accused the worst of them of indulging in 'binge legislation'. Although select committees have in recent years acquired a significantly useful role in scrutinising bills, legislation is still steamrollered through Parliament on the footing that a government has a mandate to enact every detail in its party manifesto against all odds. Provided the government has a majority in the Commons, it cannot be prevented from doing this, even though no political manifesto since World War II has been endorsed by a majority of individual voters. Lord Hailsham referred to this phenomenon in his 1983 Hamlyn Lectures as 'elective dictatorship'.[141] The exigencies of politics mean that too much legislation is loosely or impenetrably drafted, often with the vital provisions hidden away in schedules. Obscure measures slip through because they are less carefully read, and have several possible meanings which can be assented to for different reasons.[142] Constitutionally offensive measures may be protected from excision by the device of inserting in the bill even more outrageous clauses which may be withdrawn as concessions.[143] Parliament itself acknowledges the inadequacy of its products

---

[140] Cf. Serjeant Yelverton's remark, as Speaker of the Commons in 1597, that 'the price of laws is valued by the weight . . . not counted by the number': *Proc. Parl.*, iii. 299.

[141] Hailsham, *Hamlyn Revisited*, pp. 25–32.

[142] Parliamentary counsel have denied that obscurity is deliberate: J. R. Spencer, 'The Drafting of Criminal Legislation: Need It Be So Impenetrable?' (2008) 67 *CLJ* 585, 597.

[143] See e.g. Sedley, *Lions under the Throne*, p. 194 n. 5.

by regularly giving ministers the power to rewrite them when they prove not to work as intended, or by passing skeleton bills with delegated powers to pop in the substantive provisions when they have been worked out. Some statutes are alarmingly broad in scope, effectively undermining Parliament.[144] Some read more like departmental memoranda than legislation. Others are little more than statements of intention or aspiration.[145] It is not their purpose to achieve anything other than favourable press reports.

Parliamentary draftsmanship is still practised by lawyers of the highest calibre, and there is no doubting their dedication to improving the statute-book.[146] But their efforts have been frustrated both by the desire of their ministerial clients to be over-prescriptive and by the new-speak called the Plain English movement. Introducing new forms of language and legislative architecture supposed to be more easily comprehended by the person on the London Underground risks making statutes less intelligible for everyone, including

---

[144] E.g. the Localism Act 2011 (c. 20), s. 1(1), which tacitly reversed the common law by giving every local authority 'power to do anything that individuals generally may do' (i.e. without specific statutory authorisation). As if that were not sufficiently broad, s. 5 and s. 236(1) empowered the Secretary of State to amend or repeal *any* statute which he 'thinks' restricts local authorities from exercising this power. This attracted little comment at the time. See Sedley, *Lions under the Throne*, p. 224.

[145] E.g. the Autism Act 2009 (c. 15), which merely required the Secretary of State to publish a strategy and keep it under review. Parliament gave no indication of what the strategy should be.

[146] The positive case is eloquently made by P. Sales, 'The Contribution of Legislative Drafting to the Rule of Law' (2018) 77 *CLJ* 630–5.

members of Parliament. One need only instance the disappearance of the useful distinction between 'shall' and 'may', which has been cast aside as insufficiently plain. It was supposed that instances of the ambiguity of 'shall' outweighed its normal clarity,[147] and the result is that statutes now contain confusing predictions and false statements instead of imperatives.[148] Far worse than linguistic infelicity, however, is obscurity. Bad legislation reached a low point in 2003, under a Home Secretary who did not understand legal principles or trust judges.[149] His Sexual Offences Act 2003 (c. 42) created fifty new offences, some with prurient specificity, while failing to deal with elementary legal questions such as the requirement for *mens rea*.[150] Even worse was his Criminal Justice Act 2003 (c. 44), passed on the same day, which contained 338 sections and 28 schedules and was condemned in the Court of Appeal as being 'at best obscure, and at worst impenetrable'.[151]

---

[147] There was once a paper on the website of the Parliamentary Counsel (Drafting Techniques Group) entitled 'Shall' (2008), which set out at length the tortured internal debates over this.

[148] E.g. Constitutional Reform Act 2005 (c. 4), s. 23: 'There is to be a Supreme Court' (a prediction) and 'The Court consists . . .' (a false statement, until the prediction came to pass). The introduction of a new Supreme Court required a new name to be found for the old Supreme Court, and someone decided it should be 'Senior Courts', apparently unaware that the County Courts (1846) were senior to the High Court (1875). The correct comparative between high and supreme is 'superior'.

[149] He resigned in 2004 after the powers of indefinite detention which he introduced in 2001 were held by the House of Lords (in the case of the Belmarsh Nine) to be contrary to human rights law: Ch. 4, n. 75.

[150] See Spencer, 'The Drafting of Criminal Legislation' (n. 143 above) at p. 590.

[151] R. v. *Campbell* [2006] EWCA Crim 726, *per* Rose LJ.

These were extreme examples of binge legislation, but they are not the end of it. Most criminal offences nowadays are not created by a parliamentary decision at all. Of the 2,106 new criminal offences created in the single year 2014 – of which 638 were punishable by imprisonment – 92 per cent were introduced by statutory instruments, with minimal parliamentary scrutiny.[152] Then again, constant revision means that it is often necessary to join several enactments together, along with the various instruments bringing different parts into force at different times, taking care to note that parts of the statute as printed may have been deleted or adjusted by subsequent amending statutes. In 2007 Sir Igor Judge (as he then was), President of the Queen's Bench Division, gave the example of a case which required detailed submissions in court on the effect of five different statutes to discover whether a convicted defendant had committed any criminal offence at all, and the problem was so complicated that judgment had to be reserved; by that time the defendant had already served his sentence of imprisonment.[153] It is a serious affront to the rule of law when even the judges, assisted by learned counsel, cannot readily ascertain what the criminal law is. It is even worse when, as the Law

---

[152] J. Chalmers and F. Leverick, 'Criminal Law in the Shadows: Creating Offences in Delegated Legislation' (2018) 38 *Legal Studies* 221–41.

[153] Lecture in Lincoln's Inn, 29 Oct. 2007, quoted in Spencer, 'The Drafting of Criminal Legislation' (n. 143 above) at p. 585. Professor Spencer also cited a judicial complaint that, since it had taken all afternoon to explain the relevant sentencing provisions to the court, it was impossible to comply with the statute which required them to be explained to an offender in ordinary language.

Commission recently reported, penal legislation is so convoluted that sentencing decisions are 'routinely unlawful'.[154] The problem is by no means confined to criminal statutes, or even to recent legislation.[155] But these examples show that Coke was right. When the common law is believed to be wanting, legislation can be a far from adequate instrument for reforming it.

Despite all this, the Elizabethan approach to legislation survives in an important way. Statutes still have to be interpreted against the background of the common law.[156] With the exception of the land law and common-law procedure, few statutes have in fact overturned basic principles of common law.[157] It is generally accepted that there is a sensible division of responsibility between what is best left to judges, sometimes called 'lawyers' law', and what has to be left to Parliament.[158] Questions of social policy which involve the balancing of claims upon the national purse, or the invention

---

[154] Law Commission, *The Sentencing Code, Volume I: Report* (2018) Law Com. no. 382, at pp. 8, 11, 58. Out of a sample of 262 criminal appeals from 2012, 95 involved sentences which were held to be unlawful.

[155] See e.g. the diversity of views on the Limitation Acts of 1939 and 1980 in *Williams* v. *Central Bank of Nigeria* [2014] UKSC 10.

[156] *Bennion on Statutory Interpretation* (7th edn, 2017), pp. 650–1.

[157] Cf. Dyson, *Justice*, p. 56 ('Parliament rarely shows any appetite for changing the common law').

[158] See further T. [Lord] Bingham, *The Business of Judging: Selected Essays and Speeches* (Oxford, 2000), pp. 25–34; Lord Dyson, 'Where the Common Law Fears to Tread' (2013) 34 *Statute Law Review* 1–11; 'Are the Judges too Powerful?' (Bentham Lecture, 2013), printed in Dyson, *Justice*, ch. 3; *Craies on Legislation* (11th edn, 2017), pp. 664–71; Burrows, *Thinking about Statutes*, pp. 74–85; Ch. 4, n. 53.

of new criminal offences, are obviously not for judges. The same is true of some newer conceptions of human rights – such as the right to undergo an abortion, or the right to die, or the right to change gender – on the different ground that judges have neither a democratic mandate nor an exclusive expertise to decide such questions. No one doubts that there is such a boundary, or that it is of constitutional importance, though there is a controversy about where to draw it.[159] On the other hand, the principles of the law of contract, tort and restitution, and of judicial review, are creatures of the common law and best developed incrementally through legal reasoning.[160] Likewise, the law of homicide and the general principles of criminal law. Such statutory changes as have been made in these areas build upon the common-law framework without replacing it.[161] For instance, the Sale of Goods Acts 1893, which was in force until 1979 and still mostly

[159] J. Sumption, 'Judicial and Political Decision-Making: The Uncertain Boundary' (2011) 16 *Judicial Review* 301–15, with a response by S. Sedley, 'Judicial Politics' (2012) ibid. 95–100; N. W. Barber, R. Ekins and P. Yowell eds., *Lord Sumption and the Limits of the Law* (Oxford, 2016); *Craies on Legislation* (11th edn, 2017), pp. 664–71; Sedley, *Lions under the Throne*, pp. 182–3. It was also the subject of Lord Sumption's Reith Lectures (BBC) in 2019, which provoked similar responses.

[160] See *Patel* v. *Mirza* [2016] UKSC 52, at pp. 71–2, para. 226, *per* Lord Sumption ('The common law is . . . a body of instincts and principles which . . . is developed organically, building on what was there before. It has a greater inherent flexibility and capacity to develop independently of legislation than codified systems do').

[161] There is still a presumption against a legislative intention to alter clearly established principles of common law: *Craies on Legislation* (11th edn, 2017), pp. 672–6; *Bennion on Statutory Interpretation* (7th edn, 2017), p. 665.

survives in substance,[162] was a codification of the common law of sale, and it was once thought helpful to look at the case-law from which it was derived for the meaning of its well-worn language.[163] Whether or not such recourse to the common law is appropriate,[164] the legislation applies only where there is a contract of a certain kind, and some of it works by deeming contracts to contain terms which were not expressed by the parties. If there was no common law of contract, the Act would have no meaning or effect. The partial abolition of privity of contract by the Contracts (Rights of Third Parties) Act 1999 is likewise predicated on the common law. It applies only when there is a contract between parties, and the parties are free to exclude its effect by agreement. Again, if there was no common law of contract, the Act would have no meaning or effect. That is equally true of all the statutes dealing with particular types of contract,[165] and most of those dealing with tort.[166]

---

[162] The Sale of Goods Act 1979 (c. 54), which replaced it, retains much of the same language; some of its provisions were modified by the Supply of Goods and Services Act 1982 (c. 29) and the Consumer Rights Act 2015 (c. 15).

[163] The draftsman published a book setting out the decisions on which it was based: Sir Mackenzie Chalmers, *The Sale of Goods Act 1893* (1894).

[164] The general principle is that, since a codifying measure is intended to replace the common law, it is undesirable to look at the previous cases: *Bank of England* v. *Vagliano Bros* [1891] AC 107, 144–5, *per* Lord Herschell LC (as to the Bills of Exchange Act 1882); *R.* v. *Platt* [2016] EWCA Crim 21, *per* Lord Thomas LCJ.

[165] The same point is made by Burrows, 'The Interaction between Common Law and Statute' in *Thinking about Statutes*, pp. 56–63.

[166] P. Mitchell, 'Patterns of Legal Change' (2012) 65 *Current Legal Problems* 177, 188.

As was mentioned earlier, the majority of statutes and orders nowadays – as in Elizabethan times – are regulatory and deal with matters which were not dealt with, and could not be dealt with, under the common law. If and when they are repealed, the common-law void necessarily returns. Most of them are never made the subject of litigation and do not acquire a judicial gloss. If they have an intelligible and unambiguous meaning, and do not collide with basic rights or the rule of law, that is what they must mean. People will have relied on that meaning, and it is not appropriate for courts to tell them they were wrong. But when statutes do require judicial interpretation, the techniques are still those of the common law. As Sir John Laws said in his Hamlyn lecture, legislation is mediated to the people by the common law: 'It only has effect through the methods of the common law. The common law is the interpreter of our statutes, and is the crucible which gives them life. The process of interpretation is intensely coloured by the common law's insights of substantive principle: reason, fairness and the presumption of liberty.'[167] That control on statute law is a valuable legacy from the time of Elizabeth I, and it is likely to prove increasingly necessary as the statute-book continues to deteriorate. Indeed, its survival suggests that the movement from an age of common law to an age of statute, though real enough in the sense explained earlier, has been greatly overstated.

[167] Laws, *The Common Law Constitution*, pp. 3–4. See also Burrows, *Thinking about Statutes*, pp. 68–74. It is a two-way relationship, for sometimes the common law has been developed by analogy with statute: J. Beatson, 'Has the Common Law a Future?' (1997) 56 *CLJ* 291, 303–13; Burrows, op. cit. 45–56.

4

The Elizabethan Inheritance

In attempting a comparison between the law of today and that of Elizabeth I's reign, there is a difficulty beyond the mere distance of time and the quantity of change. Not only are the forty-five years of Elizabeth I's reign long enough to have a legal history of their own (not yet written), but Elizabeth II has already reigned for sixty-eight years of unremitting legal change. When the writer entered the Inner Temple in 1963, it was still frequented by a few benchers, such as Lord Goddard, who were called to the bar in the time of Queen Victoria. That is almost a third of the way back to Elizabeth I, and not so far from the world in which Miss Hamlyn (1860–1949) acquired her deep respect for English law. The legal world now is very different. It is to be hoped that at some point the lecturers in this series will survey the legal history of the second Elizabethan period. For the time being, the comparisons will have to be made with a broad brush, and with more emphasis on the present century than on the rest of the reign. But 1952 is the point at which to begin.

When the queen came to the throne, many features of the common law system were outwardly similar to those of 1558. Substantial cases were still tried at the assizes, where the judges were received with the full pomp of cathedral bells and trumpets, sheriffs girt with swords, and javelin men, and their commissions under the great seal were produced and solemnly proclaimed in open court before they began work. The judges, still all men, wore the same robes as their Elizabethan precursors, albeit with the addition of headgear and neckwear from a later period. Proceedings in civil as well as criminal cases were entirely oral, including the evidence in chief, so that anyone could go into a courtroom and follow what was going on, and the judge not infrequently gave his judgment extempore at the end of the trial. Latin words and phrases, such as *res ipsa loquitur, ex parte,* certiorari and ultra vires, were still conveniently acceptable – provided they were pronounced in the old way. Authorities were produced in the form of printed books, and the relevant passages were read out and discussed. There were as yet no electronics or Xerox machines, though the pen had been replaced for many purposes by the manual typewriter. Conveyancing was still commonly effected by indentures between parties of the first part and the second part, duly sealed and delivered as their act and deed. Things were much the same when the writer was called to the bar in 1966. These were, however, only superficial continuities; and even they have now gone. The purpose of the present lecture is to indicate some of the principal ways in which the law has really changed since 1603, and in so doing to reflect upon whether anything of value has survived.

The Courts

The courts were the first major institution to be reformed. Dissatisfaction with the assizes and quarter sessions led to the appointment in 1966 of a Royal Commission chaired by Lord Beeching,[1] the axe-wielding economist. Perhaps surprisingly, his axe chopped through the courts with far less resistance than in the case of the railways. The commission recognised the value of the assizes in bringing justice to the people, in an impressive manner conducive to local pride, but thought that such factors weighed more in small communities than in the large conurbations where most crime (and commercial business) was generated, and that the price paid in efficiency was too great. It was easy to set out the case for reform. For instance, a travelling day was set aside at each location to allow papers, typewriters and other paraphernalia to be loaded into boxes, or even wicker hampers,[2] and for the judges, with their clerks and marshals, to be loaded into suitable carriages for onward transmission. But the sardonic aspersions in the report were somewhat exaggerated because, like all well-matured institutions, the assizes worked better than a cold time-and-motion analysis might suggest. The commission's own statistics showed that waiting times were actually shorter at the assizes than in London, though this may have been in part because the judges spent so much of their time on circuit. Moreover, from the economic point of view, delay was two-edged. Since it encouraged out-of-court settlements, it was feared that a more efficient system might lead to fewer

---

[1] *Royal Commission on Assizes and Quarter Sessions 1966–69: Report* (1969) Cmnd 4153.

[2] This may refer to R. C. Lancaster (1896–1981), known as 'Lanky', clerk of assize for the South Eastern Circuit, who kept up the tradition of using a hamper for indictments and other documents. The writer remembers hearing him read the commission at Chelmsford in 1961.

settlements and therefore increase pressure on the courts. The commissioners frankly acknowledged that abolishing the assizes would not save money, and would in fact transfer a considerable financial burden from the county authorities to the central government. But they recommended abolition, and the axe duly fell in 1971.[3] By a separate measure, Admiralty judges were relieved from trying divorce cases – the last bizarre legacy of Doctors' Commons.[4]

Few have questioned the reforms, but fifty years later the system is working less well than hoped. The judges did not notice, until it was too late, that the control of their courts was being handed over to the civil service.[5] The clerks of assize and clerks of the peace (usually barristers), aided by a few other clerks and secretaries,[6] were

---

[3] Courts Act 1971 (c. 23). A number of other courts, many of them virtually defunct, were also abolished.

[4] The Probate, Divorce and Admiralty Division of the High Court reflected the specialisms of the advocates in Doctors' Commons, the last of whom died in 1912. It was abolished by the Administration of Justice Act 1970 (c. 31), s. 1, and the Family Division created. Admiralty business went to the Queen's Bench Division, probate to the Chancery Division.

[5] Some blame for this was attached to Lord Widgery LCJ, but it was implicit in the recommendations. There had been only one judge on the commission, and one QC, outnumbered by a civil servant, three businessmen (if Beeching himself may be so classified) and a trade union official.

[6] The only officers beneath the clerk of assize and his deputy (if any) were the circuit associate and the clerk of indictments, usually barristers; they were assisted by a few secretaries. The writer was told that R. C. Lancaster (n. 2 above) ran the entire circuit with one deputy and one clerk. Preliminary preparations were made by the under-sheriff, invariably a local solicitor.

replaced by thousands of civil servants with a different mentality.[7] Some of the old assize towns ceased to be visited by High Court judges, throwing the burdens of travel on to parties and witnesses. In 1986 responsibility for criminal prosecutions was transferred from the police, aided by a few hundred county prosecuting solicitors and staff, to a new Crown Prosecution Service with a staff of thousands.[8] However desirable this was from a constitutional point of view, the measure seems paradoxically to have made the system far less efficient than it was before 1971. An exasperated circuit judge, remarking on a three-year delay in a straightforward case, recently described the criminal legal system as 'beyond the point of collapse'.[9] The Bar Council agrees that the system is 'on its knees'.[10] Civil justice has also suffered, not least because a disproportionate share of the available funding – much of it derived from fees paid by civil litigants – has been diverted to criminal justice and prisons, which are also in

---

[7] The Courts and Tribunals Service now employs around 17,000 staff, but it is difficult to ascertain how many of them correspond with the few who maintained the assizes and quarter sessions.

[8] Prosecution of Offences Act 1985 (c. 23). In 2018 the Crown Prosecution Service employed over 8,000 staff. See P. Rock, *The Official History of Criminal Justice in England and Wales, vol. II: Institution-Building* (2019).

[9] *The Times*, 2 Aug. 2019, p. 15 (Truro Crown Court). Cf. *The Times*, 3 Sept. 2019, p. 15 (Shrewsbury Crown Court) ('breaking at every point . . . not fit for purpose'). There is a disturbing indictment of the criminal justice system in Anon., *The Secret Barrister: Stories of the Law and How It's Broken* (2018).

[10] *Urgent Action Required: The Bar Council's 2019 Manifesto for the Justice System* (Nov. 2019), p. 4.

a poor state.[11] A select committee reported in 2019 that it had received 'powerful evidence of a court system in administrative chaos'.[12] Moreover, the central government, having acquired control of the 'court estate', has sold off many of the local courts and allowed others to decay into a state of seediness.[13] Between 2010 and 2017 the government closed down seventy-two County Court centres and over half of all magistrates' courts.[14] A further seventy-seven closures have been threatened, despite the absence of any clear analysis of the potential effect of this drastic cost-cutting programme.[15] The relative sparseness of the surviving venues means that parties and their lawyers are at the mercy of transport problems and costs, and do not always arrive for hearings on time, if at all. Of course, the deeper underlying problems would hardly be solved by restoring the assizes, but – as with the demolished railway lines – something of value was lost in terms of

---

[11] See Genn, *Judging Civil Justice*, pp. 24, 38–45. Since 2007 the budget for the prison service (formerly the concern of the Home Office) has been merged with that for courts and tribunals under the Ministry of Justice.

[12] House of Commons Justice Committee, *Courts and Tribunals Reforms: Second Report of Sessions 2019* (2019) HC 190, p.3.

[13] In the decade after Beeching there had actually been a court-building programme: Hailsham, *Hamlyn Revisited*, pp. 75–6.

[14] Figures (for 2010–17) provided by the Ministry of Justice in answer to a written question in Parliament, 23 Apr. 2018. It has been calculated that 277 courts have closed in the last decade: *Urgent Action Required* (n. 10 above), at p. 4.

[15] A damning report on this subject was published on 5 Nov. 2019 by the Committee of Public Accounts, *Transforming Courts and Tribunals: Progress Review* (2019) HC 27.

accessibility. It has recently been proposed that our so-called Circuit Judges should (for the first time) actually go on circuit, and that there should be an electronically ubiquitous Online Court – or, rather, online processing systems – to deal with all claims below a certain amount.[16] Whatever remedy is found, courts of the traditional kind have become, and are likely to remain, less accessible physically than they were in 1952 or 1558.

Civil Procedure

Next it was the turn of civil procedure to be transformed. By 1952 it was already far removed from that of the old common law, thanks to the nineteenth-century reforms. It had been a matter of pride at the end of the Victorian era that lawsuits could no longer be won or lost on technicalities, and the role of the special pleader had passed into history. Coke and his contemporaries would have found that mighty strange. They would have been even more mystified by the disappearance of the civil jury, which since the thirteenth century had insulated the judges from fact-finding.[17] Yet the system was still essentially adversarial. Parties were permitted to ambush their opponents or harass them with the prospect of unpredictable costs. Discovery of documents and the commissioning of technical evidence from experts, though necessary in principle, was making litigation protracted and

---

[16] *Briggs Report* (2016), pp. 36–64; R. Susskind, *Online Courts and the Future of Justice* (Oxford, 2019).
[17] See 'Law and Procedure' in Ch. 2; and below, at nn. 124–5.

disproportionately expensive. More robust management by the judge was recommended by the Evershed Committee in 1953.[18] This was the dawning of what is now called proportionate justice, an official recognition that exploring every factual and legal avenue in a case may be disproportionate to what is at stake and an unfair appropriation of limited judicial resources. In the County Courts, an extremely informal procedure was introduced for small claims in 1973, counsel being rarely used and an active role given to registrars (since renamed district judges). This was rough and ready but is considered to have been successful. A further report on civil justice in 1988 proposed to soften the adversarial system in the High Court as well, with a 'cards on the table' approach.[19] This led first to the compulsory exchange of witness statements before trial, and then – by a Practice Direction of 1995[20] – judges were given greater control over the preparation for and conduct of hearings by limiting discovery, imposing time-limits on counsel and dispensing with the need to read aloud documents and authorities. Counsel were to submit skeleton arguments and prepare bundles containing the pleadings and written evidence. Witness statements were to stand as evidence in chief unless otherwise ordered, so that oral evidence would begin with the cross-examination. Further reforms were introduced in 1999, following the recommendations of Lord Woolf's

---

[18] *Final Report of the Committee on Supreme Court Practice and Procedure* (1953) Cmd 8878. A successful model for this had been the Commercial Court, created within the Queen's Bench Division in 1895.

[19] *Report of the Review Body on Civil Justice* (1988) Cm 394.

[20] *Practice Direction* [1995] 1 All E.R. 385.

committee.[21] The result was a new procedural code which replaced the century-old Rules of the Supreme Court.[22] The original writ was finally abolished, after eight hundred years of service, and replaced by a 'claim form'. Just in case fictions and smoke-screens were minded to re-emerge, pleadings (now called 'statements of case') were to be accompanied by an averment of belief in their factual truth, under the sanction of punishment for contempt. Above all, the court was to be more proactive, to make sure that the parties engaged on an equal footing, and that cases were dealt with expeditiously and fairly in ways which were proportionate to the amount of money at stake, the importance and complexity of the case, and the means of the parties. This objective was to be furthered by 'actively managing cases', with tight deadlines, and encouraging the parties to submit to alternative dispute resolution.[23] Further changes were made in 2013 following Sir Rupert Jackson's report on litigation costs.[24]

---

[21] H. Woolf, *Access to Justice* (1996). For a history of the reforms, and the underlying philosophy, see J. Sorabji, *English Civil Justice after the Woolf Reforms* (Cambridge, 2014).

[22] Civil Procedure Rules 1998, made under the Civil Procedure Act 1997 (c. 12); they came into effect in 1999. An additional rule made in 2000 (r. 54) revised the procedure for judicial review as introduced in 1977 (below, n. 103).

[23] It has been suggested that sanctions should be imposed on litigants who refuse to take reasonable steps towards a settlement: Justice Council, *ADR and Civil Justice: Final Report* (2018), para. 2.3(5).

[24] R. Jackson, *Review of Civil Litigation Costs: Final Report* (2009). See also S. Clark and R. Jackson, *The Reform of Civil Justice* (2nd edn, Cambridge, 2018).

The objectives behind these reforms were obviously sensible, but opinions are divided as to how successful the procedural changes have been in achieving them. For instance, the use of witness statements as evidence in chief may have resulted in longer trials; they are prepared by solicitors and contain more detail than oral evidence, and therefore there is more to be addressed and challenged in cross-examination. At any rate, trials take longer than they did fifty years ago.[25] Disclosure still produces mountains of unsorted material. Costs have continued to escalate.[26] Costs management hearings have themselves become expensive and dilatory, further increasing litigation costs overall.[27] There is now a Costs Bar, and Costs Law Reports. It is not as bad as the Georgian Chancery as portrayed by Dickens, in which disputed estates were inexorably swallowed up in endless contest – much of it over costs. But one reason for the general professional reluctance to fall in with the new proportional approach to justice is an ingrained familiarity with the system devised in Dickens's lifetime. The Victorian reformers chose to follow the Chancery model, which required the thorough investigation of all available facts, whatever the cost and trouble, rather than the common-law model, which was thought to be too concerned with procedural nicety and required some over-simplification of issues. No doubt the

---

[25] There are doubtless other factors. Hailsham, *Hamlyn Revisited*, p. 76, noted as long ago as 1983 that criminal trials had become longer, but he could not explain it.

[26] Genn, *Judging Civil Justice*, p. 56.

[27] See Zanders, *The State of Justice*, pp. 41–5, where it is pointed out that Lord Woolf himself later acknowledged this. For a defence see Dyson, *Justice*, p. 295.

common law at its worst could resemble a procedural game rather than a search for the truth. But that was never its objective. A system whereby a dispute was whittled down to a single issue tried before a jury, and legal argument restricted to the facts on the record, was in many respects closer to the Woolf model of efficient, economical and proportionate justice. Certainly, as we have seen, the Elizabethan common law was more accessible and far less expensive than High Court litigation today. The ebbs and flows of procedural reform over the centuries have been driven by the eternal problem of how to balance the quest for absolute justice against the need for efficiency. But experience has shown that it is easier to rewrite rules than to change attitudes.

Reluctance to abandon the primacy of substantive justice is only one of the difficulties faced by today's reformers. It is a recurrent feature of procedural reform that attempts at improvement and simplification so often result in complexity, and the recent reforms have been no exception. The elaborate new rules, designed to cover every eventuality, require a thick book of official guidance before they can even be approached.[28] Constant revision, supplemented by streams of piecemeal practice directions, further unsettles practice and creates uncertainty.[29] Moreover, the reforms have significantly reduced the 'orality' of proceedings, so that an observer

---

[28] The Court of Appeal has criticised the 'cumbrous and confusing three-tier hierarchy of rules and guidance': *R. (Mount Cook Land Ltd)* v. *Westminster City Council* [2003] EWCA Civ 1346, at para. 67.

[29] There have now been 115 amendments ('updates') to the Civil Procedure Rules 1998. They have to be read in conjunction with the earlier rules and amendments.

present in court without access to the documents cannot expect to follow all that is happening in a civil trial or even a legal argument in the highest court.[30] Litigants cannot, of course, be expected to pay for the enlightenment of observers. Posterity will have even less hope of knowing what our courts did, since no permanent record of proceedings is now kept, even by so-called 'courts of record'. The Elizabethan and earlier plea rolls, which Coke called a great and hidden treasure,[31] are to this day freely available to all and can be read in their entirety on the Internet. But no such treasure is laid down anymore, most records being destroyed after seven years, leaving only a plethora of statistical tables compiled with current management in mind.[32] What is now called the 'judgment', which is in effect a full report by the trial judge rather than the bare order disposing of the case, serves as a relation of the facts as alleged and found, the gist of the legal arguments, the authorities relied on, the judge's own analysis and the outcome. If preserved in permanent form,[33] it is

---

[30] Counsel are discouraged from reading authorities aloud, and it is common practice to refer to a passage in the court's bundle and then observe a short silence while the court reads it.

[31] *Le Tierce Part des Reportes* (1602), sig. C.ij verso.

[32] Under the Record Retention and Disposition Schedules issued by the Courts and Tribunals Service, all Queen's Bench and Chancery files and cause books are destroyed after seven years unless deemed to be of local or historical interest (which is apparently left to the discretion of registrars); records of criminal trials (including the indictments) are destroyed after ten years. Many County Court records are destroyed after three years.

[33] Electronic formats are so ephemeral that it is already practically impossible to access documents copied onto floppy discs in the 1990s.

a kind of record, but of a new kind. It contains far more than the common-law record ever did and enmeshes the finding of facts with the disposal of any incidental questions of law. This is convenient, but it has consequences. There is no longer a general verdict. Every decision turns on the particular facts, in much the same way as decisions in the Elizabethan Chancery or Star Chamber, which were considered too fact-specific to set precedents worth reporting at length. But today's judge is combining the fact-finding function of the jury with reasoned legal analysis in the common-law manner, complete with authorities. Unlike the Star Chamber, he knows that every word and omission in the 'judgment' may be scrutinised on appeal, and therefore feels obliged to address every detail of fact and law. An awkward consequence of this has been to increase pressure on the Court of Appeal, which cannot cope with its workload.[34] In these respects, the civil legal system of today would not be readily comprehensible to an Elizabethan lawyer.

Private Law

What, then, of the law? In the reign of Elizabeth I, it was dominated by the land law. Land law is today less prominent, though paradoxically it was only in the middle of Elizabeth II's reign that – with the help of building-society

---

Parchment used to be the hallmark of a court of record, for the good practical reason that it will last for a thousand years.

[34] Cf. the *Briggs Report* (2016), pp. 12–13, which attributes the overload in the Court of Appeal to the complexity of the law.

mortgages[35] and the Housing Acts[36] – the majority of householders in England became freehold property owners.[37] But the landed property of the multitude is mostly limited to domestic residences. The well-to-do Elizabethan invested in land as a source of income, ideally whole manors with tenants, tithes and advowsons,[38] and sought to control its devolution in perpetuity for the preservation of his name and blood. Today, assets are more diversified, and land cannot be entailed; the main concern is to ensure that property passes to the living in a tax-efficient manner. A wealthy person's enduring monument is more likely to be a family business, a corporation or a charity than a portfolio of manors with rent-rolls. For most other people today, real property means simply a home, whether leasehold or freehold, and its ownership is qualified not only by mortgages and 'inheritance tax' but by the uncertainties of family law and rights of occupation.

---

[35] Around half of all houses owned by their occupiers are mortgaged, and many of those owned outright were bought on mortgage earlier. Mortgages were common in the time of Elizabeth I, but they were then used by landowners to secure short-term loans on property which they already owned outright.

[36] Under the Housing Acts 1980 (c. 51) and 1985 (c. 68) about 1½ million homes have been purchased by tenants from local authorities.

[37] The proportion reached one-half in 1971, and early in the present century approached two-thirds: Office of National Statistics, *2011 Census Analysis* (2013); Ministry of Housing, *National Housing Survey* (annual). At the time of writing, it is falling back again as leasehold housing increases.

[38] S. E. Thorne, *Essays in English Legal History* (1985), p. 200, reckoned that 'Coke owned at his death ninety-nine manors, but twice that number had passed through his hands'.

No doubt much of the land law is still incomprehensible to the lay public, but the complexity of the law surrounding future estates – the occult learning which gave Coke and Bacon the opportunity to make their reputations – has largely been dispensed with.[39] The removal of the common-law pitfalls has made the purchase of land less of a gamble with history and has enabled millions of titles to be registered, thereby removing many of the older dangers in conveyancing. Only 15 per cent of the land in England is now unregistered. The precariousness of titles which pervades the Tudor law reports, and accounted for a large part of legal practice for so many centuries, is almost a thing of the past.[40]

The great majority of lawsuits brought in courts at the present day are still governed – in essence – by the common law.[41] This is because simple debt-collection is predominant in both periods and essentially the same in nature. In most cases the law is so clear that no statute or judicial decision could make it more so. Indeed, in the County Court hardly any defendants in practice produce a successful defence,[42] and questions of basic principle rarely arise for decision. Most

---

[39] It was a long time dying. The writer recollects being asked in a Bar examination in 1966 to give an account of the esoteric rule in *Purefoy* v. *Rogers* (1671) B. & M. 95. Entails, which after 1925 could subsist only in equity, were finally laid to rest by the Trusts of Land Act 1996 (c. 47), sch. 1.

[40] The Supreme Court has recognised the public interest in the security of registered transactions: *Scott* v. *Southern Pacific Mortgages Ltd* [2014] UKSC 52, at p. 6, para. 26, *per* Lord Collins (pointing out that there are now more than 23 million registered titles).

[41] This is not true of tribunals.   [42] Genn, *Judging Civil Justice*, p. 66.

contract cases in the higher courts seem now to concern interpretation of either contracts or statutes rather than the principles of the common law, which are well established.[43] This triumph of clarity must be considered one of the common law's major achievements.

The law of torts, which accounts for a much larger share of the nation's litigation than in Elizabethan times, is less constant and less comprehensible. It has in fact changed strikingly, though it has done so through legal argument, step by step, rather than through legislation. Unlike the common law of contract, which is a common set of principles governing all contracts, there are multiple torts, each with its own body of law. Even liability for negligence, which has come to dominate the law of torts, has defied attempts to impose analytical uniformity.[44] But the main purpose of this branch of the law is the same as it was in the Tudor period, namely to provide monetary compensation for harm caused by wrongdoing. It derives from the old action of trespass, which in the sixteenth century was chiefly concerned with injuries to property rights and an embarrassing number of defamation suits. Today it is more focused on physical and economic injuries, with an ever-increasing range of situations in which duties of

---

[43] The doctrine of consideration is largely Elizabethan: Ch. 2, n. 103. But it is now practically irrelevant. Most of the other doctrine is Victorian, albeit with earlier roots.

[44] There was a short-lived movement to create a broad general principle: *Home Office* v. *Dorset Yacht Co.* [1970] AC 1004, 1026, *per* Lord Reid; *Anns* v. *Merton London Borough Council* [1978] AC 728, 751-2, *per* Lord Wilberforce; *McLoughlin* v. *O'Brian* [1983] 1 AC 410, 430-1, *per* Lord Scarman.

care have been recognised. Actions could in principle be brought in the sixteenth century for non-contractual negligence; but they were uncommon.[45] It may seem strange that four centuries ago no one would have thought of suing a driver for knocking him down, or an occupier of land for an injury caused by the state of the premises, or an employer for not providing a safe system of work.[46] The explanation is not that Elizabethan lawyers were less sophisticated than we are but that social expectations have changed, especially in the context of large organisations and insurance, which enable individual losses to be spread. Occupiers' liability and employers' liability were ruled out until Victorian times by the idea of implied consent to risk, not as a technical doctrine but as a general sense of resignation about everyday dangers. A visitor who suffered an injury, even if he had taken due care himself, would probably have been considered discourteous if he complained. And a servant, being supposed to understand any risks in his job as well as his master, shared the responsibility for his own safety;[47] perhaps in reality he had little choice as to his conditions of employment, but that was the way of the world. Even a stranger, such as a road-user, was

---

[45] See e.g. B. & M. 622–6. Walmsley J said in 1601 he had never known an action to lie for negligence without a contract: *IELH* (5th edn), p. 436.

[46] See Scarman, *English Law – The New Dimension*, 2 ('The common law has, in theory, no gaps or omissions, only a few silences . . . For instance, the common law was exceedingly taciturn for centuries on the subject of the duty of care and the tort of negligence'). Cf. *IELH* (5th edn), pp. 443–9.

[47] At common law, until 1945, contributory negligence barred any claim in tort: D. Ibbetson, *A Historical Introduction to the Law of Obligations* (Oxford, 1999), pp. 59, 127.

expected to look out for himself with respect to usual hazards. Serious accidents, in any case, more often resulted in death than they would today; and wrongfully causing death was no cause of action in tort until 1846.

In the intervening centuries, the law of tort has grown incrementally and at times rapidly, as more and more new questions have been raised, to the point where there have been judicial and legislative misgivings about a 'compensation culture' and its deterrent effect on socially desirable activities.[48] But it is the same common law, and the techniques are the same – perusing the most pertinent precedents, arguing by analogy, distinguishing any countervailing principles, exploring possible repercussions (such as 'opening the floodgates') and paying heed to general perceptions of right and wrong (or what is sometimes called 'common sense').[49] Each step forward is a logically compelling conclusion from what has gone before rather than a leap into the dark.[50] From time to time the conclusion may need adjustment, even at the cost of

---

[48] *Tomlinson* v. *Congleton Borough Council* [2004] 1 AC 46; Compensation Act 2006 (c. 29), s. 1; Social Action, Responsibility and Heroism Act 2015 (c. 3).

[49] Cf. *Robinson* v. *Chief Constable of West Yorkshire Police* [2018] UKSC 4, at p. 10, para. 29, *per* Lord Reed ('. . . the courts will consider the closest analogies in the existing law, with a view to maintaining the coherence of the law and the avoidance of inappropriate distinctions. They will also weigh up the reasons for and against imposing liability, in order to decide whether the existence of a duty of care would be just and reasonable').

[50] See *McLoughlin* v. *O'Brian* [1983] 1 AC 410, 419, *per* Lord Wilberforce ('. . . the courts have proceeded in the traditional manner of the common law from case to case upon a basis of logical necessity').

occasional divergence from precedent. When precedents are found to have illogical or unfair consequences, it is not in the interests of certainty to adhere to them, because they encourage the drawing of equally illogical or over-subtle distinctions between cases essentially alike, in order to escape their effect.[51] But it is the strength of the common law that adjustment in the light of experience is built into its method. If the courts did not apply old principles and techniques constructively to new situations and understandings, the common law would be in danger of becoming irrelevant to the provision of justice.[52] It is still generally accepted that, within the limited domain ruled by the common law, it is better for the judges to nurture and adjust the law they have in their charge than to let Parliament blunder in.[53] The approach to new problems in the law of contract and the law of tort is, for these reasons, much the same as in 1600.

Public Law

Turning to what is now called public law, the historical comparatist faces more of a challenge, given the far-reaching developments of the last half-century. Rights are now

---

[51] *Darley* v. *Reginam* (1846) 12 Cl. & Fin. 520, 544, *per* Lord Brougham; *Knauer* v. *Ministry of Justice* [2016] UKSC 9, at p. 8, para. 23.

[52] See *McLoughlin* v. *O'Brian* [1983] 1 AC 410, 430, *per* Lord Scarman.

[53] *Knauer* v. *Ministry of Justice* [2016] UKSC 9, at p. 9, para. 26. It cannot be assumed that Parliament would find time to legislate anyway: see *Patel* v. *Mirza* [2016] UKSC 42, at pp. 37–8, para. 114, *per* Lord Toulson. For the proper sphere of judicial creativity see Lord Reid, 'The Judge as Law Maker' (1962) 22 JSPTL (NS) 22–9; Ch. 3, nn. 159–60.

routinely protected outside the sphere of private law as a result of the reform of judicial review procedure in 1977, the Human Rights Act 1998 and the laws against discrimination. Dangers to public order and security have led to the wide-ranging Civil Contingencies Act 2004 (which reintroduced wartime emergency powers on a permanent footing) and the Counter-Terrorism Acts 2015 and 2019. And then there are constitutional changes properly so called: devolution, accession to the European Economic Community and European Union, and withdrawal from the same, including the use of referendums.

Much of this is so unparalleled that comparisons with Elizabethan England would be fruitless. Particularly problematic is the modern tendency to treat constitutional traditions and conventions as subsidiary to political expediency. Either there is no longer an appreciation of the unwritten understandings which served in lieu of a constitutional document or there is a new and cynical disregard for them, and a failure to foresee that new precedents may be misused by future governments of a different stamp.[54] The most striking example is the arrangement of conclusive plebiscites on constitutional issues, in the name of popular democracy. Referendums have been treated like elections, or votes in Parliament, so that a majority of one is enough to carry the day.[55] Regardless of whether the outcome is thought to

---

[54] On this topic see J. Baker, 'Our Unwritten Constitution' (2010) 167 *Proceedings of the British Academy* 91–117.

[55] A simple majority is needed in the case of elections, to ensure that the vacancy is filled. This reasoning does not apply to constitutional changes.

be in the best interests of the country, and of whether a referendum is the only practical means of achieving it, setting a bare majority of the population on a collision course with the House of Commons which represents them – even if supposedly sanctioned by a prior Act of Parliament[56] – inevitably threatens the working of the traditional parliamentary constitution.[57] It is enough to observe that such things could not have happened in Elizabethan England: democracy of that direct, unfiltered kind was considered dangerous.[58] Most of the population were not even trusted to vote for members of Parliament, though they were all deemed to be represented by them, and they were all bound by Parliament's legislative acts through their fictional consent.[59] There were fewer conventions then affecting Parliament. Although Parliament was unquestionably sovereign, Elizabeth I preferred to rule without one, except when she needed its financial support or was advised to accept an adjustment in the law. The sovereignty of Parliament did not then include continuous session, and the queen had no constitutional obligation to keep it sitting or to

---

[56] The European Union Referendum Act 2015 (c. 36), following the pattern of the Referendum Act 1975 (c. 33) (concerning EEC membership), did not in fact purport to imbue the outcome with any legal force.

[57] The prime minister's attempt to have Parliament prorogued for five weeks in 2019, after an impasse in the Commons, led the Supreme Court to override the prerogative of prorogation, formerly thought to be absolute, by treating as law the convention that Parliament sits almost continuously: *R. (Miller)* v. *The Prime Minister* [2019] UKSC 41. The convention that a new Parliament should be summoned (and a general election held) within about two weeks of a dissolution had already been replaced by law in the Fixed-Term Parliaments Act 2011 (c. 14).

[58] See Ch. 2, n. 149. [59] Below, n. 90.

assent to bills which had passed both houses. Nor was the queen obliged to accept the advice of her ministers in making governmental decisions, since she appointed them at her own pleasure; acting on advice was more a matter of pragmatic convenience and political wisdom than constitutional propriety.

Most of the other recent constitutional developments may likewise be hurried past. The Elizabethans did know of devolved government: not in Scotland, which was still a foreign country, but in Ireland, the North of England, the Marches of Wales and the counties palatine of Durham, Chester and Lancaster. Ireland had its own Parliament. The English regional governments in York, Ludlow and the palatinates did not have legislative assemblies and could not make laws, but they were left largely to themselves so long as they followed general directions from the central government. From time to time the provincial conciliar courts did overstep their bounds, by interfering with common-law rights,[60] and then they could be corrected by the King's Bench.[61] All such devolved authorities fitted into the pyramid of royal authority. Any idea of surrendering legal supremacy or legislative initiative to an overseas power would have been contrary to the Elizabethans' belief in the superiority of the common law,

---

[60] For the beginnings of conflict with the courts at Westminster see Baker, *Magna Carta*, pp. 209, 302–5; Ch. 2, n. 52.

[61] Usually by means of habeas corpus. But the palatinate courts, and the courts of great session in Wales, had the like jurisdiction to those at Westminster and were subject to writs of error. So also the courts in Dublin: e.g. *Millichapp* v. *Morreis* (1596) KB 27/1337, m. 517 (reversing a judgment to recover a debt of £1,000 in the Irish King's Bench).

the independence of the nation and the supremacy of Parliament. Parliament reasserted that belief in 1559 when it confirmed all the statutes made 'for the utter extinguishment and putting away of all usurped and foreign powers and authorities' out of the realm.[62] A similar sentiment seems to have prevailed against the European Union in 2015–20.

Terrorism and religious extremism provide more obvious parallels. The reigns of Elizabeth I and James I were the last period before the present in which religious subversion and plotting were perceived as a major threat to the nation's peace, though it was only after the queen's death that the agenda included mass murder as well as regicide. The reaction then was severe criminal legislation. It must be acknowledged that Tudor standards of severity far surpassed our own. But the Elizabethan regime put an end to the punishment of religious beliefs as such. Heresy prosecutions and burnings at the stake became a thing of the past, and no Roman Catholic (or Nonconformist) suffered death for heresy after 1558.[63] In words attributed to Queen Elizabeth herself, there was no need to make windows into men's hearts and secret thoughts.[64] Thought was now free;[65] but religious practices were another matter. The grip of religion – whatever its species – was still strong, and an orderly society under the

---

[62] 1 Eliz. I, c. 1, referring to the legislation of Henry VIII which ended the ecclesiastical jurisdiction in England of the bishop of Rome. For the contemporary belief in the superiority of English law generally see Ch. 2, nn. 167, 171.

[63] Ch. 2, n. 34. [64] Baker, *Magna Carta*, p. 125.

[65] *Att.-Gen.* v. *Boothe* (1596) Hawarde 65, 66, *per* Egerton LK. Cf. *Walton* v. *Edwardes* (1608) 13 Co. Rep. 9.

Elizabethan regime was thought to require uniform worship as settled by law.[66] It was not until the nineteenth century that people became completely free, in the eyes of the law, to choose their religion or to do without.

For present purposes, the most fruitful area of comparison in public law is that of physical and economic liberty. Just before the present reign, at the conclusion of the first Hamlyn Lectures in 1949, Sir Alfred (later Lord) Denning said that the greatest task lying ahead for the courts was to ensure that personal freedom could be preserved against increasing governmental power: 'Properly exercised the new powers of the executive lead to the welfare state; but abused they lead to a totalitarian state.'[67] In the following year's lecture, Richard O'Sullivan took up Glanville Williams's contrast between the Common-Law Man – stalwart, independent and self-reliant – and the Statutory Man, whose vigour was retarded by a mass of regulations but who was better cushioned against the buffets of life. He predicted that the future was to be a struggle between the two.[68] Seventy years later, it might seem that Common-Law Man has become extinct. But the contrast with the Elizabethans is not wholly straightforward.

---

[66] An Act for Uniformity of Common Prayer and Service in the Church 1559, 1 Eliz. I, c. 2. The Roman mass, which was thought to be tainted by magic, was expressly proscribed in 1581, with criminal sanctions: 23 Eliz. I, c. 1, s. 4. Earlier attempts to prosecute priests for sorcery had been stopped on the advice of Catlin CJ that sorcery was not an offence known to the common law: *Dyer's Notebooks*, pp. lxix–lxxi.

[67] A. T. Denning, *Freedom under the Law* (1949), p. 126.

[68] R. O'Sullivan, *The Inheritance of the Common Law* (1950), pp. 28–30. He hoped the Common-Law Man would win.

The Hamlyn lecturers in 1949–50 were focusing on the benefits and drawbacks of the seemingly autonomous regulatory state. Seventy years later, the focus has shifted to the means of meeting Lord Denning's challenge: to judicial review and human rights.

The two cornerstones of protection for individual freedoms today are the judicial review of legislation (for such it is) under section 4 of the Human Rights Act 1998 and the judicial review of executive or administrative action under the common law. Human rights are widely perceived by the general public in this country as new and alien, whether or not they are seen as beneficial. There have indeed been legal changes wrought through the influence of the international court in Strasbourg, but the underlying perception is misleading. It is true that the expression 'human rights' is modern – it was for a time fatally tainted by association with the revolutionary Rights of Man – and there is an arguable case that the judges have gradually arrogated to themselves too much power to interfere with policy decisions on their merits. It is now a familiar figure of speech that judicial review, like war, is a way of pursuing politics by other means.[69] This perception has been reinforced by a tendency to denigrate invalid or flawed decisions as 'unlawful': language calculated to give people the impression that ministers and officials who got things wrong in retrospect were behaving as criminals. Nevertheless, the core concepts of human rights are

---

[69] Cf. R. (Hoareau and Bancoult) v. Secretary of State for Foreign and Commonwealth Affairs [2019] EWHC 221 (Admin), para. 326 ('Judicial review is not, and should not be regarded as, politics by another means').

essentially English in origin. Most of the rights enumerated in 1998, in broad language derived from the Universal Declaration of Human Rights 1948, were taken from the common law. It is telling that the negotiation of the 1948 Declaration was handled by the Foreign Office. Drawn up in the wake of World War II, it was conceived to be about exporting age-old English legal concepts to benighted nations overseas rather than changing anything in domestic law. The rights as then expressed would – with only a few exceptions – have been recognised in Elizabethan times. The principal exception was the death penalty, and that was still in place in England in the 1950s; it is now outlawed throughout Europe, though killing without trial seems to be officially tolerable if carried out far enough away.[70]

The rights and liberties known to the Elizabethans were, it is true, the rights of the English rather than of mankind in general. But everyone lawfully within the realm came within their purview. Those outside the realm obviously did not, and immigration was controlled by the government.[71] Yet immigration was common, and there was some sympathy for refugees.[72] An alien, once admitted to the country, had access

---

[70] Quite apart from assassinations, which can now be managed by drone, recent governments have sanctioned the 'collateral' killing of non-enemy aliens in overseas conflicts. E.g. there was no outrage in 2003 when a restaurant in Baghdad was bombed by coalition forces, killing many civilians who were not armed or threatening violence, merely because Saddam Hussein was (wrongly) thought to be inside.

[71] See Ch. 2, nn. 25–8.

[72] See Henry Jackman's speech in the Commons (1589) against a bill forbidding aliens to sell wares by retail, urging compassion for the

to the courts and was a 'free person' within the protection of Magna Carta.[73] It is therefore accurate to say that the liberties which English men and women enjoyed under the common law and the great charter were shared by all humankind within the jurisdiction. They were, in that sense, human rights.

These liberties were defended with much the same vigour as today. If there were imperfections in their protection, so there are now. Foremost among the liberties was bodily freedom, assured for most purposes by the development of habeas corpus under Elizabeth I.[74] This has today been reinforced by the Human Rights Act 1998 and by the use of judicial review procedures to challenge powers of detention. Even so, the 1998 Act did not prevent the government in 2001 from detaining terror suspects indefinitely without trial under statutory powers.[75] Compulsory exile was forbidden by Magna Carta, and in the time of Elizabeth I it properly required an Act of

'miserable and afflicted state of these poor exiles': *Proc. Parl.*, ii. 480–3. The bill was further debated in 1593 but did not pass.

[73] Even if aliens were accused of treason, they were entitled to a jury trial, though not to a half-alien jury: *R* v. *Sherleys* (1557) Dyer 144; *Re Mary, Queen of Scots* (1572) *Dyer's Notebooks*, ii. 256; *R.* v. *Lopez* (1594) Co. Nbk, BL MS. Harley 6686A, fo. 78. The queen of Scots was not in the event (in 1586) tried by jury because of an ambiguity as to the character in which she had entered the realm.

[74] There was the significant exception that the Privy Council (in effect, the government) could imprison people without having to justify it to the King's Bench: Ch. 2, n. 58.

[75] In the *Belmarsh Nine* case it was held that the powers in question, though incompatible with the Human Rights Act 1998, had been lawfully exercised under the Anti-Terrorism Act 2001 (c. 24): *A and others* v. *Secretary of State for the Home Department* [2004] UKHL 56. The detainees did not, therefore, gain immediate release. But the statutory

Parliament;[76] yet in 2016 the Supreme Court turned a blind eye to the great charter and upheld the prerogative banishment of the Chagos Islanders.[77] Excessively harsh treatment of prisoners was illegal and punishable,[78] and in 1612 would be held contrary to Magna Carta.[79] Yet many of today's prisons are so squalid and dangerous as to constitute inhumane treatment by modern standards.[80] Torture was sometimes deemed necessary by the Elizabethan Privy Council where national security was at stake, but it was extralegal and not defended as legally right.[81] In

powers were replaced by control orders under the Prevention of Terrorism Act 2005 (c. 2) (repealed in 2011).

[76] 35 Eliz. I, c. 1 (for persistent recusants); 39 Eliz. I, c. 4 (for dangerous rogues); Baker, *Magna Carta*, pp. 250 n. 8, 509. But there were instances of prerogative banishment: Kesselring, *Mercy and Authority*, pp. 32–5.

[77] *R. (Bancoult (No. 2)) v. Secretary of State for Foreign and Commonwealth Affairs* [2016] UKSC 35; Baker, *Magna Carta*, p. 448. In 2019 the International Court of Justice held the United Kingdom's actions to have been contrary to international law.

[78] James Morice, in his reading of 1578, said that imprisonment was for restraint and custody, 'not sharply to punish': BL MS. Egerton 3376, fo. 27. Early in the next reign a gaoler was fined £100 for putting a party in a noisome prison without food or drink and ignoring writs of habeas corpus: *Att.-Gen. v. Hunnings* (1605) Baker, *Magna Carta*, pp. 310, 514.

[79] *Hodges v. Humkin* (1612) 2 Buls. 139 (putting a prisoner in a dungeon without food or drink).

[80] See e.g. H.M. Inspectorate of Prisons, *Life in Prisons: Living Conditions* (2017); *Annual Report 2017–18* (2018) HC 1245. A court in Amsterdam recently refused to extradite a prisoner to the United Kingdom because of the real risk of facing inhumane and degrading conditions: *The Times*, 11 May 2019.

[81] The Privy Council nevertheless recorded its orders to rack suspects, and the law officers (including Coke) were named in torture warrants. See Baker, *Magna Carta*, pp. 170–2; *IELH* (5th edn), p. 510.

contrast with Civil Law jurisdictions, which judicialised inter-
rogation under torture, no English court ever sanctioned it,[82]
and it did not last much longer in practice. In 2005 the House of
Lords finally decided that evidence obtained by torture is
inadmissible.[83] Yet as recently as 1988, Parliament introduced
into English law for the first time the concept that torture might
sometimes be lawful,[84] and still more recently the British government has colluded in torture by allied forces overseas.[85]
Freedom from restraints on employment was a recognised
legal principle, brought to the fore in the attack on monopolies;
indeed, this was the context in which the phrase 'liberty of the
subject' first became common currency.[86] Slavery was therefore
never part of the common law, and in Elizabethan times was
seen as an odious badge of oppression in less civilised nations.[87]

---

[82] There was a challenge in *R. v. Grevyle* (1589), but it was not argued
because the defendant refused to plead: Baker, *Collected Papers*, ii. 1068.
James Morice wrote in the 1590s that 'the common law condemneth it as
a thing both cruel and barbarous': HLS MS. 120, fos. 125–8, citing
Fortescue and Smith, *De Republica*, p. 85. Smith had gone so far as to
assert that torture was not used in England.

[83] *A v. Secretary of State for the Home Department* [2005] UKHL 71.

[84] The Criminal Law Act 1988 (c. 33), s. 134(3), introduced a defence of
'lawful authority, justification or excuse' to a charge of torture by an
official.

[85] See e.g. *Alseran v. Ministry of Defence* [2017] EWHC 3289; *The Times*,
20 May 2019, pp. 1–2.

[86] Baker, *Magna Carta*, pp. 155, 202 n. 340, 245, 312–14. There were full
discussions in *Att.-Gen. v. Joiners' Company of London* (1581) ibid.
468–76; *The Blacksmith's Case* (1587) Moo. 242; *Davenant v. Hurdys*
(1599) ibid. 576; Baker, *Magna Carta*, pp. 315–18; *Cleygate v. Batchelor*
(1601) Owen 143. For monopolies generally see Ch. 2, n. 36.

[87] Ch. 2, n. 16.

The law has not changed; and yet new forms of slavery and human trafficking are so rife in today's ethnically diverse England that between 2014 and 2017 there were 438 convictions for modern slavery offences, and the total number of suspected victims is now believed to be closer to 7,000.[88] In both periods, therefore, we must distinguish the normative from the descriptive. The ideals are not disproved by what people, and governments, actually do.

What, then, of the entrenchment of these fundamental liberties in Elizabethan times? There was no possibility that the common law could ever contradict them, because they were derived from, and part of, the common law. An Act of Parliament might in theory thwart them, and if it did so there was no machinery for declaring it to be incompatible with them. Parliament could in law do anything,[89] and its acts could not do anyone a legal wrong.[90] But that is no different from parliamentary sovereignty as still understood. What the

---

[88] See the government's *Annual Report on Modern Slavery* (2018); *The Times*, 14 May 2019, p. 9. However, the definition has changed. Under the Modern Slavery Act 2015 (c. 30) slavery means forced or compulsory labour. Under the Elizabethan poor laws, the able unemployed might be compelled to work if they declined job-offers (39 Eliz. I, c. 3; 43 Eliz. I, c. 2, s. 4), but this did not make them slaves.

[89] See Ch. 3, n. 102. But Francis Tate suggested that it could not (perhaps meaning would not) legislate against Magna Carta: *Proc. Parl.*, iii. 407.

[90] *Rudhale* v. *Miller* (1586) Co. Nbk, BL MS. Harley 6686A, fos. 263 (tr.: 'an Act of Parliament does not wrong anyone, for all are consenting, and *volenti non fit injuria*'), 302v; *R. v. Lady Gresham* (1589) 9 Co. Rep. 107 (tr.: 'an Act of Parliament, to which the queen and all her subjects are parties and give consent, cannot do a wrong'); *Digby's Case* (1599) 4 Co. Rep. 78, 79 (tr.: 'the Act of 21 Hen. VIII, to which everyone is party').

courts did possess was the power of interpretation, as explained in Chapter 3. So far as it was possible for them to do so, they would read and give effect to legislation in a way that was compatible with common-law rights because it was accepted learning that statutes which derogated from the common law would be construed strictly. In the sphere of public law, the judges' main concern was to ensure that those exercising broad statutory or prerogative authority, such as the ecclesiastical high commissioners or the commissioners of sewers, acted within the boundaries of their legal powers and (if their powers were discretionary) in accordance with 'equity' or fairness.[91] But some judges ventured further. Anderson CJ held in 1595 that an Act of Parliament which purported to do something legally improper would be 'vain and void'.[92] Six years later he said that anything in an Act which was too obscure to be understood, or was contrary to law and reason, should not be 'allowed'.[93]

Judicial Review

It was only seven years into the following reign that Coke CJ made his famous assertion that a statute would be held 'utterly void' if it was repugnant, impossible to be performed, or against common right or reason, as where it

---

[91] Ch. 3, nn. 81–2.

[92] *Germyn* v. *Arscott* (1595) LI MS. Misc. 491, fos. 99 (vain), 100 (vain and void). This is absent from Anderson CJ's own report: 1 And. 186; 2 And. 7.

[93] *Mildmay* v. *Mildmay* (1601) LI MS. Maynard 66, fo. 168 (tr.: '. . . and this rule he wished to be kept in all Acts of Parliament, deeds and writings whatsoever').

authorised proceedings contrary to the principles of natural justice.[94] That was indeed a declaration of incompatibility; but whether it was really judicial review of legislation, or merely a strongly worded form of strict interpretation[95] – a declaration of inefficacy – was controversial then and remains controversial in England. Although the word 'void' would not today be used in this context, and was a source of misapprehension at the time,[96] Coke's approach has recently resurfaced. Given that Parliament is, in reality, an instrument through which a government with a working majority in the Commons exercises unrestrained power for the time being, the courts have begun to indicate that it may not have an unlimited ability to oust the most fundamental principles of law.[97] At any rate, the mere fact that the government responsible for promoting a statute intended it to displace the rule of law, as for instance by excluding the jurisdiction of the ordinary courts, is not enough in itself to defeat the presumption that Parliament cannot have

---

[94] *Dr Bonham's Case* (1610) 8 Co. Rep. 114. The other judges decided the case without invoking so broad a principle. For discussion see Baker, *Magna Carta*, pp. 90–1, and the articles cited there.

[95] For the meaning of 'void' in this context see Ch. 3, n. 60.

[96] Lord Ellesmere LC asserted that only the king in Parliament could judge whether an Act of Parliament was void: speech to Coke's successor, Montague CJ (1616) Moo. 826, 828.

[97] E.g. *R.* v. *Secretary of State for the Home Department*, ex p. *Pierson* [1998] AC 539, 591, *per* Lord Steyn; *R.* v. *Secretary of State for the Home Department*, ex p. *Simms* [2000] 2 AC 115, 131, *per* Lord Hoffmann; *Thoburn* v. *Sunderland City Council* [2003] QB 151, 186–7, *per* Laws LJ; *Jackson* v. *Att.-Gen.* [2005] UKHL 56, at p. 47, para. 102, *per* Lord Steyn; Sedley, *Lions under the Throne*, pp. 147–50.

intended it.[98] If Parliament does intend a particular statute to override the rule of law, it must say so expressly in order to rebut the presumption. Even when it appears to have done so, the courts are prepared to construe the wording as narrowly as possible.[99] Indeed, the opinion was expressed in the Supreme Court recently that 'it is ultimately for the courts, not the legislature, to determine the limits set by the rule of law to the power to exclude review'.[100] That opinion is not, however, universally shared.[101] As yet, the judicial policy has been to apply the presumption of Parliament's intention to respect the rule of law rather than directly to challenge its supremacy. And Parliament has, so far, wisely accepted this equipoise of power. A direct clash between Parliament and the queen's courts of law could not easily be resolved and would diminish both institutions.

While judicial annulment of legislation has not taken root in the United Kingdom, as it has in the United States, the judicial review of administrative action has become commonplace. It now seems remarkable that, until the present reign, administrative law was not widely recognised as a discrete

---

[98] Sedley, *Lions under the Throne*, pp. 146–7.

[99] *R. (Privacy International)* v. *Investigatory Powers Tribunal* [2019] UKSC 22. The Supreme Court was here divided 4:3 as to whether the language was sufficiently unequivocal to oust judicial review.

[100] Ibid. 56, para. 131, *per* Lord Carnwath.

[101] Lord Wilson expressly denied it: ibid. 108, para. 237. Cf. ibid. 99, para. 209, *per* Lord Sumption ('The rule of law applies as much to the courts as it does to anyone else, and under our constitution, that requires that effect must be given to Parliamentary legislation'); *AXXA General Insurance Ltd* v. *Lord Advocate* [2011] UKSC 46, at p. 23, *per* Lord Hope ('The question . . . is still under discussion').

branch of English law.[102] At that time only two or three dozen prerogative writs were issued every year, and few cases in the High Court had a public-law element. Since then, judicial review has become a field of dramatic growth, especially following the streamlining of procedures in 1977.[103] It is true that only 1 per cent of applications achieve a judgment for the applicant, but this statistic seems not to diminish hope, and the number of cases reached a peak of over 15,000 in 2013. The cases were transferred from the Queen's Bench Divisional Court to the High Court in 1977 so that they could be heard by single judges, and in 2000 the Crown Office list of the Queen's Bench Division was renamed the Administrative Court. Over two-thirds of the applications by then concerned immigration or asylum, and a separate immigration tribunal had to be introduced in 2013 to deal with them.[104] The sheer scale of this business was novel and largely unforeseen, but its ultimate origin is Elizabethan. It was in the 1560s that habeas corpus was first developed as a means of freeing individuals

---

[102] The first significant English textbooks were J. A. G. Griffith and H. Street, *Principles of Administrative Law* (London, 1952), and H. W. R. Wade, *Administrative Law* (Oxford, 1961). Cf. the pamphlet by W. I. Jennings, *Administrative Law and the Teaching of Public Law* (1938).

[103] RSC 1977, Ord. 53; Supreme Court Act 1981 (c. 54), s. 31; Civil Procedure Rules, Rule 54 (2000). The procedural change in 1977 followed the Law Commission's recommendation in their *Report on Remedies in Administrative Law* (1976) Law Com. No. 73.

[104] Ministry of Justice, *Civil Justice Statistics Quarterly . . . October to December 2014* (2015), p. 7. The new court is formally called the First-tier Tribunal (Immigration and Asylum Chamber). The term 'chamber', in this new sense, was imported from Europe in 2007.

who were wrongfully imprisoned. At that time, its importance lay not in the context of immigration and deportation, which did not give rise to litigation, but in reviewing imprisonment by prerogative courts and councillors.[105] Since most forms of government, including taxation, were enforceable in the last resort by imprisonment, the writ of habeas corpus gave the King's Bench a broad power of surveillance, extending not only to the provincial councils in Wales and the North but also to the queen's dominions outside the realm.[106] The court could use the ancient writs of prohibition and *quo warranto* in challenging other excesses of jurisdiction or authority.[107] Prohibition was used mainly against the ecclesiastical courts, especially in tithe cases, but also increasingly against the Admiralty.[108] The two other prerogative remedies of certiorari and mandamus existed in embryo, but their emergence into everyday life belonged to the next reign. They were used chiefly to control local government: certiorari in the case of counties (whose governance then belonged to the quarter sessions) and mandamus in the case of towns.[109]

[105] Baker, *Magna Carta*, pp. 155–70.

[106] This was established in the case of Berwick-upon-Tweed: *Brearley's Case* (1601), discussed in Baker, *Magna Carta*, pp. 299–302, 338.

[107] Besides its more traditional uses, Coke Att.-Gen. used *quo warranto* to challenge monopolies: e.g. Public Record Office, E 159/413 (rolls of the queen's remembrancer), Mich. 1597, Recorda, mm. 432–9.

[108] This caused much resentment from the doctors of law who practised in those courts: see M. J. Prichard and D. E. C. Yale, *Hale and Fleetwood on Admiralty Jurisdiction* (108 Selden Soc., 1993), introduction, pp. li, lxxxv, lxxxviii–lxxxix, xci–xcix.

[109] In Elizabethan times, overbearing mayors who arrested their opponents had already been subjected to some oversight by means of habeas

The new remedies received such encouragement under the chief justiceship of Sir Edward Coke in the following reign that Lord Ellesmere LC accused him of having effectively claimed for the King's Bench a 'superintendency' over the government itself.[110] That was more or less true. Coke CJ had asserted that 'no wrong or injury, either public or private, can be done, but that it shall be reformed or punished by due course of law'.[111] This was unacceptably shocking to Ellesmere and James I. Yet the rule of law was a principle so appealing to the minds of English lawyers, and the people they served, that it survived Coke's rude dismissal from office in 1616. With great astuteness, Coke CJ had represented the jurisdiction of his court as an exercise of the king's prerogative rather than a challenge to it. The new remedies, which were already (or very soon would be) called 'prerogative writs',[112] were in fact most often used to question abuses of the royal prerogative; but this was justified by the higher prerogative of preserving the rule of law, a prerogative entrusted to the judges of the king's own bench. Showing the independence which Elizabeth I allowed him, Coke had already begun to

corpus. In addition to the King's Bench remedies, the Star Chamber was available to deal with abuses of office by persons in authority, including magistrates and sheriffs: Ch. 2, nn. 67–70.

[110] *Law and Politics in Jacobean England: The Tracts of Lord Chancellor Ellesmere*, ed. L. A. Knafla (Cambridge, 1977), p. 307.

[111] *Bagg's Case* (1615) 11 Co. Rep. 98. This case, concerning the restitution of an alderman, established mandamus and linked it with Magna Carta.

[112] The original sense of 'prerogative writ' was an Exchequer writ to recover the queen's debts: e.g. *Hoe v. Boulton* (1600) 5 Co. Rep. 89. But already by 1619 habeas corpus was characterised as a 'prerogative writ': *Bourn's Case* (1619) Cro. Jac. 543, *per* Montague CJ.

develop this thinking while he was attorney-general in the 1590s,[113] and he soon saw the strategic advantage of linking the prerogative writs with Magna Carta. The great charter had acquired the sacrosanct authority of a higher law which bound even kings and their ministers. It was powerful enough to protect the prerogative writs, even if it did not protect Coke himself, in facing up to the absolutist inclinations of James I. It was habeas corpus which brought matters to a head under Charles I, first in the case of the five knights imprisoned for refusing to pay a forced loan (1627), and then in Hampden's case for refusing to pay ship-money (1638). It helped to preserve the idea of constitutional monarchy in England, while absolute monarchies rose and fell on the Continent. And judicial review continues to keep governments and their agencies within the rule of law today. The five prerogative writs became embedded in written constitutions across the world, from Africa to Asia and Latin America. Coke has not been given enough credit for this. Indeed, he suffered badly at the hands of historians who failed to understand what he was about. Yet his lasting achievements as a law officer and a judge have no obvious parallel. Some of the principles which he promoted in the time of Elizabeth I, enabling the judicial review of prerogative powers and statutory discretions alike, were almost forgotten and had to be found again in the present reign.[114] The prerogative writs themselves remained

---

[113] Baker, *Magna Carta*, pp. 291–2, 338; Ch. 2, n. 52.

[114] For the prerogative (cf. Ch. 2, n. 163) see *R. v. Criminal Injuries Compensation Board*, ex p. *Lain* [1967] 2 QB 864; *Council of Civil Service Unions* v. *Minister for the Civil Service* (the GCHQ case) [1985] AC 374;

in use in England until 1977, when their workings were sensibly merged into a single procedure. Since then, judicial review proceedings have become the mainstay of the Queen's Bench Division, as ordinary civil litigation there has diminished.[115] That is a recent development; but the change is in the sheer volume of applications rather than the underlying principles, which had simply been sleeping.

The Operation and Public Perception of the Law

Today's armies of claimants are encouraged by a still larger change than those already mentioned. Sir Leslie Scarman, as he then was, called it The New Dimension. In his Hamlyn Lectures of 1974, Scarman drew attention to numerous challenges facing the common-law system. Quite apart from human rights, the new European connection, and devolution, everyday matters such as social security, the environment and industrial relations did not fit with traditional English jurisprudence, which was essentially concerned with interactions between individuals.[116] The strength of the common law had been its universality, but it was now being pushed into corners and was in retreat, not challenged but simply abandoned – 'remaindered', as he put it – and left to die in a forgotten

---

R. (Miller) v. *Secretary of State for Exiting the European Union* [2017] UKSC 5. For discretionary powers see Ch. 3, nn. 81–2.

[115] See e.g. the letter of Sir John Laws in *The Times*, 20 Sept. 2019, p. 30 ('Their elementary task is . . . to keep governments and other public powers within the functions allotted to them by Parliament').

[116] Scarman, *English Law – The New Dimension*, p. 40.

corner.[117] He warned that if the common-law system could not meet these challenges, they would destroy it.[118] Welfare law, for instance, was not about contract, tort or property but about need; and it was governed not by law, and causes of action by plaintiffs against defendants, but by policy and its administration.[119] The old techniques of the law did not apply, and lawyers were in danger of becoming irrelevant.[120] The business of the civil courts was already falling away. The question, he thought, was partly constitutional. The universality of common law was being discarded. Public law was becoming no more than an exercise in statutory interpretation, so that people's rights and liabilities were determined by governmental machinery which was subject not to the rule of law but to administrative and political controls beyond the reach of the law. Much of it, he thought, would soon be managed through computers. The men who pushed the buttons would be the same men who manipulated the parliamentary majority.[121] Where were the safeguards against such power?

---

[117] Ibid. 71. Cf. ibid. 74 ('. . . the common law system is in retreat: it is being remaindered to corners of the house which are unvisited by most members of society. The basis of the system is not only challenged: it is being abandoned').

[118] Ibid. 1.

[119] Hailsham, *Hamlyn Revisited*, pp. 57–61, characterised it as a movement from contract to status, reversing Maine's thesis that the process of legal evolution had been from status to contract. However, Maine's thesis was demonstrably mistaken in respect of English legal history: *IELH* (5th edn), p. 207.

[120] Scarman, *English Law – The New Dimension*, pp. 40–3.

[121] Ibid. 73. Similar fears predated the computer: G. W. Keeton, *The Passing of Parliament* (1952).

An analogous point may be made from a longer historical perspective.[122] Between the thirteenth century and the
nineteenth, the common law, like Roman law, had been predicated on the affairs of individuals who dealt with each other
on the same footing. In place of the vertical nature of feudal
management, it had come to operate horizontally between
legal equals. Mere expectations of fair treatment by a lord,
according to customary norms, had given way under Henry II
or soon afterwards to rights enforceable against others in
royal courts with professional judges. The final stage in that
process occurred in the Elizabethan period, when the copyholder's upward claim to seignorial protection in a manorial
court was replaced by a horizontal action at law.[123] In the
Victorian age the whole body of horizontal law arrived at an
almost mathematical clarity, which could be reduced to the-
orems by the textbook writers. Since then, however, there has
been an adventitious transformation.

The most far-reaching cause was the disuse of juries
in civil cases. Judges and lawyers had always been astute to
prevent juries from tackling questions they might not understand, and after 1854 it was possible for parties in common-
law suits to bypass the jury altogether and elect for trial by
judge alone. By the 1960s the balance had changed so far that

---

[122] The following two paragraphs are heavily dependent on S. F. C. Milsom,
'The Past and Future of Judge-Made Law' (1981), reprinted in *Studies in
the History of the Common Law* (1985), pp. 209–22. Milsom had
addressed the same subject in his unpublished inaugural lecture at
Cambridge in 1978. The thoughts had been evolving for much longer:
'The Vitality of the Law' (1969) 119 *New Law Journal* 607–9.

[123] See Ch. 2, n. 77.

the courts were unwilling to allow civil juries at all, save in exceptional cases.[124] There were good reasons for allowing the civil jury to slip away.[125] However, breaking down the boundary between investigating the facts and applying the law to the facts brought two unintended consequences. One was that the law began a descent into ever-lower levels of detail, with a loss of the clarity that had been essential when a judge had to explain it to a lay jury: 'Longer judgments cite more cases to settle smaller questions less clearly.'[126] The other was that it removed the element of discretion enjoyed by a jury, and the consequent 'index-linking' of decisions to the reasonable man or woman of the day.

Another change was in the modus operandi of legislation. Parliament no longer thought of itself as adjusting the existing law, but chose rather to withdraw matters from it and

---

[124] *Ward* v. *James* [1966] 1 QB 273 (effectively reversing *Hope* v. *G.W.R.* [1937] 2 KB 130); *Williams* v. *Beesly* [1973] 1 WLR 1295; P. Devlin, *Trial by Jury* (Hamlyn Lectures, 1956), pp. 181–5. The principal survival was in defamation cases, but since 2013 these too are tried without a jury unless the court orders otherwise: Defamation Act 2013 (c. 26), s. 11. Juries may still be used in cases of fraud, malicious prosecution or false imprisonment: Supreme Court Act 1981 (c. 54), s. 69(1).

[125] Devlin, *Trial by Jury*, pp. 129–65. Even in criminal cases, the Supreme Court has opined that 'trial by jury can in certain circumstances be antithetical to a fair trial': *In re Hutchings* [2019] UKSC 26, at p. 12. But cf. J. I. H. Jacob, *The Fabric of English Civil Justice* (Hamlyn Lectures, 1987), pp. 156–60.

[126] Milsom, 'The Past and Future of Judge-Made Law', p. 217. Cf. M. Arden, 'Are Shorter Judgments Achievable?' in *Common Law and Modern Society* (Oxford, 2015), ch. 16. See also above, at nn. 33–4.

hand them over to managerial bodies and tribunals. Milsom concluded that

> [a]t different speeds, much of the Western world is moving back to dependent structures of which the feudal unit was a simple model. In such a structure the obligations of society are not between man and equal man: they are, as it were, in the vertical dimension, between manager and managed, between those with the power to allocate and those with some entitlement to allocation.[127]

The consequence was a parallel world of vertical dispute-resolution alongside the old legal system. The range of statutory tribunals is now so wide that there are few, if any, lawyers who could enumerate them all; and besides them there are the ombudsmen, the regulators, the public inquiries, the disciplinary bodies and the various species of arbitration,[128] not to mention eBay's worldwide online dispute resolution system, which is said to process forty times as many cases as the County Court.[129] The horizontal is also being overtaken by

---

[127] Milsom, 'The Past and Future of Judge-Made Law', p. 221.

[128] The rise of commercial arbitration is not without its critics. J. D. Heydon, a former justice of the High Court of Australia, wrote in 77 CLJ 212 (2018): 'Modern arbitration, made compulsory by many ill-advisedly entered contractual clauses, is in many respects a scandalous institution. It is a procedure dominated not by the parties, but by their grasping lawyers, who secure delays and financial advantages connived at by arbitrators ... And the "law" enforced by arbitration is often not the actual law of the land against which the contract was written, but some new and unpredicted departure from it ...'.

[129] In 2015 it was reputed to handle 60 million disputes a year: Civil Justice Council, *Online Dispute Resolution for Low Value Civil Claims* (2015), pp. 11–12.

the vertical as a result of the massive surge in judicial review proceedings. The Human Rights Act 1998 is so vertically oriented that there seems to be no protection under the Act against fellow humans and corporate bodies, as opposed to public bodies.

Contrary to Scarman's fears, none of this has harmed the legal profession or the ethos which it traditionally represents. The number of practising barristers has risen from around 2,000 at the beginning of the present queen's reign to around 16,000 today – three-fifths of them women – even though the number of High Court actions has declined. The number of practising solicitors has increased at much the same rate, from under 20,000 to over 140,000, of whom half are women. There are also various new ancillary professions providing legal services, such as chartered legal executives, licensed conveyancers, patent attorneys and costs draftsmen. Indeed, the varieties of legal and paralegal activity are now so many that in 2007 it was thought fit to regulate them by a labyrinthine statute, wholly unintelligible to the outsider, which includes forty-four sections on the regulation of the regulators.[130] The proportion of lawyers to population, at the beginning of the present reign, was about ten times that in 1558. Without even counting the new professions which have sprung up in the interim, that has today increased by a factor of five, just as under Elizabeth I the number of attorneys quadrupled and was further swelled by the new breed of paralegals (as they then were) called solicitors. It seems, therefore, that there are still about ten times as many lawyers today

---

[130] Legal Services Act 2007 (c. 29).

per head as there were in Elizabeth I's reign.[131] Part of the explanation is that much of today's business is generated by corporate clients rather than people: the huge City firms which serve them are themselves an innovation of the present reign, fuelled by the demands of modern global trade and finance. Until 1967 partnerships between solicitors could not exceed twenty, and many firms were handed down in the families whose names they bore. The large changes began soon after that rule was rescinded.[132] The City firms now contain around 15 per cent of all practising solicitors, acting for clients worldwide. Another part of the explanation is that much of the business is transactional rather than litigious. The increase in private-client work is doubtless attributable to greater general prosperity: there are, for instance, nearly one million domestic conveyancing transactions every year.[133] In the contentious sphere, another factor is that many of the new kinds of claim, and the new ways of

[131] See the estimates in Brooks, *Pettyfoggers and Vipers*, p. 264 (1:20,000 in 1558, rising to 1:2,100 in 1913); Ch. 1, n. 88. The population in 1951 was around 39 million and has risen to about 55 million today, so that, during the present reign, the proportion of practising solicitors to the population has risen from about 1:1,950 (slightly below Brooks's figure for 1913) to about 1:393. The Elizabethan figures are for attorneys; the number of solicitors is unknown.

[132] R. L. Abel, *The Legal Profession in England and Wales* (1988); R. G. Lee, 'The Rise and Rise of the City Law Firm' (1992) 19 *Journal of Law and Society* 31–48; M. Galanter, 'From Kinship to Magic Circle: The London Commercial Law Firm in the 20th Century' (2009) 15 *International Journal of the Legal Profession* 143–78. Sets of barristers' chambers have also grown ever larger and swallowed up smaller ones.

[133] *Scott v. Southern Pacific Mortgages Ltd* [2014] UKSC 52, at p. 27, para. 86, *per* Lord Collins (who gave the figure as 900,000).

dealing with them, outside the courts of law, have been aligned with old-style legal processes by appointing professional chairmen, allowing representation by lawyers and the testing of evidence, and requiring reasoned decisions which can usually be challenged elsewhere.[134]

The need for legal assistance in coping with this new world is evidently greater than it was under the older law. The biggest stumbling block for the litigant in Elizabethan times was the mass of arcane procedures, many of which used Latin forms, though it was overcome by forbidding litigants in person to act in the higher courts and exempting from fees those too poor to afford them. Although formalism as such has gone, finding and following the right procedure is still a major difficulty for the lay complainant who cannot afford legal advice at the outset. And the common law itself is fast descending into the depths of complexity which disfigured the Tudor land law, for reasons already touched upon.[135] A bigger stumbling block today, though, is the complexity, obscurity and sheer volume of written law in the regulatory state.[136] Statutes are bad enough, but they are more or less finite. A greater source of perplexity nowadays is the almost infinite

---

[134] The first step was the creation of a unified tribunal system as proposed by A. Leggatt, *Tribunals for Users – One System, One Service* (2001). The transformational measure was the Tribunals, Courts and Enforcement Act 2007 (c. 15): see R. Carnwath, 'Tribunal Justice – A New Start' [2009] *Public Law* 48–69; M. Elliott and R. Thomas, 'Tribunal Justice and Proportionate Dispute Resolution' (2012) 91 *CLJ* 297–324.

[135] Above, n. 126. The Tudor land law had been largely removed from juries by means of special verdicts and demurrers to special pleading.

[136] See Ch. 3.

corpus of statutory instruments, directives, regulations and codes of practice which potentially govern our lives.[137] Most of them do not in fact govern our lives, but only particular activities which are unlikely to concern us, some of which we may never hear about. No one, not even the most assiduous practising lawyer, has read all of them. They are tracked down via the ether rather than in libraries. Even when the right texts are found – and it may be that several have to be read in conjunction – they are probably long-winded. The desire to provide for every eventuality and to reduce the room for discretion has led to more and more written detail, and more detail inevitably requires more frequent amendments, probably with yet more detail, backed up by sheaves of notes and guidance which have little or no official authority. It is no wonder that there is an increasing demand for legal services. Only a specialist can confidently know how to find the relevant rules on any subject, and one may need professional advice to know what kind of specialist to go to. It is therefore a fair guess that most of today's law is unfamiliar to most lawyers, let alone the public.

This is not meant merely as a lament but as another point of comparison with the law of Elizabeth I's day. The mystification of legal rights and obligations may be the largest difference between our world and that of the sixteenth century. It is true that the Elizabethans complained, as we do, of

---

[137] Over 80,000 statutory instruments are listed on the government website, and around 1,400 are added every year. (The number has exceeded 3,000 in some years.) A similar number of regulations and directives have been issued by the European Union.

too much legislation and too many lawyers. Yet, as was noted in Chapter 2, they lived and breathed law and legal language. So much is evident from the allusions in Shakespeare. Many of the men in his audiences would have resided for a while in the inns of court and chancery, since some basic knowledge of law was considered a necessary accomplishment for every gentleman.[138] No doubt some of them – like Justice Shallow and his swashbuckling former companions[139] – did not get far beyond the first few pages of Littleton. But as men of the world they knew about remainders and reversions, trusts and mortgages, final concords and common recoveries, manors and copyholds. They attended the assizes as jurymen and witnesses, or merely as interested onlookers, and they attended lesser courts as well. Awareness of the law and its workings percolated down beneath the Shallows, Pickbones and Squeals of Clement's Inn to the humblest countrymen. In a fictitious dialogue of 1602, William Fulbecke makes a poor country yeoman declare that his neighbours 'are so full of law points that . . . when they breathe, it is perfect law; when they dream, it is profound law . . . Littleton's *Tenures* is their breakfast, their dinner [and their supper]. Every plough-swain with us may be a seneschal in a court baron; he can talk of essoins, vouchers, withernams and recaptions . . . .'[140] This was, of course, a facetious exaggeration. But the parody worked because of the undoubted truth that legal knowledge was

---

[138] Speech to the new serjeants (1594) Poph. 43, 44, *per* Popham CJ.

[139] *Henry IV, Part Two* (*c.* 1596–99), act 3, scene 2. Shallow was, of course, only a country justice.

[140] W. Fulbecke, *The Second Part of the Parallele* (1602), sig. B2. The author was a member of Gray's Inn.

pervasive. Not that this was necessarily considered a good thing. Contemporaries blamed the general obsession with law for the ever-increasing number of attorneys and lawsuits. (Little did they know what was to come when people knew less.) They were right that lawyers and lawsuits were on the increase.[141] But whether they were right in their explanation is questionable, since the ultimate cause is more likely to have been – as in our own age – a greater general prosperity.[142] Nor is it easy to judge whether the litigation really was excessive, in the sense that it was unmerited and vexatious, rather than that it could have been averted by sensible discussion and compromise.[143] There was no obvious decline in the proportion of successful plaintiffs. What may be accepted as fact is the Elizabethan perception that too much interest in the law was a mixed blessing.

The pervasiveness of legal knowledge still to some extent survived, at least among the readers and subjects of novels, in the England of Jane Austen and Charles Dickens. The processes of justice felt more stable – in bad ways as well as good – because they were governed by seemingly ageless law, fondly supposed to have descended from the time of Henry II and from Magna Carta, improved by occasional tweaking. Even the sweeping reforms of the next generation

---

[141] Ch. 1, nn. 87–94.

[142] So thought Coke: 4 Co. Inst. 76. The most detailed study of fluctuations in litigation is in C. W. Brooks, *Lawyers, Litigation and English Society since 1740* (1998).

[143] A bill presented to Parliament in 1589 would have prevented plaintiffs recovering damages for trespass where a sufficient recompense had been offered and refused: *Proc. Parl.*, ii. 496.

did not diminish the general sense of continuity and steady improvement. The Victorians took pride in the reformed system of civil justice, and their confidence was embodied in the impressive and costly neo-gothic architecture of the Manchester Assize Courts (1864) and the Royal Courts of Justice (1882), major landmarks in their day and designed, like the law, to last for ever. But that world is long gone, and the belief in an evolutionary legal system of prestigious splendour now seems as quaintly remote as the belief in a flat earth or purgatory. People in general – not counting lawyers as people – do not read about law, except for newsworthy trials and appeals, and many of them seem not to understand legal concepts or how the law works.[144] People only have a one-in-three chance of ever serving on a jury and are unlikely ever to attend a civil court. Even if they do see a civil court in action, they will only be able to see half of what is going on, the other half hidden in bundles and skeletons. Their knowledge of private law may well be derived from older works of fiction rather than real life; and they are surprised, if not disappointed, when told that we no longer have writs and plaintiffs, or judges in traditional robes in the higher civil courts. The level of understanding may be changed by the televising of important cases. The experience can nevertheless be a shock. Viewers now know that leading barristers address the highest court in the land wearing identity tags labelled 'Lawyer'

---

[144] The need for more public legal education, 'to equip people to avoid, recognise and resolve disputes', was acknowledged in the *Briggs Report* (2016), pp. 21–2, 60–1; and by the House of Common Justice Committee, *Courts and Tribunals Reforms: Second Report of Session 2019* (2019) HC 190, at pp. 21–2, 69.

instead of professional costume.[145] They are rightly impressed by the consummate skill of the advocates. But they have learned how difficult it is to follow even a purely legal argument when they cannot see or hear the materials to which counsel refer.

It is not only the public image of the law which has shrunk. Lawyers do not influence public thinking in the way they once did. There are no Cokes, Bacons, Fleetwoods or Pophams in today's House of Commons. It is no longer practicable or appropriate for members to pursue full-time parallel careers, as it was when parliaments were special events. The Commons has not for forty years had a lawyer as Speaker,[146] as it always did in Elizabeth I's reign, and even the lord chancellor (now consigned to the lower House[147]) is not always a lawyer. Legal advice is rejected or ignored by ministers when it does not suit them or their unqualified special advisers. The newspapers have pared down or abandoned legal reporting, having decided that their readers would rather learn about attacks on the judiciary than be given full accounts of what the courts are doing. Arguments about bills before Parliament are also generally ignored by the press. The professional judiciary has expanded with the tribunal system to encompass a wide range of talents, and

---

[145] Even the justices sit gownless, as if they were still a judicial committee rather than a supreme court. Gowns appear to be required only for the otherwise casually dressed ushers.

[146] The last was John Selwyn-Lloyd (1971–6).

[147] Elizabeth I's lord chancellors and lord keepers presided in the House of Lords, though none of them were peers. Egerton LK only became Lord Ellesmere LC in 1603.

newspapers are keen to report the aberrations of anyone who can be called a 'Judge'. Since there are now over 1,600 people accorded this title, the cumulative effect of such reports is to tarnish popular perceptions of judicial calibre. But even the superior judges, who were once accorded the same formal respect as the monarch whom they represented, are subjected to much uninformed criticism and hostility from the news and social media, and from politicians.[148] As long ago as 1983, Lord Hailsham declared such attacks to be a threat to judicial independence, and held it the duty of the lord chancellor to defend the judiciary.[149] Since then the attacks have become still more strident, especially in the area of public law, and it is becoming evident that the judicial role is simply not understood by the public, the media or the politicians who make the law. In consequence, judicial morale is said to be lower than it ever was in the past and there are difficulties of recruitment. This is another phenomenon which would have mystified the Elizabethans.

---

[148] Lord Burnett LCJ, in a press conference on 5 Dec. 2017, reported that judges were facing a 'torrent of personal abuse . . . and a growing number of cases where judges are threatened and physically abused'. This was reaffirmed in *The Lord Chief Justice's Report* (2018), p. 10. It is said that a majority of judges now have concerns about their safety in court: C. Thomas, *2016 Judicial Attitudes Survey* (2017), p. 22. For ill-informed attacks on judicial decisions see Dyson, *Justice*, pp. 17–34.

[149] Hailsham, *Hamlyn Revisited*, pp. 45–6, 48, 54–5. One of Coke CJ's complaints about Lord Ellesmere LC was that he failed to defend the judges from political hostility, which then came from the king rather than the people: Baker, *Magna Carta*, p. 439 n. 168. By 1616 Coke CJ had become a popular hero.

5

Comparing Then and Now

Numerous comparisons have been made in the foregoing chapters, pointing to some of the differences and similarities between the law of the two Elizabethan eras. The obvious concluding question must be: 'To what extent, if at all, is today's law better?' To this, the obvious first response must be that it depends on the criteria. Thanks to an emerging literature on the evaluation of legal systems, there are many and various criteria to choose from.[1] If the question were rephrased, 'Would anything be improved if some of the law was put back?', that would be an unrealistic and vain question because society has changed. Only religions cling to archaic rules designed for different societies. Then again, the substantive law must be distinguished from the legal system. There is no obvious way of measuring the quality of substantive law.[2] In any case, whatever law professors might wish, the main purpose of a civil legal system is not to improve or develop the

[1] Zander, *The State of Justice*, pp. 4–5, suggests that the criteria should be: accessibility, the absence of serious delay, the encouragement of settlements, the efficiency of enforcement, and (above all) fairness. See also F. Wilmot-Smith, *Equal Justice: Fair Legal Systems in an Unfair World* (Cambridge, MA, 2019).
[2] Professor Zander concluded that there are no means of measuring the 'justice quotient' in judicial decisions: *The State of Justice*, p. 2.

law, or even to produce judgments, but rather to provide a framework within which disputing parties can resolve their difficulties in a satisfactory manner. Only a tiny proportion of cases taken to court proceed as far as judgment, let alone result in a new principle of law. So it was in the sixteenth century. But there has been a reorientation in the overall patterns of litigation, characterised in Chapter 4 as a shift from horizontal to vertical. Even the law of contract is largely for public bodies, commercial organisations and debt-collectors, and the law of tort is for insurance companies or public authorities battling over claims at levels which only insurers or large entities could possibly afford to pay. The ordinary person's assessment of justice is more likely to be focused on the means of challenging discretionary decisions than on jurisprudence of the older kind. It must also be remembered that most people – as opposed to organisations – have an aversion to using formal processes at all. Although those who have legal problems usually take some steps to resolve them, only a small minority use the civil justice system, and of those only a small minority pursue cases to the end.[3] Going to law is an unwelcome, and intimidating, last resort. It is also beyond most people's means. Many lawyers would still agree with the Dickensian advice that it is better for private persons to suffer almost any wrong than to litigate.[4]

---

[3] Zander, *The State of Justice*, pp. 32–4.

[4] C. Dickens, *Bleak House* (1853), ch. 1, referring to the Chancery ('there is not an honourable man among its practitioners who . . . does not often give the warning, "Suffer any wrong that can be done you, rather than come here!"'). More recently, Alexandra Marks, head of the Centre for Effective Dispute Resolution, suggested that every judge should tell the

Whether that represents an advance from Elizabethan litigiousness is an esoteric philosophical question, and the answer may depend on subjective notions of satisfaction with the processes, and the alternatives, rather than on legal thinking. At any rate, it befuddles any direct comparison.

The Rule of Law

Given all these difficulties, the criteria proposed for the present purpose are those which have come to be associated with the 'rule of law'. Coke, in a passage recently quoted with approval by the Supreme Court, suggested that justice should be free, open and expeditious.[5] That, however, does not go quite far enough. Lord Bingham identified seven basic principles underpinning the rule of law.[6] To simplify matters, they may here be reduced to three (which incorporate Coke's): accessibility, efficiency and fairness.[7]

Accessibility was Lord Bingham's first principle, though he used the word to refer to the ease with which the substantive content of the law can be accessed: its clarity, intelligibility and predictability. However, there is a second

---

parties, 'If you really think that your day in court is going to deliver what you want out of this … think again': *The Times*, 6 Dec. 2018, p. 60.

[5] 2 Co. Inst. 55 (in the commentary on Magna Carta, c. 29); *R. (on the application of Unison)* v. *Lord Chancellor* [2017] UKSC 51, at pp. 22–3, para. 75.

[6] T. Bingham, *The Rule of Law* (2010). Cf. Hailsham, *Hamlyn Revisited*, pp. 33–4 (referring to due process).

[7] A fourth, the adequate protection of personal liberty, was considered in Ch. 4.

important aspect of accessibility, which is the effective availability of legal remedies to those who need them.[8] The right of
access to the courts is now regarded as a constitutional right,
guaranteed by chapter 29 of Magna Carta, which can be
impeded only by the clearest expression of a statutory intention to override the rule of law.[9] The Supreme Court has
indicated that the right will be vigorously enforced with
respect to disproportionately high court fees, though little or
nothing has been done to moderate the spiralling fees charged
by lawyers and expert witnesses on hourly rates. The fear of
heavy costs, especially in cases where there is little hope of
recovering them in the event of success, may not only deter
meritorious claimants but may also drive defendants to pay
damages to unmeritorious claimants rather than incur the
unpredictable cost of defending.[10] The recent review conducted by Lord Justice Briggs (as he then was) concluded
that 'the single, most pervasive and indeed shocking weakness
of our civil courts is that they fail to provide reasonable access
to justice for the ordinary individuals or small businesses with
small or moderate value claims'.[11] And the Law Society in 2017
expressed concern that 'increases in court fees, court closures,

---

[8] This was an aspect of Lord Bingham's seventh principle: *The Rule of
Law*, p. 85.

[9] *R. (on the application of Unison)* v. *Lord Chancellor* [2017] UKSC 51, at
p. 20, *per* Lord Reed; ibid., p. 22, referring to Magna Carta, c. 29. See also
R. v. *Lord Chancellor*, ex p. *Witham* [1998] QB 575, 580, 586, *per* Laws J;
Dyson, *Justice*, pp. 57–8.

[10] Dyson, *Justice*, pp. 74–5.

[11] *Briggs Report* (2016), p. 28. The problem is perceived to have worsened as
the result of reducing legal aid in recent years: Zanders, *The State of
Justice*, pp. 6–25; Dyson, *Justice*, p. 12. See further below, at n. 16.

and legal aid cuts, are progressively eroding access to justice for ordinary people in England and Wales, undermining their ability to exercise their rights'.[12] For the reasons given in Chapter 1, our Elizabethan precursors were well ahead of us in that regard. And they were probably at least level with us in respect of intellectual accessibility as well.[13] Elizabethan procedure and land law were fraught with recondite learning, it is true, and law reports were not even in English. But the books were far fewer, and a body of law which evolves from reasoned argument in real cases yields answers to legal questions more readily than masses of constantly changing and often ill-drawn legislative rules.

Efficiency is more difficult to evaluate. The most obvious negative factors in a legal system are delays in getting before a court, time-wasting in court, and lack of adequate enforcement once a court has pronounced. In respect of all three, the balance between the two periods is about even. Small claims are now heard expeditiously, though no more quickly than in Elizabethan local courts, which could dispatch cases in a matter of days. For instance, in a 1567 contract case in the Canterbury piepowder court, a plaint was made on Saturday morning; the defendant was summoned to appear at 2 p.m. and finally appeared at 6 p.m.; Sunday being *dies non*, he was given till 8 a.m. on Monday to answer, when he failed to plead; a jury to assess the damages reported at 1 p.m., and

---

[12] The Law Society, 'Access to Justice: Making the Legal System Accessible to All' (General Election briefing, 2017).

[13] Cf. Scarman, *English Law – The New Dimension*, p. 7 ('The law is very much the esoteric business of lawyers. It is neither accessible nor easy to understand when found').

judgment was thereupon given to recover £94. 17s. 4d. (about £¼ million today); finally, at 5 p.m., the defendant was committed to gaol to enforce payment.[14] In higher courts, trials in both periods usually took place within a year of commencement. If there were difficult points of law, there might in the sixteenth century be numerous adjournments for judicial reflection and discussion at Westminster; but there is a modern equivalent in the two-year wait for a hearing in the Court of Appeal. One cause of delay and expense nowadays is exhaustive preparation. In Elizabethan times there was little or no discovery, limited written evidence and probably no expert witnesses. Trials were in consequence much swifter, though whether they led to a better or worse result is impossible to know. Equally time-wasting, if not more so, is inadequate preparation, and loud complaints are heard today about both the poor preparation of criminal cases by the Crown Prosecution Service and the lack of legal representation in many civil as well as criminal cases. In Tudor times there was no prosecution service, and usually no prosecuting counsel. This sometimes caused cases to collapse unnecessarily; but defendants were not prejudiced, because a gaol delivery meant just that: if no evidence was forthcoming against an accused on the appointed day, he was entitled to be discharged. We know little of the conduct of civil trials in the same period; but in Westminster Hall, where the law was argued, only learned counsel could be heard. That would

---

[14] *Smyth* v. *Hyckes* (1567) KB 27/1224, m. 24. James Morice nevertheless observed of these courts that 'their expedition is . . . sometimes with more haste than with good speed': HLS MS. 120, fo. 183.

now be prohibitively expensive for most self-funded private litigants. The remedy found in the present age was legal aid, first introduced for civil cases in 1949. The ideal, as formulated by the Benson Commission in 1979, was that financial assistance out of public funds should be available for every individual who would suffer an undue financial burden in properly pursuing or defending his or her rights, and that individuals receiving such assistance should have the same standard of services as those who pay for them.[15] But this goal has never been achieved. It is an expense which governments have found it impossible to meet, and in recent years the expenditure on legal aid has been significantly diminished,[16] though other ways of funding litigation are being sought.[17] The decreasing availability of legal assistance for a substantial part of the population has led to the courts being seriously troubled by litigants in person. Through no fault of their own, unrepresented lay litigants are not equipped to assess whether their case is worth starting, do not understand the relevant law and practice, do not know how to produce or deal with evidence, are not bound by professional conventions, and are unable to take an objective view of the merits of their various

---

[15] Royal Commission on Legal Services, *Final Report* (1979) Cmnd 7648, para. 5. The first measure introducing civil as well as criminal legal aid was the Legal Aid and Advice Act 1949 (c. 51).

[16] Especially after the so-called Access to Justice Act 1999 (c. 22). The total legal aid bill was in fact increasing in real terms, until by 2010 it reached £2.2 billion per annum, which some claimed to be the highest per capita provision in the world. Since then it has been steadily reduced in real terms.

[17] E.g. lawyers' contingent fees (no win, no fee), speculative investment in litigation, and crowd-funding.

points. Much of this is also true of unrepresented defendants in criminal cases. The consequent inefficiency and the added expense compare unfavourably with the Elizabethan civil legal system. This may seem remarkable, given that Tudor governments spent nothing at all on legal aid; but lawyers then were required by law to act pro bono for the truly indigent, trials and legal motions were generally short, and costs were much lower.

The efficiency of pre-trial preparations depends to a large extent on effective case-management. How far interlocutory case-management orders should be enforced strictly – following the new emphasis on efficiency and proportionality – is now controversial, particularly where lay litigants are concerned.[18] The Elizabethan common-law courts managed their proceedings by means of 'rules', for instance rules to plead by a certain day, or to show cause why judgment should not be entered, and these were enforced with discretion unless made peremptorily. Most litigants had attorneys at Westminster, paid their forty pence a term to ensure compliance. As to the enforceability of judgments, a comparison depends to a large extent on the view one takes of the effectiveness of imprisonment for debt, the last vestiges of which lingered until 1970.[19] Paradoxically, it

---

[18] See Dyson, *Justice*, pp. 338–40. The new approach was explained in *Mitchell* v. *News Group Newspapers Ltd* [2013] EWCA Civ 1537; and clarified in *Denton* v. *T. H. White Ltd* [2014] EWCA Civ 906.

[19] O. R. McGregor, *Social History and Law Reform* (Hamlyn Lectures, 1981), pp. 33–63. Since 1869 an element of contumacy was a prerequisite, but even so, debtors constituted 14 per cent of the prison population in the 1960s: ibid. 38.

worked best for the creditor when the debtor escaped, because liability was then transferred to the sheriff.[20] Leaving that aside, the methods are broadly similar, and indeed the writ of *fieri facias*, executed by the under-sheriff, was the last of the old forms of routine process to be abolished. As with pre-trial procedure, however, recent reforms have made the law of execution more complex than it used to be.

The third element in the calculus, fairness, has two principal aspects. One is fairness in exercising authority, whether by the government and its agencies or by courts and tribunals. It requires conformity with the dictates of natural justice and, above all, independent and competent judges and officials. The other is fairness in the process of lawmaking: whether it is properly thought through, whether it takes account of legitimate general concerns, and how far it is susceptible to influence from single-issue pressure groups and trendy dogmas which briefly enthuse the media.[21] If we like to think that the legal system aims to embody both aspects of fairness, so did the lawyers of the first Elizabethan age. Elizabethan language did not include such phrases as natural justice and the rule of law, but the root concepts were well known. The government could not change the law without Parliament, in which everyone was supposed to be represented. It is true that everyone could not yet vote for the representatives; but it is equally true that a Commons filled with lawyers, landowners and leading men of business could

---

[20] See Ch. 3, n. 67. The sheriff's liability for debts was ended in 1887.

[21] Single-issue campaigns ignore the need to weigh all desiderata against the available resources: Hailsham, *Hamlyn Revisited*, pp. 31–2, 62–3.

bring some effective influence to bear on the government of the day – a government which did not then, of course, depend on election – and perhaps more effective than today in finding and implementing remedies for defects in the law. The rule of law was preserved by the courts. The right of parties to be heard by counsel in civil cases was unquestioned; indeed, in the superior courts, they had more opportunities to re-argue difficult cases on successive occasions than would be allowed today. Judges were sworn to administer equal justice to all the queen's subjects, rich and poor alike, and judicial independence was assumed. They may have allowed private predilections to sway their opinions more freely than the judges of today. But their autonomy was more tightly circumscribed. They were not allowed to find facts at all, and single trial judges could not (in civil cases) decide on the law either. Although one judge was dismissed for criticising the government extrajudicially,[22] security of tenure would not become a serious issue until the Stuart period, and courts could and did decide points of law against the Crown. Bribery was unacceptable. Bias or corruption in inferior decision-makers was an acknowledged problem,[23] and it was difficult to challenge since certiorari

---

[22] Monson J, who in 1580 had criticised the savage treatment of a political pamphleteer as possibly illegal: Baker, *Magna Carta*, p. 174.

[23] There was an indignant reaction when Edward Glascock MP, a recently called barrister, suggested in the Commons in 1601 that there were JPs who 'for half a dozen chickens will dispense with a whole dozen of penal statutes'. He had to qualify his remark, and explained that he only meant 'basket justices' of the meanest sort: *Proc. Parl.*, iii. 416, 425–7, 483–5. For punishments imposed on erring magistrates see Ch. 2, nn. 67, 69, 70; below, n. 28.

was still restricted to criminal cases; but a start was made with the important decision of 1598 that a discretionary statutory power had to be exercised 'equitably' (or reasonably).[24]

Criminal Law

The most negative feature of Elizabethan justice, in comparison with today, was the criminal legal process.[25] The accused in ous criminal case did not have many of the safeguards, aken for granted, which have been developed in the intervening centuries. Counsel usually played no part, on either side, and it was left to the judge to defend the interests of the defendant. If counsel were allowed, so the King's Bench warned in 1602, 'it would be a dangerous precedent, for every prisoner would demand it'.[26] Indeed they would. It was in the judge's discretion whether to respite judgment so that a point of legal difficulty could be discussed with other judges back in Serjeants' Inn. There was little to be done if he did not see a point worth arguing; and few defendants would have been able to find one without legal assistance. Judge and jury doubtless believed that they knew a serious crime when they saw one. But the uneducated and undefended prisoner, overawed with terror, was at

---

[24] See Ch. 3, nn. 81–2. Certiorari was used from the time of James I to challenge fines imposed by administrative tribunals, and later in the century to challenge other decisions: *IELH* (5th edn), pp. 159–60.

[25] See also 'Criminal Law' in Ch. 2.

[26] *R. v. Boothe* (1602) Coventry's reports, BL MS. Add. 25203, fos. 569v-570 (tr.); Baker, *Collected Papers*, ii. 1048. Counsel were permitted to argue a point of law, but the defendant himself had to indicate the point of law first.

a serious disadvantage. There were no exclusionary rules of evidence, such as the rule requiring direct evidence as opposed to hearsay,[27] other than that the defendant (like the parties in civil cases) was disqualified by self-interest from giving sworn testimony himself. Trials were so swift that many a prisoner, even when on trial for his life, could barely have grasped what was happening before he was convicted and sentenced.

Sanctions were available in the Star Chamber in case of any reported misconduct by officials or magistrates which sullied the criminal process,[28] and if a trial judge thought a verdict unsafe there were several ways to avoid its consequences.[29] But the determination of guilt was entrusted exclusively to ordinary people, with only elementary directions. This at least meant that the criminal law was kept simple and unsophisticated. How much we have gained by making it complex and juristically subtle is a question upon which views may be divided. The ruthlessness of the Tudor

---

[27] In R. v. *Hall* (1571) 110 Selden Soc. 242, the defendant objected to the evidence of the bishop of Ross being given in writing; but the objection was overruled, following a decision by all the judges in 1556. Hall was convicted of treason and executed.

[28] E.g. in 1599 a sheriff was fined £500 for telling the under-sheriff to return a jury favourable to the prosecutors: *Hawkins* v. *Kemeys* (1599) CUL MS. Dd.8.48, pp. 107–8. Procuring an acquittal was perhaps seen as worse: *Jorden* v. *Willoughby* (1595) Star Cha. Rep. 124, no. 922 (sheriff and JP fined £2,000); *IELH* (5th edn), p. 128. Note also Hawarde 108 (Richard Lechford JP fined £2,000 in 1600), 145 (Richard Broughton JP fined £200 in 1602).

[29] E.g. Ch. 2, nn. 67–70. Error and certiorari were of little use because the factual details which might raise questions of law were hidden behind the routine phrases in indictments.

law of treason horrifies us today. On the other hand, the routine creation of hundreds of new criminal offences by ministerial order, albeit under statutory powers, would have appalled the Elizabethans. It is also worth remembering that our present age has done away with many of the protections thought necessary when accused persons faced death: in the Elizabethan period a defendant could challenge up to twenty jurors without giving reasons, a verdict of guilty had to be unanimous, and there could be no retrial after a verdict of acquittal.[30] Without question, however, a defendant today receives a fuller and more careful hearing, and will even find prosecuting counsel safeguarding his just interests against the failings of an overworked prosecution service.[31]

Legal Continuity and Social Change

The most difficult obstacle in the way of a final conclusion is the inconstancy of general social attitudes. Some of our understandings of rights, wrongs and obligations change significantly over the centuries, while others do not. Murder, rape and robbery have always been serious offences,[32] and fair bargains

---

[30] Majority verdicts were introduced in 1974; peremptory challenges were reduced from seven to three in 1977 and abolished in 1988; retrials after acquittal became possible in some situations after 2003.

[31] E.g. the failure to disclose relevant evidence in a notorious rape trial in 2017 which received much press attention: see Metropolitan Police, *A Joint Review of the Disclosure Process in the Case of R. v. Allan* (2018).

[32] In the time of Elizabeth I, they were among the offences punished by death, benefit of clergy having been withdrawn from them by Tudor legislation: Ch. 2, n. 120; Ch. 3, n. 118.

have always been morally binding. Most of the fundamental personal freedoms recognised today, such as freedom from slavery, from arbitrary imprisonment or confiscation of property, and from restraints on employment, were also understood by the Elizabethans in much the same way as now. So were recognition as a person before the courts, with judicial remedies for infringements of rights, a presumption of innocence until proved guilty according to law at a public trial, and an opportunity to be heard in one's defence. And yet, on other matters, there have been complete reversals in general attitudes. For example, in the present age there is an aversion to the death penalty even for terrorists and mass murderers,[33] and all judicial corporal punishment – frequently imposed by Elizabethan magistrates – has been abolished.[34] At the same time, property has become less sacrosanct. The guarantee of property rights vis-à-vis the Crown in Magna Carta has been replaced by a human right not to be deprived of possessions 'except in the public interest'.[35] Whereas for Coke it was axiomatic that 'no one shall be forced to sell his own property, even at a fair price',[36] powers of compulsory purchase have become acceptable and have been considerably extended since 1960.

[33] The death penalty was abolished for murder in 1968, and its last vestiges (for treason and piracy) went in 1998.

[34] Criminal Justice Act 1948 (c. 58) s. 2. It was permitted in prisons until 1967.

[35] Human Rights Act 1998, Sch. 1, Part II, art. 1. Cf. Magna Carta 1225, c. 29 ('No free person shall be . . . disseised of any free tenement'). Taxation, however, had always carried the possibility of enforcement against a person's possessions in the public interest.

[36] Co. Nbk, BL MS. Harley 6686B, fo. 211v (1597) ('Nemo cogitur rem suam vendere etiam justo precio'); 4 Co. Inst. 275.

A person's home is no longer his 'castle and fortress'[37] and may actually be taken away from him to enable a motorway to be built. He is also subject to planning laws, and may need official permission to replace his own windows. Moreover, there is a generally resigned attitude to the thousand or more powers of entry given to enforcement officers and public authorities.[38]

Another change is in the autonomy of the family, and especially of the father as paterfamilias. Chastisement – of wives as well as children – was not only lawful in the sixteenth century but widely considered (by men) to be meritorious. There was no jurisdiction to take children into care or to make them attend school, only gross abuse being punishable, whereas today the child's interest, as viewed by the courts, is paramount and prevails even over the parents' wishes. Young children in Elizabethan landed families could be under pressure to consent to arranged marriages.[39] This is now seen as

---

[37] For this principle see Ch. 2, n. 72.

[38] The Protection of Freedoms Act 2012 (c. 9), ss. 39–53, was intended to facilitate the abolition of unnecessary rights of entry, and made a start by abolishing fifteen of them. A government report then found that over 1,200 powers of entry were still vested in various authorities (not counting court enforcement-officers): Department for Communities and Local Government, *Review of Public Authorities' Powers of Entry* (2014). It identified only six which might be abolished.

[39] The consent was revocable. If girls were married under the age of twelve, or boys under the age of fourteen, the de facto marriage could be repudiated by either party at full age. See J. Baker, 'Some Elizabethan Marriage Cases' in *Studies in Canon Law and Common Law in Honor of R. H. Helmholz*, ed. T. L. Harris (Berkeley, CA, 2015), pp. 181–211, at 189–95.

child abuse, though cultural diversity has brought back arranged and even forced marriages in some communities.[40] Valid marriages could not be dissolved in Tudor England, however intolerable, and an ill-treated wife was unlikely to receive much assistance from the Church courts. Now divorces are frequent and hardly ever contested; there is widespread support for the introduction of divorce by consent, or by the judgment of one party that the marriage has broken down irretrievably;[41] and it is common for matrimonial assets to be divided equally when a marriage ends. Not only is the matrimonial home no longer the man's castle, but the law no longer treats the father of the family as lord and master of those within it. The right to respect for private and family life, as enshrined in the Human Rights Act, has therefore come to have a very different meaning from what would have been understood in the sixteenth century.

Other changes have occurred in popular understandings of individual autonomy. Freedom of thought did not in Tudor times extend to unbridled freedom of speech. Nor is the freedom of expression guaranteed by the human rights

---

[40] The problem is so widespread that the government in 2008 established a Forced Marriage Unit. Coercing someone into marriage against their consent became a criminal offence under the Anti-Social Behaviour, Crime and Policing Act 2014 (c. 12), s. 121.

[41] This was provided for by the Family Law Act 1996 (c. 27) but never brought into operation. It was reintroduced, while this book was in the press, by the Divorce, Dissolution and Separation Act 2020 (c. 11). Until this Act is brought into force, marital breakdown as judged by only one party is still not a ground for divorce: *Owens* v. *Owens* [2018] UKSC 41. Divorce by consent is commonly achieved by making fictional allegations of adultery.

legislation an absolute right. But the bearings of free speech have shifted dramatically.[42] Open criticism or ridicule of the queen or her government was not appreciated four centuries ago,[43] whereas nowadays it is tolerated even when it is ill-mannered and unrestrained. Spreading false news about the state of the economy was punishable then,[44] but normal today. On the other hand, the expression of adverse sentiments about religious or ethnic minorities was then regarded as normal, whereas now it is criminalised by statute. Even non-criminal 'hate speech', which seems to include anything to which someone takes offence, is supposed to be recorded by the police.[45] The chief brake on secular speech in the sixteenth century was not the criminal law but the law of defamation, which was so widely used that the Elizabethan judges tried to water it down to discourage discord. Even so, it was not concerned with insults.[46] A related change of mindset has

---

[42] The common-law freedom was stated in the broadest terms in Sedley LJ's stirring judgment in *Redmond-Pate* v. *DPP* [2000] HRLR 249, 255 ('Freedom only to speak inoffensively is not worth having').

[43] One of the queen's first proclamations was aimed against satirical plays in which she was 'taken off': *TRP*, ii. 115. Most prosecutions for sedition, however, were for attacks on the religious settlement: see Emmison, *Elizabethan Life: Disorder*, ch. 3.

[44] *Utting's Case* (1566) 101 Selden Soc. 76, 77, *per* Browne J ('by such rumours ... the commonwealth has been greatly disturbed').

[45] This was revealed in *R. (H. Miller)* v. *Chief Constable of Humberside* [2020] EWHC 225 (Admin). It was held that merely recording such complaints was lawful, even when there was no evidence of a criminal offence; but it was unlawful for the police to try to dissuade the claimant from repeating his views on a controversial issue of public interest.

[46] E.g. merely calling someone an arrant papist was not actionable since the words did not necessarily import criminality: *Dyer's Notebooks*, p. xxii.

occurred with respect to discrimination on grounds of personal predisposition or prejudice. Not long ago, it was the freedom to engage in discrimination, however unworthy or even
immoral, that was regarded as something approximating to
a human right: the right, that is, to make contracts, or to
refrain from making them, at one's own free choice.[47] Now,
since 2010, declining to make a contract may in some situations be illegal.[48] Freedom of contract, though never completely unfettered,[49] has also given ground in recent times to the
protection of reasonable expectations – even when they are
contrary to the terms of a contract[50] – and the demands of
fairness.[51] This shift has the different explanation that the

[47] An ancient exception was the duty of innkeepers to accept any bona fide
traveller if there was a room available: *White's Case* (1558) Dyer 158. This
paved the way for a new approach to racial discrimination: *Constantine
v. Imperial Hotels Ltd* [1944] KB 693; tacitly confirmed as to hotels by the
Hotel Proprietors Act 1956 (c. 62), s. 1; cf. Race Relations Act 1965 (c. 73).

[48] Equality Act 2010 (c. 15), ss. 29, 33, 39.

[49] E.g. contracts in restraint of trade were invalid in Elizabethan times: Ch.
4, n. 86. Penalties in contracts were unenforceable: Ch. 3, n. 133. And
contracts to lend money at interest were until 1854 subject to the laws
against usury. Usury was an invention of medieval theologians, who held
that it was proper to speculate with money but a sin to accept
a reasonable consideration for a fixed loan. After 1571 it was permissible
in English law to contract for interest, but not above 10 per cent: 13 Eliz.
I, c. 8.

[50] E.g. Unfair Contract Terms Act 1977 (c. 50), s. 3(2)(b); J. H Baker, 'From
Sanctity of Contract to Reasonable Expectation?' (1979) 32 *Current Legal
Problems* 17–39.

[51] E.g. the concept of unfair dismissal in employment law, and of a fair rent
in landlord and tenant law. Equity began the process at any earlier
period, but only in respect of contracts which were not merely unfair but
unconscionable.

mass of people who work for big employers, rent property, travel and take holidays, or buy cars and manufactured appliances, have no freedom to negotiate the printed standard terms which they must sign in order to take part in everyday life. Their contracts are not vitiated by duress at common law, or by undue influence as defined in equity, and yet it is no longer thought realistic to view them solely in those terms. In many of these respects, 1952 was closer to 1558 than to 2020.

The conclusion must be that a detailed comparative evaluation of the two legal systems is beyond reach. There are too many variables. But the paradox of the common law is that it remains essentially the same while undergoing adjustment to suit changing attitudes. It has a genuine continuity because it has been able to adapt gradually over the centuries, through a process of reasoning, as social conditions and public opinion change. By way of contrast, legislative interruptions or additions have been more instantaneous and inflexible, justified by democratic consent (or majority rule) rather than legal logic, and therefore modifiable only by further legislation. Yet this contrast is nothing new. Social and economic regulation through the statute-book was well under way in the Tudor period. Much of it dealt with the same kinds of issue as today, and complaints were already being voiced about the excessive number of regulatory statutes and their complexity. If we were to ask an Elizabethan nobleman whether he would prefer to live under the present legal system, we can be fairly sure that his answer would be negative. If we were to put the same question to a well-informed country labourer, the answer would undoubtedly be more positive. The middle-ranking classes in each period would probably elect to stay where they were. No doubt they would all be right. Human reason does not alter, only the world upon which it has to operate. And the biggest factual alterations affecting the law have been in people's attitudes to individual autonomy and how far it should give way to the common good or to the majority view as to how people should live.

It is obvious that the complexities and comforts of life today were utterly unforeseeable in 1603. Many were unforeseeable in 1952. But comparison of the two periods reveals that the past is not such a foreign country as it is sometimes made out to be. Making due allowance for the differences engendered by four centuries of social evolution, English law under both Elizabeths is in essence the same organism facing similar challenges. It is embedded in the precious heritage of constitutional monarchy, parliamentary democracy, objective rationalism and judicial integrity. And that, no doubt, was the lesson that Miss Hamlyn had in mind when she established these lectures.

children, 41, 208–9

Church. *See* ecclesiastical courts;
    heresy; High Commission;
    religion

circuit judges. *See* assizes; County
    Court

civil justice system, evaluations of,
    147–8, 196–202

Civil Law. *See* Roman law

civil procedure
    common law replaced by statute,
        128, 149, 152–3
    formalism, complexity and
        technicality in, 36–9, 153, 187
    orality of, 144, 150, 153–4,
        191, 192
    pre-trial proceedings, 10, 151, 201
    proportionate justice, 150–1
    reforms of, 149–55, *See also* jury
        trial; nisi prius; pleading

clergy. *See* benefit of clergy

Coke, Edward, 7, 11, 15–16
    as attorney-general, 50, 82–3, 97,
        133, 178–9
    as Speaker, 80, 95
    founder of administrative law,
        178–80
    on antiquity of common
        law, 34–5
    on Magna Carta, 116
    on sanctity of property, 207
    on statute law, 95–6, 97–8,
        123–4, 133
    on the requirements of
        justice, 196
    on void statutes, 173–4
    on wills and perpetuities, 61

pleading and, 38

commercial litigation, 24–5

commissioners of sewers, 110–11,
    122, 173

common law
    antiquity of, 34–5
    compared with statute, 87–8,
        119–20, 132–3, 139, 166
    immortality of, 1, 122–32
    limits of, 119–20, 139–42
    method of, 35–6, 39, 160–1
    social change and, 212–13
    sources of, 16–17

Common Pleas, 3, 4, 13–14,
    23, 48

common recovery, 56, 113, 114

compensation culture, 160

competition law, 121, *See also*
    monopolies

compulsory purchase, 207

computers, 149, 181, 188

constitution.
    called the 'covenant of the
        commonwealth', 78–9
    conventions of, 162–4, *See also*
        monarchy; judicial review;
        Parliament; royal prerogative

contract, freedom of, 211–12

contract, law of, 63–5, 157–8
    unfair contracts, 211–12

conveyancing, 29, 56, 157, 186

copyhold, 54–5, 182

corporal punishment, 72, 207

corporations, 24, 186

cost of litigation, 19–25, 152, 197–8

Council in the Marches, 47

Council in the North, 47

Lightning Source UK Ltd.
Milton Keynes UK
UKHW022237050721
386699UK00013B/168